'Gosh, you mean you actually *TOUCHED* Barry John!'

WHEN LIONS
ROARED

WHEN LIONS ROARED

THE LIONS, THE ALL BLACKS AND
THE LEGENDARY TOUR OF 1971

TOM ENGLISH
PETER BURNS

POLAR*S
PUBLISHING

First published in 2017 by

POLARIS PUBLISHING LTD
c/o Turcan Connell
Princes Exchange
1 Earl Grey Street
Edinburgh
EH3 9EE

in association with

ARENA SPORT
An imprint of Birlinn Limited
West Newington House
10 Newington Road
Edinburgh
EH9 1QS

www.polarispublishing.com
www.arenasportbooks.co.uk

2

ISBN: 9781909715523
eBook ISBN: 9780857903433

British Library Cataloguing-in-Publication Data
A catalogue record for this book is available on request from the British Library.

Designed and typeset by Polaris Publishing, Edinburgh

Printed in Great Britain by Clays, St Ives

CONTENTS

In memory of
Carwyn, Doug, Gordon, Mervyn and Alastair

Legends forever

ACKNOWLEDGEMENTS

In the late summer of 2016, at a book signing at O'Mahony's on O'Connell Street in Limerick, it was pointed out that it was forty-five years since the great Lions tour of 1971 – and perhaps it was time for a retrospective on that incredible rugby crusade to New Zealand. *When Lions Roared* is the result.

Over the months that followed that conversation, we rewatched every available piece of footage and read everything we could lay our hands on about the tour, the years leading up to it and the years afterwards. We got in touch with as many Lions, All Blacks and provincial New Zealand players as we could. And every second of it was both a pleasure and a privilege.

We are indebted to our fantastic colleagues in New Zealand, Tony Johnson and Lynn McConnell, for all their work in helping to piece the jigsaw together from the Kiwi side of things, often conducting interviews on our behalf and putting us in touch with former players, as well as sending through a treasure trove of newspaper cuttings and scans from old magazines and books that were produced in New Zealand in the aftermath of the '71 tour. John Griffiths was able to do much the same from Wales and thanks go to him for all his help with our research.

Thanks also to Elspeth Orwin in the Sir George Grey Special Collections department at Auckland Libraries; the archivists at the

National Library of New Zealand; Dave Barton at the British & Irish Lions; and photographers Ans Westra and Peter Bush whose images brought the tour to life for us. Thanks also to Katie Field and Julie Fergusson and everyone involved at Polaris Publishing.

Thank you to Stephen Jones, David Barnes and Nick Cain, who worked with us on *Behind the Lions: Playing Rugby for the British & Irish Lions*, which provided a strong foundation when we set out to write this book. Furthermore, both John Reason's *The Victorious Lions* and Terry McLean's *Lions Rampant* were invaluable to our research. They provide a ringside seat to each match on the tour and are brilliantly insightful accounts.

Most importantly, thank you to all the players who so generously gave up their time to speak to us; it was wonderful to be able to relive the great adventure with you. We hope that we have captured the essence of the tour as you remembered it.

Finally, thank you to our loved ones (Lynn, Eilidh and Tom; Julie, Isla and Hector) for putting up with us during the mad months while we wrote this book. Tom would also like to thank the greats of Court Brack, Castleconnell and Rintulla for their love and support.

Tom English & Peter Burns

BOY, COULD THEY PLAY

BARRY JOHN was in the bath when the intruder entered his bedroom and made away with the watch which had been given to him by his wife as a departing gift. Barry never heard him, never saw him, and by the time he noticed that the watch was gone, it was too late. It was a moment in history – the one and only occasion the New Zealanders got the better of the King during that storied summer of 1971.

The Lions were in the town of Pukekohe, fifty kilometres south of Auckland, and Carwyn James' tourists were about to begin their three-month, twenty-four-match trek around New Zealand against some obliging rural fodder: Counties-Thames Valley. The following day, the Lions put twenty-five points on them. For the New Zealand press, it wasn't enough. If the Lions were any good, they wrote, they'd have scored fifty.

After one game, conclusions were drawn. The All Blacks should beat this lot 4–0 in the series. Anything less would be an affront to the jersey, an insult to the legacy of their former coach, Fred Allen, who had taken charge for sixteen Tests up until 1968 and who, by winning sixteen out of sixteen, had sent a message to the wider world that New Zealand was the greatest rugby nation on earth.

After two games, the clean-sweep conclusion was being tweaked. The Lions had just hammered King Country and, though the local media maintained that 4–0 was still likely, it was no longer an absolute certainty.

On it went. The Lions ran amok against Waikato in Hamilton, a John Bevan hat trick at the heart of the rout. The Maori got heavy in Auckland, but they were seen off, too. At every turn the Lions were told, 'Wait until you get to Wellington,' as if the Wellington boys were the ones who would categorically put the visitors back in their box.

When the time came, the Lions beat Wellington 47–9, and all of New Zealand gasped as one. Bevan got four more tries, Mike Gibson got two and Sandy Carmichael, John Taylor and Barry John got one apiece. Nine scores against one of the pre-eminent provincial sides in the land. The country had never seen anything like it.

'Onslaught crumbles capital!' ran the headline in the *Dominion* the morning after. 'Athletic Park watched in stunned disbelief as much as admiration,' the newspaper reported. The bravado of the 4–0 prediction had now been obliterated, replaced with something approaching fear and awe.

When it was all over, months later, the *Dominion* produced a magazine of the tour, detailing every cough and splutter of what had happened in each city and one-horse town the Lions had gone to. They hailed them as the greatest team that had ever set foot in the land of the long white cloud, better even than the celebrated men who had beaten New Zealand at home not once but twice in 1937 – the Springboks of Danie Craven, Boy Louw and the splendidly named flanker, Ebbo Bastard.

The *Dominion*'s final reckoning was that Barry John was the greatest number ten, Gareth Edwards was the greatest number nine, Mike Gibson was the greatest centre and JPR Williams was the greatest full-back. The starting point of the New Zealand media in those innocent early days in Pukekohe in late May was that the Lions were going down; the end point, in mid August, was that the Lions were going down all right – in history.

The documenting of the Lions' greatness went on for page after page, the last headline encapsulating how the rugby nation felt having watched them in full flow. It simply read, 'Thank you'.

Joe Schmidt: In 1971 I was only about five years old.

Warren Gatland: I must have been nearly eight.

Vern Cotter: I was eleven.

Warren Gatland: You kind of get brainwashed about the All Blacks. You think the All Blacks are the best team in the world. I thought rugby was invented in New Zealand. I didn't know that anyone else around the world played it. So, when the Lions came to New Zealand in 1971 and won, it had a significant impact on me. That red jersey has had a profound effect on me throughout my whole life.

Joe Schmidt: My memories are a little hazy, but I remember some of the flying players: JPR Williams, Gerald Davies and David Duckham, the guys who got on the end of the ball and just caused havoc; the likes of Mike Gibson and Barry John, who kicked it, ran with it and did a lot of pretty amazing things. Those are the images that I can recall.

Vern Cotter: My whole school was taken to see them play and I remember it clearly because it was my first big game of rugby. It of Plenty at Domain Park in Tauranga. We all trooped ... the school bus, walked single file down the touchline and sat on the edge of the field. I was so close to the paddock I could hear the thundering of bodies and feel the wind on my face as these players ran past me. Because we were sitting on it, you could feel the ground moving. I was in awe of that day. It wasn't just a game of rugby, it was a cultural event and one of my biggest memories as a kid.

Sean Fitzpatrick: My first rugby heroes weren't All Blacks, but members of the 1971 Lions team. Gareth Edwards was my hero. I even bought myself a red jersey so that when my brother and I played in the garden he would be the All Blacks and I would be the Lions.

Joe Schmidt: I grew up in a country where you start playing rugby in bare feet in the backyard as soon as you can get out of your nappies. Rugby is everything in New Zealand. For a group to come over and remain unbeaten through the provinces and then win a Test series is something that is incredibly difficult to do and it's a measure of the quality of the individuals that were on that team, and also a measure of the camaraderie that they shared, that they were able to accomplish that feat. In these days of science, where everything is tracked and measured and analysed, where you have GPS to see how far players run, how hard they hit and so on, these guys had the number of empty glasses on the table to see how many pints they had drunk. But boy could they play.

Sean Fitzpatrick: JPR Williams, Gerald Davies, David Duckham, Mike Gibson, Barry John, Gareth Edwards, Gordon Brown, Willie John McBride – just thinking of them makes me smile. All the boys of my age loved the Lions and the way they played. Prior to that tour, everyone had tried to kick like Don Clarke, who was a legend as far as we were concerned. You ran up to the ball and hoofed it as hard as you could, as he did. Then along came Barry John and he kicked around the corner. It wasn't just that it was different – it was that it worked so well. After that, it was farewell to Don.

Graham Henry: The Lions tours of 1959 and 1971 had an intense effect in our household when I was growing up. My father and I used to talk for hours about those teams. The 1971 Lions changed the face of New Zealand rugby. They helped lay the foundations of the All Blacks side that won the 1987 World Cup and that style of counter-attacking play that we've seen from All Blacks sides ever since. That was a tour that had a huge impact on how I coached the game. We got beaten by a team who played fifteen-man rugby. They shook the foundations of New Zealand rugby and from the top down things changed.

Steve Hansen: My father was Des Hansen, the coach at Marist rugby club in Auckland from way back. The 1971 Lions had a big influence on my dad's coaching philosophy and left a big impression on me as a young lad. Dad's big thing wasn't about coaching rugby skills, but getting players to think. When he was coaching, most coaches were 'Do it as I say' dictators, but Dad challenged us to think 'Why did that work?' or 'How could it work better?' When I became an All Blacks coach we'd often discuss the game, and Dad wasn't shy about coming forward with his opinion. He was a massive influence on me. I've been lucky in coaching, being associated with other people as well, but the basics definitely come from him. And a lot of his whole view of coaching, which he passed on to me, came from that 1971 Lions tour and the attitudes of Carwyn James and his players. Their influence on New Zealand rugby in the years since can't be underestimated.

Graham Henry: After 1971, guys like George Simpkin at Waikato and Frank Ryan at Wellington took on the fifteen-man game as well. They took on a lot of the Lions' backline set-up, the way their centres stood in defence and how they created space for the players on the outside. I took a lot of that on board. The coaching culture in New Zealand changed, from the grassroots upwards. By the mid eighties and going into the 1987 World Cup, New Zealand boasted a generation of outstanding, modern-thinking, quick-witted players.

I wonder if I would have been as successful as I have been, or if I would have become a coach at all, without that tour. Before Carwyn arrived with a host of new ideas, coaching patterns in New Zealand had become sterile. Everyone was doing the same thing, no one dared to be different. The game had moved on. You have to understand, New Zealand is a very young country, and rugby has put our country on the map. This country earned respect from the rest of the world for three things: what we did in two world wars and, to a lesser extent, what we've done on the rugby field. So, over time, rugby has become a major part of our national identity. And in 1971, the Lions showed us how to play.

CHAPTER ONE

WE ALL WANTED TO BE CARWYN JAMES

RAIN ROLLED in over the Gwendraeth Valley in the heart of South Wales, a swirling wind sweeping across the field of the village rugby club, with its hand-cut steel goalposts lovingly painted in Cefneithin's yellow and green colours. It was a late-summer night in 1957 and there was little sound to be heard other than the intermittent thump of leather on leather as rugby ball was struck by boot. Carwyn James raised a hand in signal to a small group of boys who were huddled behind the posts, all shivering with the cold and who immediately punted the balls back to him.

It had become a tradition that, come rain or shine, whenever Carwyn came out to practise his kicking, the boys from the village would stand beneath the posts to collect the balls and kick them back to their hero, the famous fly-half for Llanelli, hoping to impress him with the shape of their spiral punts and to snatch a few words with him at the end. One of them was a small, wispy boy of twelve, with dark hair and a puckish expression. His name was Barry John.

*

Carwyn James was born in the winter of 1929. A thoughtful, shy child, he not only grew up during the height of the Great Depression, but also in something of an unconventional family set-up. His father worked long, hard hours at the Cross Hands Colliery in Cefneithin, while his mother was forced to pour most of her energy into caring for Carwyn's brother, Dewi, who had contracted diphtheria.

Carwyn's sister, Gwen, became something of a surrogate mother to him. He was an insular child, but he found creative outlets with a love of poetry and literature, and then through his talent for sport. He excelled at football and cricket, but it was rugby that stole his heart.

Carwyn became captain at Gwendraeth School, winning six caps for Welsh Schools and making his debut for Llanelli while he was still a pupil. Later, he went to Aberystwyth University to study Welsh. He immersed himself in politics, becoming president of the college branch of the Welsh nationalist party, Plaid Cymru. Later still, he became a Welsh language teacher. All the while, he established himself as the fly-half at Llanelli, and a player that could quicken the pulse. At Stradey Park, he would glide and dance and dictate play in the number-ten jersey. In 1958, at the age of twenty-nine, he won a long-overdue first cap for Wales in a 9–3 victory against Australia. It was a result that was celebrated far and wide throughout Wales, but nowhere more wildly than in Cefneithin.

Barry John: Can you imagine what it was like to be a boy from a little village like Cefneithin and to see Carwyn out there playing for Wales? He was the king. The hero. He was everything rolled into one. There were a lot of boys in the village when I was growing up and sport was always a big thing for us – Liverpool, Manchester United and all the rest of it – but rugby was the biggest. And to get one of the blokes from the village playing for

Wales – it was unheard of. And then he went and dropped a goal against Australia. It was like Christmas for us all. We all wanted to be Carwyn James.

His parents' house backed onto the rugby field and he'd go in there to practise his kicking. The road where we lived was on the opposite side and we'd all go out to watch him. We'd be like little disciples, running around and catching the ball and kicking it back to him. We didn't have to rely on comic books for heroes. We had our own hero.

Carwyn may have been the master of Stradey Park, but he would only play once more for Wales – a 16–6 loss to France in Cardiff in the 1959 Five Nations. It was Carwyn's misfortune to be born in the same era as Cliff Morgan, one of the finest fly-halves of the twentieth century. 'I often wondered why I played more times for Wales than Carwyn,' reflected Morgan. 'I think it was because I was stronger. My schoolmaster always used to say, "You've got to have strength." He wrote in one school report, "Not very good in class, his biggest asset is his buttocks." He believed you had to have big buttocks to be able to ride tackles. And Carwyn was naturally slim and elegant and I was squat and rather nasty. I loved playing against him – he always had a smile. He'd always show you the ball as he was running at you, creating space because you had no idea where he was going to put it.'

For Carwyn, Test-level success wasn't to be, but his influence didn't end there. It wasn't just Barry John and his friends in Cefneithin who worshipped him. In Llansaint, a small village that overlooked the Carmarthen Bay, another young boy would play rugby in the streets, pretending to be Carwyn James.

Gerald Davies: Carwyn was my hero. He had this magical quality of being able to accelerate and sidestep, the ball always in two hands – an electrifying thing to see done so cleverly. I loved watching that. He was the first player I ever saw sidestepping, and he always seemed to have time on the ball. He had a huge influence on how I played.

He teased opponents, almost daring them to tackle him, persuading them to go one way when he had made up his mind to go the other. He was a marvellous player, a delicate player, a whippersnapper, a will-o'-the-wisp. The kind of player who would start the game with his shorts white and pristine and would end the game with his shorts white and pristine. Nobody could touch him.

As a child, I'd loiter after Sunday chapel to listen to the village pundits voice their opinions on the game. Arguments always raged and at no time were they fiercer than when it came to who should play outside-half for Wales. Cliff Morgan played twenty-nine times for Wales, Carwyn James only twice, but to every adult man in the village, it should have been the reverse.

Barry John: I was first picked for Llanelli when I was eighteen. I was still at school, yet here I was being asked to play for one of the greatest clubs in the world. When Carwyn finished playing, he came to coach us. He was such a breath of fresh air and his attitude to the game was very similar to my own. I just loved the way he thought about playing. He'd prowl around the changing room before kick-off and would always encourage us to play it as we saw it. 'Take a risk or two, make a few mistakes,' he'd say. 'As long as you are adventurers, I won't mind.' His changing room mantra was always, 'Think, think, think – it's a thinking man's game.'

*

After the horrors of the Second World War and the deprivation that stretched on for the years that followed, the generation that rose from the ashes of the conflict began to come together as ambitious young rugby players in the latter years of the 1960s. Many of them were implored by their parents to do anything but follow them into the heavy industries that dominated so many of the rugby heartlands around Britain. From the soul-destroying darkness and danger of life in the mines in South Wales, the middle and north of England and the central belt of Scotland to the long, laborious and perilous work of life in the shipyards of the Clyde and Belfast, life had been hard for many of them. This had, in turn, created hard men.

Gareth Edwards: My father was away for five years during the war and lost a great part of his life to it. He was a talented singer and there were opportunities for him at the end of the war to continue with that as a career, but he came back to the village and he got a job as a miner. People say to me now, 'Gareth, you've got to slow down, you're doing too much,' but I often think of my father and the life he led, and of all the opportunities that he missed out on.

He used to get up at four in the morning to be in work at six. He would work his eight-hour shift and somebody might say, 'Glan, there's a chance for you to work a doubler,' and he would take it and carry on. I never appreciated how hard it was until I went underground and visited a mine many years later. You couldn't see your hand in front of your face. It was a bloody gruesome thing.

Barry John: My father was a coal miner. Every morning at 4.30 a.m. he would rise and get ready to catch the bus to the Great Mountain Colliery at Tumble, just a few miles from our home. He would work relentlessly once he got there, only occasionally breaking for his sandwiches hundreds of yards underground – if the rats hadn't got to them first. Not only would he come home utterly exhausted and flop into his armchair, but there were times – if he was doing a double shift – when he'd not even see any daylight for ten days at a time. He would go to work in the dark, come home after six in the evening when it was dark, and in the meantime would be working down there in the pitch dark.

The natural role for me, and for anyone growing up in our village, for that matter, was to follow our fathers down the mines. But I promised my father I would never go underground. 'Barry,' he would tell me, 'if you don't do your homework, you know where you'll end up, don't you? Down the mines with me. And believe me, you don't want to be doing that.'

Gerald Davies: My father was a miner, too. Saturday afternoon's rugby match was the time for my father to get some of the floating coal dust out of his lungs, to stretch his limbs that had remained cramped and closeted for hours on end in a tiny, dirty black hole. For me, rugby was a recreational leisure activity; for him it was a great escape.

My father spent most of his working life underground. He had to get up very early in the morning, walk a mile and a half down to the railway track and then catch a train to Glynhebog Colliery. There were times during the winter when he literally did not see daylight at all, except for the weekends. As a result, he never wished anything of the kind on me. For the most part, my parents did much to protect me from any awareness of many of the hardships they had suffered. But they never failed to emphasise that if I didn't stick to my education then I would invariably follow my father down the pits.

Barry John: My school was near the colliery and I'll never forget the time of the wailing hooter. Our classroom overlooked the pit and I remember looking down and seeing a scene of just utter panic below us. As the hooter wailed, the teachers ran out of the classrooms and into the playground to try to see what was going on. We were running up and down corridors and in the distance we could hear the wailing sirens of the emergency vehicles.

We were like ants, rabbits, rats – just running into one another in blind panic, asking, 'What is it? What's happened? Is everyone okay?' There had been a huge blast down the pit. My father was so shell-shocked by the incident that he didn't speak for three days.

Mervyn Davies: My father loathed life underground. To him, the call to arms during the war was a godsend, a chance to flee from the pit. He once said the mines would have killed him if he'd stayed there a moment longer – he preferred taking his chance against the Germans. He was shipped out to North Africa with Montgomery's Eighth, was taken prisoner and bundled off to Germany where he spent his war trapped behind barbed wire. Although in many ways his war could have been much, much worse, it was an ironic fate to befall a man who had joined up because he felt imprisoned in the pit.

My parents made sure I worked hard at school. If I was going to get anywhere in life, if I wanted to avoid a dirty, dangerous future, if I wanted to get well away from the acrid smoke of the smelters' yard or the blackness of the mine, then I would have to 'think' my way out. My father didn't want either one of his boys toiling away like him.

Ian McLauchlan: I was born in the mining village of Tarbolton in Ayrshire. My father was a miner and a very strong man, but I also worked on the local farms in the summers from the age of thirteen – no shite about how old you were then. My dad had had vague ambitions that I should be a doctor. I wanted to be a teacher. He was happy for me to do anything to avoid that life down the pit.

Willie John McBride: I was brought up in a wee farm in Moneyglass in Antrim and sport was the last thing on our mind. My father died when I was four and we had to work on the farm. I didn't play rugby until I was seventeen, and the 1940s were tough. We went to school, came home and helped our mother. Sport wasn't a part of it for a long time. The first athletic thing I ever did at school was pole-vaulting. I was a pole-vaulter. Tall and skinny. I won the Ulster Schools Championship twice. Then I got too heavy and the pole broke and I was enticed out to play this game called rugby. And it turned out I was pretty good at it. Farming makes you tough.

John Pullin: Our family farm is in Aust in Gloucestershire, and I can't remember a time when I wasn't working. As Willie John says, farming makes you tough – which was just as well, because playing hooker for Bristol put you in the firing line in some fairly tasty Anglo-Welsh clashes over the years. Our farm is on the banks of the Severn and the view is all of Wales. I made my debut for Bristol against Newport in September 1961 and I was up against Bryn Meredith, the Wales and Lions hooker. It was a hell of an introduction. And we won. After that, I never looked back. I'd work on the farm from dawn until dusk and then run to training. It was hard, but it was good for me. It gave me a base fitness and strength that lasted my entire career.

Barry John: To earn money when I was eighteen, I had a seven-week spell working at the colliery during the summer holidays. I only worked up at the top, cleaning up a couple of huge pipes and giving the guys underground a helping hand by supplying them with tools. Those seven weeks underlined to me why my father was right to get me to do my homework. Suddenly I was up at the crack of dawn and on the same bus with him. I was young, fighting fit, playing a good standard of rugby and had just started a teaching course at Trinity College, Carmarthen. Every single morning I looked around the bus and saw men in their early twenties and thirties with their eyes shut who would suddenly jerk awake coughing, spluttering and wheezing – a legacy of breathing in coal dust every day. Many of them had been at school with me. All I knew at the end of that summer was that my career path would go in another direction. It had to.

CHAPTER TWO

AM I BORING YOU, YOU BIG PRICK?

IN THE autumn of 1967, the rugby machine that was Brian Lochore's All Blacks toured the northern hemisphere on the back of two years of blistering form. They had won eight of their previous nine Tests, beating the Springboks 3–1 in a four-match series in 1965 and walloping the Lions 4–0 in 1966. Over those nine matches, they had scored twenty-two tries and were, unquestionably, the most feared team on earth and one of the finest in the history of the game.

They were coached by Fred Allen, otherwise known as the Needle for his refusal to tolerate bullshit. He had captained the All Blacks on twenty-one consecutive occasions from 1946 to 1949 and then moved into coaching, guiding Auckland to twenty-four successive defences of the Ranfurly Shield, the most coveted trophy in New Zealand provincial rugby.

Colin Meads: Fred was a dictator. If you let him down, say, socially, you were cast out, you were gone. Other coaches would say, 'Come on, we need you back in this team. You've got to pull your horns in.' That wasn't Fred.

Chris Laidlaw: I was an All Black half-back under Fred. Once, shortly before a Test and in the middle of an Allen monologue, Colin Meads let slip a nervous yawn. Allen came at him like a cobra. 'Am I boring you, Colin?'

Colin Meads: He actually said, 'Am I boring you, you big prick? There's a bus leaving in ten minutes if I am.'

Chris Laidlaw: If Allen had Meads in his pocket, it's not difficult to imagine his effect on the lesser souls of the team.

Colin Meads: Fred often used me as a means of showing the young ones that he had no favourites. He was straight and I liked that. Before he arrived, we used to be pretty dour and forward-orientated. Backs were a necessary evil. Then along came Fred and changed it all. He said, 'You're going to change and if you don't, you're out.' He convinced us that there was a better way to play the game. Fred told us what was going to happen: 'We're going to run the ball, it's going to get out to the wings and you big bastards up front are going to get there and there'll be no taking shortcuts.' He used to get into us terribly, which was good for us. And we took to his philosophy. It wasn't hard – we had good players, we were fit.

The All Blacks were a wrecking ball when they had to be and a thing of beauty when they wanted to be. In their squad they had hard-core leaders in Lochore, the captain from Wairarapa, Meads, the great icon from King Country, Kel Tremain, the fearsome openside from Hawke's Bay, and Ken Gray, the tighthead rock from Wellington. They also had a cavalry of other players who hadn't yet made their mark, but who would emerge soon enough – Ian Kirkpatrick, the flanker from Canterbury, his teammate, Alister Hopkinson, a prop with a reputation for badness, Jazz

Muller, another prop from Taranaki, and Sid Going, a scrum-half from North Auckland.

En route to Europe, they played two matches in Vancouver and Montreal and knocked the spots off British Columbia and Eastern Canada. Then they started taking the Brits to the cleaners. They won three provincial matches in Manchester, Leicester and Bristol before they fetched up at Twickenham and did a number on England, scoring five tries in a 23–11 win. The gulf in class was ridiculous.

They played fifteen matches on their northern hemisphere tour, winning fourteen – including all the Tests – and drawing one, the penultimate match against East Wales at Cardiff Arms Park.

Brian Lochore: Fred indicated right at the beginning of the tour that he wanted a fifteen-man game, which absolutely suited us. It was great rugby to play. Fergie McCormick was a magnificent running full-back.

Ian MacRae: I was a centre. I won seventeen All Black caps between 1966 and 1970 and most of them were with Fergie. He was outstanding. He was the only full-back selected for the tour and was indestructible. No one ever got past him.

Gareth Edwards: I was twenty years old when they came over, and I have to admit that the fables about the past and all the great New Zealand teams completely intimidated me before the game. They began their tour in Manchester, beating the North of England 33–3, and then they rolled over the Midlands and Home Counties, the South of England and then England itself at Twickenham. I sat in the crowd in Swansea as they beat West Wales 21–14 and I remember being amazed when I saw Colin Meads and realised he wasn't ten feet tall with one eye in the middle of his forehead. He was much smaller than my nightmares had told me – but he was about as good. There is something about the blackness of the New Zealand jersey that sends a shudder through your heart.

Gerald Davies: Ever since the days when my father talked about them, I had held the All Blacks in awe. Any discussion about them was in hushed, almost reverential tones. From the way he talked, they were indestructible. And from the way the 1967 team played, they *seemed* indestructible. They were the best side I ever played against.

Gareth Edwards: Wales played them on Saturday, 11 November – a horrible day of high winds and pouring rain. The Welsh selectors decided to pick as big a pack of forwards as they could find, and I remember Norman Gale, our captain, prowling around the dressing room like a caged bear before kick-off. There were a load of new caps that day and I was only winning my third cap at that stage, so we were all pretty callow.

I only have fleeting memories of the game. I remember my second pass to Barry – I remember it because Kel Tremain stamped down on my arm afterwards. It was like it had gone through a laundry press – the pain went all up my back, it was horrendous. If the ground hadn't been so soft he would have broken it. A huge bruise came up on it later, stud marks and all.

I remember getting up and running off in agony, telling myself it was an accident, but I looked at Tremain more carefully at the next lineout. There he was, seventeen stone, playing as a wing forward. He'd had a cortisone injection in order to play so I knew he must be pretty important. He was massive, ears on him like hydrofoils. After going down under a ruck, their other flanker, Graham Williams, rolled over close to me, close enough

AM I BORING YOU, YOU BIG PRICK?

to talk. He grabbed my shirt and pulled me just underneath him. 'Get under there, son,' he said, 'and keep your head in or you'll get hurt.' He was right – the All Blacks ruck was like some giant combine harvester. Bodies were booted around like chaff.

Barry John: You knew that when you played a side like that, if you made a cock-up you were going to get punished. So don't make cock-ups, make the right decisions. Don't be overambitious, get your kicks in nicely, get the right weight on them. Do the basics. That's what you had to do when you played a team of that calibre. It was the end of the year and Cardiff Arms Park was like a paddy field, so I decided to put in little dinks here and there and little grubbers, making them turn on the heavy ground, making it difficult to get back to cover the ball. We were playing well, keeping it steady and tight, but then late on they took a penalty shot at goal and it hung in the air and then fell down short, next to the upright. And one of our new caps, John Jeffrey, made a mess of it and they jumped on it to score a try. And that one mistake knocked the stuffing out of us because with that try we were ten points behind and there was no way we were going to overtake that deficit in the time left. I got a drop goal, but it was too little too late.

Gareth Edwards: I tackled Ian MacRae and cut his eye open with my head. Later, at the dinner, I went over and apologised to him. He said it was okay. The blood was dripping down his dinner suit as he said it.

Fergie McCormick: Fred was especially keen that the All Blacks should beat Wales. I'll never forget Needle after we beat them. He was out on the ground with mud over his shoes, congratulating the guys.

The All Blacks juggernaut just kept on rolling. They travelled to France to face the Five Nations champions, scoring four tries in a 21–15 win, and beat Scotland at Murrayfield despite Colin Meads being sent off for kicking the ball out of fly-half David Chisholm's hands.

Sandy Carmichael: I was partly to blame for Meads getting sent off. I kneed him in the gut because he'd been punching one of our guys. He lashed out with a foot and caught Davie.

Fred Allen: To watch him walk off the pitch like that, it just didn't feel right. To me, Colin Meads was the greatest rugby player ever. They threw away the mould when they made Pinetree.

Brian Lochore: We beat everybody. The only team we didn't beat was Ireland, and that was because there was an outbreak of foot-and-mouth disease and the game was cancelled. A Grand Slam hadn't been done before and we had a great opportunity to do it. We missed out.

For the two years that Fred Allen was in charge, the All Blacks never lost a match. He looked untouchable in his position, but his reign was to come to a sudden end.

On 15 June 1968, the first Test of the year, between the All Blacks and the Wallabies, was about to be played at the Sydney Cricket Ground. Allen and manager Duncan Ross had agreed to let Alex Veysey, a reporter from the *Dominion* newspaper in Wellington, gain access to the All Blacks changing room so that he could write about the sights and sounds of a team preparing for battle.

Veysey wrote how Allan had rapped his fist on a table before addressing his players. 'I've approached a lot of games very frightened,' he said quietly. 'But I'm terrified by today.' There was silence in the room. He looked over at Colin Meads. 'Pinetree, the Australians were using a sack of sawdust for rucking practice yesterday. D'you know what they called it? *Piney.*'

One by one he went around the team, telling each of them to front up. Finally he came to his captain, Lochore. 'Brian, I'm relying on you for strength and leadership today and I know you won't fail us.' Then he walked from the room, leaving his players in silence.

Sid Going: Fred's team talks were like being positioned in front of a firing squad, not certain whether the guns are loaded or not. He had you on the edge of your seat. He had an alarmingly accurate memory of previous matches and used to spear you to the wall by recalling your errors. Those tactics might not have worked with all the players, but they inspired me.

Veysey's report offered a wonderful insight into the inner sanctum of the All Blacks' changing room, but it was met with icy disapproval by certain members of the New Zealand Rugby Union. At seven the following morning, Duncan Ross was woken by a phone call from Wellington. At the other end of the line was an irate Tom Morrison, the chairman of New Zealand Rugby, who had just read Veysey's piece in the paper. Morrison felt that Veysey's presence had betrayed the sacred confidences of the All Blacks environs and should never have been allowed. Ross was instructed to pass on Morrison's deep displeasure to Allen.

When Ross relayed the message, the coach was furious in his own right. He felt that Morrison should have had the courage to speak to him himself rather than use Ross as an envoy, and he didn't appreciate being berated like a schoolboy.

Fred Allen: There was nothing in the article about moves or tactics or anything like that. It was about self-belief and confidence, about dedication and courage. It was about patriotism for your country and what the game meant to everyone back home. I knew how those players sitting in front of me were feeling with the minutes ticking down. I'd been through it myself a hundred times. Fear and anxiety were striking at the very heart of most of them and I wanted to bring them back to reality and convince them that they were the best.

For all Allen's protestations that there was nothing wrong with Veysey's piece, a group of administrators at NZR had been growing increasingly disgruntled with the head coach, and this latest escapade added grist to their argument that he was the wrong man for the job.

Fred Allen: It just didn't make sense. I'd been entrusted to coach the All Blacks and we hadn't lost a game. Why would they want to harm a winning coach who was now even better equipped to carry on than ever before? The situation finally reached a point where I wasn't going to let them walk all over me. So I told them to stop interfering with the coaching. I told them to get on with their business and let me get on with mine. No one had ever spoken to them like that before – and they didn't like it. But I wasn't going to hold back any longer. I'd had enough of their bickering and backstabbing. That's not the way I like to operate.

They never had the guts to speak to me directly. I got it all second-hand. They wanted to get rid of me. There's no doubt about it. That's why I resigned. I wasn't going to carry on in that sort of atmosphere. Several papers suggested I was dumped, but that wasn't the case. I formally advised them I would not be standing as All Blacks coach the following year. That's a fact. I voluntarily gave up coaching, but I could never give up my love of the game.

Brian Lochore: That Test in Australia was Fred's last.

Ian Kirkpatrick: I remember him saying, 'I'm getting out of here before they kick me out.' We couldn't believe it.

Chris Laidlaw: Many of the leading All Blacks contemplated retirement after Fred went.

Fred Allen: One of the things I have always cherished is the fact that there wasn't a man in the All Blacks who wanted me to go. When they realised what I intended to do, the entire team presented me with a cup to celebrate our achievements together. That cup is the most precious thing I have.

In Tests and non-Tests, Fred the Needle had guided his teams through thirty-seven matches in eight countries without defeat. His perfect record remains the best in New Zealand rugby history. He was replaced by Ivan Vodanovich, a former prop out of Wanganui on the west coast of North Island. Vodanovich had played three Tests for the All Blacks, but he had more of a name in the world of coaching where, according to Sid Going, he pushed his players until their 'brains were fuzzy'. Vodanovich didn't have Allen's charisma or his off-the-cuff ability to inspire his players with oratory of the first order, but he still had a Rolls-Royce team.

New Zealand rugby was still mourning Allen's loss when, in 1968, the cream of the northern hemisphere ventured south for a three-Test series. France had won the Five Nations championship in 1967 and had taken the Grand Slam in 1968 before heading to Christchurch, Wellington and Auckland to face the All Blacks. This was the France of Pierre Villepreux, Jo Maso, Jean-Pierre Lux, Benoit Dauga and Walter Spanghero. The visitors were gallant, but defeated at every turn. In the first and second Tests they were beaten by Fergie McCormick's boot. In the third Test they lost to two Sid Going tries and four more kicks from the redoubtable Fergie.

Allen may have gone, but the powerhouse he created was still causing destruction, no matter what was put in its way.

CHAPTER THREE

A FAIRLY RUDE AWAKENING

IN THE spring of 1969, Wales took over France's crown as the northern hemisphere's pre-eminent rugby country, winning the Five Nations with three wins, one draw and a whole lot of style. Two new players came into the team that season: a fearless and outrageously talented full-back called JPR Williams and a number eight of world class, Mervyn Davies. They joined a side that already had Gerald Davies in the centre, Barry John at ten, Gareth Edwards at nine and John Taylor at seven.

They put seventeen points on Scotland, twenty-four on Ireland and thirty on England. It was the most points they'd scored against the Scots since 1947, the most points they'd scored against the Irish since 1920 and their biggest victory over England since 1922.

With a team of speed and wit and power, Wales thought they were ready for a step up. In the summer of 1969 they went to the ultimate testing ground to find out precisely how good they were, a place they had never toured as a country before – New Zealand.

Mervyn Davies: The tour schedule alone should have set the alarm bells ringing – flying to the other side of the world with your knees around your neck, turning up in Taranaki at 2 a.m.

Barry John: Whoever organised the itinerary for that tour should have been shot. We took nearly two days to get there. We stopped in every bloody petrol station on the way – Delhi, Singapore, Hong Kong. Fuck me. Everywhere.

Sid Going: They were out of their minds accepting the itinerary. Completely insane.

Mervyn Davies: Five days after our arrival, we played the All Blacks in Christchurch. It was rugby GBH. It was the end of innocence. Stuffed 19–0.

Sid Going: It was the attitude of the Welsh that inspired us. They weren't content just to be Five Nations champions; they arrived in New Zealand like a squad of Muhammad Alis.

Barry John: Rubbish.

Sid Going: They couldn't stop telling us how good they were.

Gareth Edwards: Complete nonsense.

Sid Going: And that sort of thing doesn't impress New Zealanders. It only made us more determined to shut them up.

Ian MacRae: There was a lot of interest in Wales that summer, that's true.

Sid Going: Gareth Edwards came into the series with a big reputation, which made me pretty determined to get one over on him. His mere presence made me go better. That 19–0 was one of the most complete All Blacks performances I was involved in.

Mervyn Davies: I couldn't believe it when I first saw Ian Kirkpatrick; I thought he was a lock forward until he turned away and I saw a number six on his back. They were a magnificent sight.

Gareth Edwards: That All Blacks team was the best side I'd ever played against – Meads, Lochore, Kirkpatrick, Going, McCormick, MacRae, Kirton. Jesus, they were good.

Mervyn Davies: We got our act together in the next two games and put two fine wins on the board against Otago and Wellington. The Wellington match erupted into a brawl, but by then we had been kicked, raked, penalised and beaten into action. There is only so much a team can take, and going toe to toe did wonders for our morale. We genuinely felt we could level the series at Eden Park, Auckland. We lost 33–12. Fergie McCormick set a record of twenty-four points.

Fergie McCormick: One drop goal, three conversions and five penalties.

Barry John: Another kick in the guts.

Sid Going: We beat them even more heavily in the second Test than we did in the first, and Eden Park really belonged to Fergie. The Welsh got pretty upset with the referee, but I thought he was good. The real problem was that they came with a giant reputation and had it smashed to bits.

Brian Lochore: We gave them a real pasting. We overpowered them and it was the forwards' ability to run with the ball that actually blew them away. It was the forwards who did the damage.

Gareth Edwards: On the way home I remember wondering if British and Irish forward play could ever meet the standards being set by the All Blacks. Their speed on the ball made tackling almost a worthless sacrifice. It was a black summer.

JPR Williams: A fairly rude awakening.

Mervyn Davies: A large part of the steel that was so evident in the Wales of the 1970s was fired in the New Zealand tour of 1969. Tours offer priceless insight into the workings of a squad, and as much as the All Blacks played us off the park, a core of younger players were left with the knowledge of what we had to achieve if we were to be regarded as a real force. We learned a lot about the All Blacks, but we learned more about each other as players and men.

Gerald Davies: I had eleven caps in the centre before that tour to New Zealand and it was on plane trip from Christchurch to Auckland that we decided on the move to the wing. Clive Rowlands, our coach, asked if I'd do a shift on the wing because of injuries. 'You don't want to get involved with the heavy mob in midfield anyway, Gerald,' he said. 'We've got to use your genius on the wing.' There was no answer to that. A winger I was and a winger I stayed.

Barry John: If you take the 1968 Lions tour and that 1969 Wales tour into account, I think all the players who were involved with the Lions and with Wales hardened up over the next two years. We improved a lot, individually and collectively, and we had a harder mindset about winning and how to achieve success. And you had guys like Willie John McBride who had been on Lions tours since 1905 or something. He couldn't get enough of those bloody tours. He was around forever.

Willie John McBride: I was one of nine new caps when I made my Ireland debut against England at Twickenham in 1962. Myself, Ray McLoughlin and Mick Hipwell came into the pack on the same day. You have to have a sense of humour to choose nine new caps for any game, let alone when you go to Twickenham. I'd never been to London before. I'd never even been to an international.

Ireland lost an awful lot of matches. We played New Zealand at the end of 1963 and we'd won only one of our previous dozen games. There were a couple of draws in there, but we weren't exactly favourites going in against the All Blacks. Ignorance is a great thing. I knew that the All Blacks had a great name and that they normally won and that, apparently, there was a great aura about them, but I didn't care about that. Aura wasn't a big thing around Moneyglass. I remember I hit Colin Meads that day and put him down and I didn't know who the hell he was. He pushed me out of the first couple of lineouts and I warned him not to do it and then I hit him a belt. Noel Murphy [the Ireland back-row forward] says to me, 'Do you realise who you hit? Meads! We're all dead now.' Five minutes later I got one back from him. That was the end of it.

Mick Hipwell: Mike Gibson came into the Irish team against England at Twickenham in 1964, and from the off he was just one of those players. He had intensity and power and was so influential. He was a marvellous footballer. He was aloof. Very much reserved. A good northern Protestant. We all have our own idiosyncrasies. He kept himself to himself but he was a smashing guy. He'd do anything for anybody that needed it. And on his debut we beat England at Twickenham, which was huge, because we'd almost forgotten how to win.

Mike Gibson: I'd play games on my own where I would just kick with my left foot or just kick with my right foot and develop a strength in each area, and then concentrate on the simple things in rugby – the ability to take a pass and deliver a pass, and then the thinking bit, which is making decisions. If you can go out and make the right decisions throughout a match then your side is likely to be successful. I've always highly regarded the ability to anticipate and to read situations. I often watch players and see them drift around the field and then suddenly the action takes place close to where they are and I smile and think, 'Well done, that was class.'

Ray McLoughlin: I had no dealings with the IRFU until I became captain in 1965 – and then I had a lot of dealings with them. Before I was captain, the team would get together on a Friday, we'd have a team meeting in the Shelbourne at two o'clock and there'd be five selectors and three sub-selectors and everybody would give their opinion. That always extended the time by at least forty-five minutes and so we'd have to rush out to Anglesea Road for a run. Bill Mulcahy was an excellent captain but he wasn't given the tools to work with. We'd have a couple of scrums, a couple of lineouts and then we'd go into the shower and sing 'Ireland Boys Hurrah'. We'd then go back to the hotel and off to the cinema that night. The following morning, we'd get up and there'd be a bunch of drunks there from the night before telling you how to play the match. Ten minutes before kick-off we were brought out onto the pitch for the team photograph. We went out on the field totally under-prepared and the match could be ten minutes old before we adjusted to it.

I went to the chairman of selectors and said, 'If you want me to be captain, I want the following things. I want us to have a room at the Shelbourne on the Thursday night so we can have a meeting. I don't want any selectors or sub-selectors to attend. On the morning of the match, I want us to go to the Marine Hotel in Dún Laoghaire at 10 a.m. I want no selectors, sub-selectors or committee men on the bus with us. Or if they're on the bus, they cannot speak. When we eat, we want to eat alone. We don't want any committee men near us. If they are, they cannot speak. When we leave the Marine and head for Lansdowne Road, we don't want selectors, sub-selectors or committee men with us. If they are, they cannot speak. We go to the ground an hour and a quarter before kick-off. We'll have a photograph when we get there, not ten minutes before we go out to play. That's what I'm looking for.' And the IRFU said, 'Oh, we couldn't have that. The things you want to get rid of are all part of the international game.' I said, 'Okay, get another captain.'

The chairman was a very courteous man. He was just saying it the way he saw it. This created a bit of a crisis. Charlie Harte was the president of the IRFU that year. Charlie was a good man. He came to me to discuss it and I said, 'Charlie, this thing is a farce. This is it, take it or leave it. If you want me as captain, it has to happen this way.' So Charlie went away and delivered the whole lot. He got it all done.

My style of captaincy wasn't every player's cup of tea. I considered it really important to focus on the game and imagine the things that might happen. Visualisation, I suppose. I wanted the players to concentrate on the match and think of situations that might arise and imagine how they would react. I wanted them to stop going to the cinema the night before and instead to think about what we would have to do in the match. Not going to the cinema probably upset some people.

Willie John McBride, Mike Gibson and Ray McLoughlin were hard-bitten veterans. McBride had been an international player for seven years and had been on three Lions tours by the end of the 1960s. His record could not exactly be described as stellar. He'd appeared in two Tests in South Africa in 1962, three in New Zealand in 1966 and four in South Africa in 1968 and he'd yet to experience the sensation of winning – losing eight and drawing one.

Gibson, as good a centre as there was in world rugby, was in his pomp for Ireland, but his Lions record had a McBridesque bent – seven losses and one draw from his eight Tests. McLoughlin, the prop, former captain and rugby visionary, had played one Lions Test against New Zealand in 1966 and, of course, he had lost. John Pullin, the England hooker, was another who had been routed in South Africa in 1968. John Dawes, the Welsh centre, hadn't yet become a Lion, but he was another experienced operator and an accomplished leader who was helping to spark a revolution at his club, London Welsh.

Other players were emerging: Sandy Carmichael, Ian McLauchlan and Gordon Brown out of Scotland; Fergus Slattery and Sean Lynch out of Ireland; and David Duckham and John Spencer out of England.

Ian McLauchlan: I was capped first in 1969. You never know how you are going to cope with becoming an international player until you've lived through it. I've seen people freeze up, I've seen others who couldn't stop talking as they tried to overcome their nerves, but for me the feeling was of complete exhilaration. I couldn't wait to get into the dressing room and get my hands on the blue jersey, and when we got in there I grabbed it off the peg and pulled it down over my shoulders as quickly as possible, just in case the selectors changed their minds. I was twenty-six years old and had waited all my life for that moment.

David Duckham: I was always pretty emotional about playing for England and although, in all honesty, our national anthem is not the most inspiring piece of music, every time I hear it I immediately find myself back at Lansdowne Road in 1969 when I made my debut against Ireland. A big part of it for me was living the dream and connecting with my hopes and inspirations as a youngster.

Sandy Carmichael: In September 1969, Scotland toured Argentina. Being in Argentina was the closest I've ever been to a war.

Mick Hipwell: We were there a year later with Ireland. It was a lovely country but we weren't aware of what was really going on in Buenos Aires at the time. We hadn't a notion that all these political activists were disappearing. They were throwing the bodies of the protestors into the fucking Atlantic.

Sandy Carmichael: Things were crazy out on the streets – and pretty crazy out on the field as well. One game had to be postponed for two days due to snipers, which was a first. The Argentines had a guy called Raul Loyola who was basically the contract man. Their team would point to you and he'd come in for a whack.

Ian McLauchlan: That tour to Argentina was absolutely brutal. But the thing I liked about the Argentineans was that you could hit them as hard as you liked and they would never bother. They would dish it out, but they'd take it as well – and they'd never complain because as far as they were concerned it was all part of the game. For a lot of guys on that tour, they went out as boys and came back as men. When the Pumas came out the tunnel for that first match you would have thought someone had tied a bit of elastic to their backs and then let it go. They came out of the tunnel with their legs and arms pumping and their eyes bulging. Our guys weren't small, but these guys were built like brick shithouses. The Argentinean guy I was playing against was an Olympic rower, a strong, strong boy. And there was a bit of jiggery-pokery going on early doors, so I smacked the hooker then turned to him and said, 'You're next.' This guy spoke pretty good English, and he said, 'No, no, I don't play like that.' I said, 'Great. I do.'

Gordon Brown: I made my debut against the Springboks on 6 December 1969. The dressing-room atmosphere was very emotional. When I pulled the Scotland jersey over my head I caught a glimpse of myself in the far corner mirror. I was nearly in tears. When I took up position to field the kick-off, I could hardly see it because of the tears in my eyes, such was the emotion of the moment. I caught the ball and the whole Springbok pack caught me – and the emotion evaporated.

Fergus Slattery: I made my debut against the Springboks when they came to Dublin a few weeks later, in January 1970. There were protestors everywhere, all of them saying we shouldn't be playing South Africa. I can't really say what I'd like to say about that match. Most Irish people hadn't a clue about South Africa or apartheid. I met an eminent surgeon around that time and he had a couple of jars on board and he was giving it to me big time about playing against South Africa. 'You fuckers are a disgrace, shame on you!' Next time I saw him was in a bar in Cape Town on a rugby tour. The hypocrisy of it.

The 1970 Five Nations was shared between Wales and France, and the feeling in northern hemisphere rugby was that the nucleus of a fine Lions team was emerging. There was the brilliance of Williams, Gerald Davies, John, Edwards, Gibson and Duckham, the leadership of McBride, McLoughlin, Dawes and Pullin. There was Mervyn Davies and Gordon Brown, Ian McLauchlan and John Taylor. There was hope, but it was tempered by realism. If they were going anywhere else on earth bar New Zealand in 1971 they would have been considered a shoo-in for victory. New Zealand was different. They all knew that. What they didn't know was that, coming up to the summer of 1970, New Zealand was changing. In the post-Fred Allen era, all was far from well.

CHAPTER FOUR

THAT WAS THE END OF ERNEST GRUNDELINGH

NEW ZEALAND first tried to win a Test series in South Africa in 1928, drawing 2–2, then tried again in 1949, losing 4–0, and again in 1960, losing 2–1. In the summer of 1970 they had another go and this time, from Whangarei to the north, Invercargill to the south, Gisborne to the east and Te Anua to the west, their supporters felt that a moment of history was about to arrive.

The Springbok team was a severely wounded beast. From December 1969 through to January 1970 they'd been coursed around Britain and Ireland, off the field and on. The apartheid regime brought out the protestors from all corners. Everywhere the South Africans went they were reminded, sometimes viciously, how unwelcome they were and how despised their political system was.

In London, the mayhem reached its zenith when an activist hijacked the Springboks' team bus with half the squad on board, speeding away from their Park Lane hotel and only coming to a halt after crashing into a row of cars near Green Park underground station – one of the players had grabbed him by the neck in an attempt to wrestle him out of the driver's seat.

The rugby was a calamity, too. South Africa lost to Oxford University early in the tour, then lost again to Newport – the first time they'd been beaten by Welsh opposition since 1912. A week later they lost to another Welsh side, Gwent in Ebbw Vale, and only escaped from a game in Belfast against Ulster with a 0–0 draw.

They played four Tests and didn't win any of them, going down 6–3 to Scotland and 11–8 to England before drawing with Ireland and Wales. This was New Zealand's chance. Behind the scenes, the All Blacks had issues with their new coach, Ivan Vodanovich, but a series win in South Africa would blow those concerns to kingdom come.

Ignoring all the protests in New Zealand about touring South Africa, they travelled. From the third week of June through to mid September, they went in pursuit of greatness. And with them they had a nineteen-year-old winger of Samoan descent who was threatening to shake up the world – Bryan 'Beegee' Williams.

Williams' heritage was something of a melting pot – his maternal grandfather was South African, an agricultural official who had been on his way to work in the Bahamas when he diverted to New Zealand and ended up marrying Beegee's Samoan grandmother. This diverse genetic composition produced an astonishingly gifted athlete, with the kind of muscle-bound thighs that had rarely been seen before in the game. He had it all – speed, strength, balance, sidestep, strong defence and great handling skills – and looked, to the outside world, like an ace being added to an already unstoppable team.

Bryan Williams: I first played at Eden Park when I was ten years old. It was a curtain-raiser, and Colin Meads and some of the

All Black greats of the 1960s were playing in the big game, and when they walked out onto the field in front of me I remember being so overawed by the whole experience. Nine years later I'm playing in a Test match with him. When I first made the team I was absolutely terrified of all of them. Was I going to call them Mr Meads and Mr Lochore? That's how I felt. Imagine trying to come into a team like that. The All Blacks of the 1960s were my heroes. Even now, whenever I'm in Pinetree's presence I still feel overawed. I don't say that lightly. I'm sixty-six years old and even when I meet him now I still get goosebumps and don't know what to say.

Sid Going: It was some baptism for Beegee. We flew into East London and Ivan wanted to get rid of jet lag so he decided to beast us.

Ian Kirkpatrick: Guys were falling over.

Sid Going: We went round and round the field for an hour in searing heat – jogging, sprinting, jogging, sprinting. My feet were numb, my mouth went white and dry. I had to undo my boots to get circulation into my feet.

Ian Kirkpatrick: He was running us up sand dunes, carrying guys like Jazz Muller on your back. Jazz Muller is a big unit to be carrying up a sand dune.

Bryan Williams: That was my first experience of the All Black environment. I'd never played under Fred Allen, so I didn't really know what it had been like before. All I was worried about was proving that I was good enough to be there.

Brian Lochore: Good enough to be there? Bloody hell, I'd never seen anything like him before.

Bryan Williams: I was only there because the apartheid government in South Africa had made me an 'honorary white'. New Zealand toured South Africa in 1960 and had I been around back then I wouldn't have been allowed into the country. They relaxed their warped system in 1970 and made me an 'honorary white' so I was deemed acceptable. I was allowed in. It was complete bloody nonsense. I wasn't an 'honorary white'. I was who I was.

South Africa needed the All Blacks to tour, but the All Blacks needed Williams to tour with them, so this 'honorary white' title was hit upon. It meant he could travel and so could Sid Going, a Maori, whose ancestry would also have precluded him from playing for New Zealand in South Africa had he been on the scene the last time the All Blacks went there in 1960.

The compromise was deemed outrageous by black South Africa. They didn't want Williams or Going in their country. They wanted them to stand up to the concept of 'honorary whites' and shine a light on the sickness of apartheid. The players were, according to a leading activist of the time, 'hated and despised for selfishly looking at their aspirations whilst trampling on those of black South Africans'.

Bryan Williams: I suffered a panic attack when the plane touched down. Suddenly, it all hit me and I just thought, 'I can't go through with this, I don't want to get off the plane.' I just sat there, shitting myself. I took it one step after another and suddenly an hour has gone by, then a day and suddenly you are pulling on a jersey and getting ready to play.

Ian MacRae: We roomed together a lot and I thought he was so relaxed. He would sit around playing his guitar. He seemed to just take everything in his stride.

Brian Lochore: I can't think of a game on that tour where Bryan Williams wasn't absolute perfection. Some of the tries he scored, and the breaks he made, were superb. It was just a shame that the rest of us struggled to emulate that kind of form.

Everything began well enough. En route to South Africa, the All Blacks stopped off in Perth for two warm-up games, and put fifty points apiece on the unfortunate locals that were thrown at them like fresh meat to hungry wolves.

Their early performances in South Africa were of a high order as well. They beat Boland 28–3 in their opener and then pulverised a combined provincial team, Paul Roos XV, 43–9. 'Bryan Williams,' wrote the local press, 'always ran with bursting vitality, breaking many tackles with a great flick of his powerful hips while also having the feet to deceive on his way to scoring two tries.'

Colin Meads: Brian Lochore broke his thumb in Perth and I took over as captain for the second game and the other side were so mad they went away to a camp for a fortnight before. No papers, not a bloody thing were they allowed to see about the All Blacks. They probably didn't even know how we got on against Boland in our first game. I went out to toss the coin and I've never forgotten the guy's name – Toy Dannhauser. I went to shake hands but he wouldn't. He was frothing at the mouth. I'm marking this bastard Dannhauser in the lineout. Keith Murdoch was playing for us. I said to Murdoch, 'I could have a bit of a problem with this fella. I might need you to help me out'. Then I said, 'Don't do anything until I tell you, I'll try him out first.'

We'd been going about quarter of an hour when all of a sudden Murdoch hits him. I said, 'I told you not to do anything until I said so,' and he said, 'I couldn't be bothered waiting.' He set the seal. In South Africa, word goes through the system very quickly. They were coming for us after that.

Ian Kirkpatrick: We were probably conned a bit by Danie Craven [legendary South African player, coach and administrator]. He spoke after a few of the games as the chairman of the South African Rugby Union and was really talking us up and saying we were the greatest team he had ever seen. We didn't want to believe that, but when you keep hearing it and the scores are indicating it . . . We just needed someone to call us back into line and say, 'Listen, you show ponies, it's not all about running around scoring tries.' I know exactly what Fred would have done – he would have told us we would get a fright when we came to the first Test.

In their third game they put up another big score against Griqualand West in Kimberley. 'Colin Meads has become indefinable,' it was reported. 'He is emphatically the greatest forward in world rugby.'

The game was a prelude to the violence that would follow later in the tour, with Ron Urlich, the New Zealand hooker, having to leave the field after getting his ear damn near shoed off at a ruck. Then there was mayhem on the full-time whistle.

Not all black South Africans resented Williams' presence in their country. Far from it. When Williams started to run amok and make the locals look inferior, the black South Africans in the crowd basked in his glory – or in the humiliation of the hosts, more to the point. After that game in Kimberley, a jubilant black fan ran onto the pitch and tried to chair Williams off. He was then clubbed to the ground by a white police officer and kicked repeatedly by a white supporter who had appeared on the scene, full of hate. Another coloured fan weighed in and attacked the white man. It set off a chain reaction of racial rioting.

In the midst of all of this, the godfather of South African rugby, Danie Craven, sent out a message of hope that one of the provincial sides would be strong enough to soften up the All Blacks before the first Test in Pretoria. In game six, the bruisers of Eastern Transvaal stepped up to the plate, 'like gladiators intent on the kill', as the local paper in Springs put it.

The match started with an all-out brawl, then Alan Smith, the New Zealand second row, was knocked unconscious and Meads had his arm broken. Only six minutes had been played.

Colin Meads: I went to the sideline and the doc looked at it and said, 'I think you've just pinched a nerve.' I wasn't going off for a bloody pinched nerve. So I carried on playing.

Earle Kirton: He played seventy-four minutes with a broken arm. What a beast he was.

Pinetree refused to be felled and the All Blacks delivered another beating, despite Eastern Transvaal putting twelve New Zealanders out of the tour for a week or more. As one report put it, 'They climbed into the All Blacks like they were hooked on some sort of drug which turned them into fighting dervishes insensitive to hurt.'

The All Blacks carried onwards to Johannesburg to play Transvaal at Ellis Park. Again, the atmosphere was extraordinarily hostile. The non-playing members of the squad had to sit on an embankment near the southern touchline and were within easy range of the home support, who promptly pelted them with oranges.

Even without Meads, the All Blacks were immense, scoring four tries in the opening twenty-two minutes. Fergie McCormick got twenty-two points, and Bryan Williams scored yet another try in a 34–17 win.

Bryan Williams: We had a lot of players at the peak of their game. The forwards were laying down a good platform, the grounds were hard and fast and I knew I could run and I knew I could step and with the opportunities I was getting I was able to pull out the bag of tricks. I felt really confident going into the Test series.

Williams was hardly alone. New Zealand had won ten from ten on tour and were on a Test-match run of seventeen wins from seventeen going back five years. Even without the great Meads they had hardly missed a beat. The South African writer Chris Greyvenstein put it well when he spoke of the All Blacks' 'aura of almost mystical invincibility'.

Colin Meads: I warned them. Because my arm was broken and I couldn't play, Vodanovich sent me to have a look at the Springbok trial up in Rhodesia. When I went back, I don't think the players believed me when I told them to look out. I said the South Africans were going to hit them with everything going. They were fired up by the apartheid thing. The opposition to it was getting stronger and they were thinking that if they didn't win they might never play again. They were driven by fear.

Bryan Williams: Then, *wham*! Along came the Springboks with the kind of intensity I'd never experienced before.

Ian MacRae: The ferociousness they came at us with in the Test was incredible. I'd never experienced the sort of fervour they had or the speed they had. Their forwards were tearing around like mad things.

Early in that first Test in Pretoria, the Springbok lock, Frik du Preez, hit All Blacks scrum-half Chris Laidlaw with a tackle that was a borderline assault. Laidlaw was concussed, but stayed on the pitch for forty-two minutes. The Springboks' opening try was a consequence of Laidlaw's confused state.

The All Blacks were rattled. Soon after, another howitzer tackle landed with the subtlety of a dump truck. Joachim Scholtz Jansen, a big hitting Free State centre who went by the name of Joggie, levelled the All Blacks fly-half, Wayne Cottrell, with one of the most exquisitely timed and venomously effective tackles the game has ever seen.

Jansen tackled Cottrell into a semi-conscious state, the play carrying on furiously around him on the floor. This was the way of it for the day. New Zealand tried to play fifteen-man rugby and South Africa bludgeoned them at every turn.

Not even Beegee's brilliance could turn things around. He scored another try – of course he did. Pure artistry, the South Africans called it. He sped down the left touchline and went in and out of three defenders with such pace that they fell over each other trying to stop him. They literally sat on the ground staring at each other as he motored away to score.

It wasn't enough. Finally, New Zealand had been toppled.

Fergie McCormick: After the first Test, we had a bit of a drinking session, and the following day we really paid for it. It started at Kruger Park. We went out into a sun as hot as fifty thousand bastards and Ivan put us through a run. Our manager, Ron Burk, had ripped into us for hitting the grog too much and it was maybe his call that we were put through the hoops. Or it might have been an overreaction to the Test loss. But my God, we hadn't lost the Test because we weren't fit or because we were slopping with beer. We'd lost it because the Springboks had out-thought us, planned more intelligently than us and then outplayed us. At Kruger, we deserved a couple of days of relaxation. What happened was unwarranted. It was brutal. It was insane. The players would have appreciated the opportunity to mull over tactics with Ivan and Ron, but there was none of that. The relationship between the management and the players took a sharp downturn.

Bryan Williams: It would be fair to say Ivan wasn't a great coach, but he was a very nice person, a very caring sort of guy who wanted the best for the team – but he'd been thrown in at the deep end as well, because once Fred Allen retired, I don't think the New Zealand Rugby Union had much of a succession plan in place. He was just kind of dropped into the head-coach role because he'd been one of the selectors and had been around the team. One of the things he struggled with most was getting his message across. When it came to explaining exactly what he wanted, he would struggle.

In the days leading up to the second Test in Cape Town, Winston McCarthy, a New Zealand rugby commentator, wrote a column about things he was supposedly hearing coming from inside the All Blacks camp. He wrote that there was player dissatisfaction with Vodanovich, a claim that the captain, Brian Lochore, thunderously denied.

The All Blacks made five changes for the second Test. Into the team for his debut came an enforcer from Canterbury, an openside flanker by the name of Alex Wyllie – or Grizz, for short. New Zealand's game plan was obvious. They weren't going to be bullied like they were before; they weren't going to stand around waiting for South Africa to set the agenda. They were going to get there first. And Grizz was just the man to help them do it.

The Test was so furious that it was said that some spectators in the pavilion were upset at what they saw. It wasn't long before Piston van Wyk, the Springbok hooker, was being escorted off the pitch with blood streaming down his face. Later, little Fergie McCormick thumped the Springbok wing, Syd Nomis, and knocked him out.

Fergie claimed he didn't mean to smash his arm into Nomis' mouth, but that's what happened. When Syd woke up, he was helped to his feet by referee Wynand Malan and promptly spat a couple of teeth into his hand.

With three minutes left, McCormick had a penalty to put New Zealand into a 9–8 lead. It was written by the famous Kiwi journalist Terry McLean that just as McCormick lashed over his kick, a watching Afrikaner, an old man by the name of Ernest Grundelingh, dropped dead with a heart attack.

The series was level at 1–1 and New Zealand were unapologetic about the ferocity they'd brought to the table. 'They asked for it,' one of them said of the Springboks. A cartoon in a Cape Town newspaper the following morning had an image of a man reading a newspaper to his wife, the caption saying, 'The All Blacks lead by 16 stitches to 6 in the second Test'.

Ian MacRae: There was a lot of blood and guts involved in getting the win. The dressing shed was like an ambulance ward afterwards.

Colin Meads: I eventually had a guard fitted to my arm that I could take on and off and meant that I could play with it on. It wasn't ideal, but it was good enough. I had to get the thing checked by what seemed like every referee and official in South Africa to make sure they didn't think I could use the bloody thing as a weapon, but it eventually got the okay and I was able to play in the third and fourth Tests. Looking back, you have to wonder whether it was the right decision.

Sid Going: At the time, the players wanted him to play, but he didn't play well after his return. And who could blame him? It became a psychological thing with us and the opposition.

Fergie McCormick was a major part of the narrative leading up to the third Test in Port Elizabeth. The Nomis incident was not forgiven nor forgotten. He was public enemy number one. While having a quiet drink in a hotel bar one day, he was taunted by an Afrikaner. Fergie ignored him. Then the barman joined in. Fergie ignored him, too.

He got up to leave and another loudmouth appeared. He caught up with Fergie alongside the water fountain in the hotel lobby. After a few more verbals from the South African, Fergie shoved him in the drink – and walked away.

Between the second and third Tests, New Zealand played five more provincial games and won all five, easily. Before one of them, McCormick was informed by an opposition forward that he was a marked man and would be leaving the pitch on a stretcher for what he did to poor Syd.

He got abusive phone calls and telegrams and words of warning from a hotel receptionist in Port Elizabeth that the Springboks were going to get him. She wasn't wrong. Within minutes of the kick-off, Syd Nomis directed an up-and-under right down Fergie's throat. When he took the catch, the three Horsemen of the Apocalypse descended upon him. In that moment, Jan Ellis, Piet Greyling and Hannes Marais were a human combine harvester, chewing up Fergie and spitting him out of the other side of a ruck. 'They cleaned me up,' he said, later. 'That's all there is to it.'

South Africa won that third Test 14–3. They'd win the fourth Test as well, a 20–17 victory in Johannesburg, where rumours of discontent about Vodanovich cranked up another notch. There was an incident in Potchefstroom that caused rancour in the camp. Grizz Wyllie and his Canterbury mate, the prop Alister

Hopkinson, pulled a prank on Vodanovich that cost them their place in the Test side.

The players were standing at the bottom of the hotel stairs having a chat when Vodanovich came rushing through, heading for the revolving doors. For reasons known only to himself, Grizz stuck out a leg and tripped him, and Vodanovich ended up in a heap on the floor.

The coach said that, by way of punishment, no Canterbury player would be selected for the fourth Test. Everybody presumed that Vodanovich was joking, but he was serious. Wyllie and Hopkinson were dropped, as was their Canterbury mate, Fergie McCormick. It caused a rift, and that rift needed to be healed.

Earle Kirton: We'd have won that series if Fred had still been head coach – and that's no disrespect to Ivan. He was a passionate rugby man, a good and wonderful friend, but we needed the Needle.

Brian Lochore: We failed in what was the most fiercely burning ambition of my time – to beat South Africa in a series in South Africa. I experienced such a deep depression at the end of the tour. I came home and I didn't have the enthusiasm for another four Tests against the Lions in 1971. I was walking around in the paddock one day and I just decided I was retiring. I went home and told my wife Pam.

Ian MacRae: At the end of the tour I retired. I had a mortgage and needed to work. I was also frustrated with the injuries. I'd had my share of pulled muscles and felt it was time to look after my family.

Chris Laidlaw: That was the end of the road for me, too – and for a few of the other boys. Bill Davis, Bruce McLeod, Malcolm

Dick, Earle Kirton, guys like that, they never played another Test. It was a hard way to go out, but we'd given it a good crack. I don't think any of us had it in us to hang in there for another year to take on the Lions.

The playing records of the departing heroes were extraordinary. Bill Davis had won all eleven of his Tests matches for the All Blacks, Dick had won eleven out of fifteen, Kirton twelve out of thirteen, MacRae fourteen out of seventeen, Laidlaw seventeen out of twenty, Lochore nineteen out of twenty-four and McLeod twenty-one out of twenty-four. They were going to take some amount of replacing.

Bryan Williams: I went from being an absolute novice in 1970 to being one of the more experienced players in the squad. I was just twenty. And the next time I put on an All Blacks jumper, it wasn't the South Africans I was looking at any more, it was the Lions.

CHAPTER FIVE

A THINKING MAN'S GAME

THE HISTORY of the Lions had been full of men who were promoted above their station – players, coaches and managers. Politics reigned, deals were done and so often the decisions were wrong. While the selectors should have been in the business of picking the best people for the job, self-interest got in the way and the Lions suffered as a consequence.

It was John Tallent's job to make sure that petty parochialism didn't get in the way of the expedition to New Zealand. Tallent had been an England centre back in the day, a pre-war player whose international career amounted to five caps – and four defeats – but whose real mark on the game came in administration. In the summer of 1970, he was chairman of the Home Unions selection committee. That meant the task of appointing a coach and a manager for the Lions tour in 1971 was down to him and one man apiece from Ireland, England, Scotland and Wales. If there was stalemate, Tallent had the casting vote. He had power, but he also had strength.

He knew his history. He knew that between the first tour to New Zealand in 1904 and the most recent in 1966, the Lions had played twenty Test matches on Kiwi terrain and had won just two of them, with two more ending in a draw. For the Lions to have any chance of turning around sixty years of failure, Tallent knew that he couldn't afford to make bad appointments.

The job of Lions manager went to Aberdonian doctor Doug Smith, a former Scotland winger and a Lion in New Zealand in 1950. Smith was a gregarious sort, a bundle of charisma and wisdom – the perfect profile for a tour of this magnitude.

There was agreement on the coach, too. Carywn James might have been a god in his own backyard in west Wales, but he was hardly a rugby figure of international renown. He'd never been a Lion, and had never toured with Wales. Because of the emergence of the great Cliff Morgan, he'd only ever played twice for his country, and both of those games were in Cardiff. But just because he hadn't seen the rugby world didn't mean he was without a world view. There was something about Carwyn that appealed. He had a capacity to bring his skills as a teacher to the rugby field. As coach of Llanelli, he banged home the mantra of not just winning but winning with style. As an inquisitive and cultured man, he moved effortlessly between the worlds of arts and politics. It was said that he spoke with lyrical brilliance about everything from Beethoven to Barry John, from Samuel Beckett to Phil Bennett. Amongst the committee, there was no doubt that he was the man most capable of combining the best of four countries into one concerted unit while also giving freedom to the individual brilliance at his disposal. There was a problem, though. As much as Tallent and the boys wanted to make Carwyn the coach of the 1971 Lions, they were concerned about one of his other pursuits – politics.

Carwyn was a passionate believer in Welsh independence. He had appeared at demonstrations while a student, he opposed the official investiture of Charles, Prince of Wales, at Caernarfon and there is evidence that Special Branch were keeping an eye on his activities. Years later, he would turn down an OBE. At the time of his hat being in the ring to coach the Lions, he was simultaneously running for political office. He was a Plaid Cymru candidate in the Llanelli constituency in the 1970 general election, with a polling day of 18 June.

Llanelli had been staunchly Labour since the early 1920s, hoovering up around seventy per cent of the vote with the Conservatives usually in second place. And it was expected to stay that way, despite Carwyn's popularity. The committee weren't sure what to make of all of this, though. A fortnight before the election they asked to meet Carwyn at the East India Club in London.

Carwyn James: I made two points to the committee when they asked about my political ambitions. The first was that I was competing with all my might to win the seat, even though the Labour majority was well over 20,000 and even though the odds quoted in the current issue of the *Llanelli Star* for Plaid Cymru were 10,000–1 against me. So I offered to take a pound from each of the committee back home with me so that they could all make a quick £10,000. No offers were forthcoming.

Labour won Llanelli, but it was a measure of the respect that Carwyn was afforded there that he polled nearly seventeen per cent of the vote, the highest in Plaid Cymru's history in the constituency. He lost, but he won. There was now no barrier to him becoming the coach of the 1971 Lions.

Carwyn James: The first thing I felt when I was named coach was a feeling of humility. I'd not been good enough as a player to represent the Lions and to find myself in the position of coaching the side was something that I looked forward to enormously. I spent weekends with Doug Smith at his home in Essex. We were able to discuss previous Lions tours. We talked about the All Blacks in depth. I watched as much film of the All Blacks as I could, so that I was able to come to certain conclusions about their patterns of play. We picked the brains of everyone who knew something about the New Zealanders. We invited John Dawes to talk us through his thoughts. We talked to Don Rutherford [the RFU technical adviser and national coaching organiser] and Ray Williams [his Welsh counterpart] and we had papers from other people. Any ideas that I had about New Zealand scrummaging, about New Zealand lineout play, about every last detail, all needed confirmation from other people who thought in depth about the game.

Doug Smith: Carwyn and I must have travelled about 12,000 miles each in the build-up, going to games, getting to know the contenders. We knew what we wanted.

Wales were kings of Europe again in 1971, winning their first Grand Slam in nineteen years in a season of undiluted genius. They began with a 22–6 victory over England in Cardiff, their second biggest win against the English since 1951. Gerald Davies scored two tries, and there was one for a debutant on the other wing, a lethal finisher by the name of John Bevan.

Next, Wales went to Murrayfield, and what took place there has gone down in legend. The lead changed hands seven times during the course of the game. JPR set up John Taylor for one try and Gareth went down the short side of a ruck for another. Scotland responded through Sandy Carmichael. Wales came back through Barry John. Scotland went again with Chris Rea.

With a few minutes remaining, Scotland led 18–14. They had a lineout deep in their own half, and Delme Thomas, the

Welsh second row, stole it. This was Wales at their glorious best. Needing to conjure up a converted try to win the match, they put the ball through the hands with pace and accuracy: Gareth to Barry to Dawes to JPR to Gerald, who sped around the outside of the Scottish defence to touch down in the corner. It was his third try in two games.

Wales needed the conversion to win. John Taylor, the openside flanker – or 'that ratbag Taylor' as Ian McLauchlan, Scotland's loosehead prop, soon christened him – lined it up from wide on the right-hand side and 105,000 people fell silent. Taylor calmly stepped towards the ball and belted it between the sticks for a 19–18 victory.

Nineteen points was the most Wales had managed in Edinburgh since 1947.

The Triple Crown was secured with yet more brilliance against Ireland, Gerald once again scoring twice with Gareth adding two more of his own in a 23–9 rout. Wales hadn't handed such a beating to the Irish since 1955.

The Grand Slam was won with their first win in Paris since 1957, Gareth and Barry getting the history-making scores in a 9–5 win. All in all, Wales had scored thirteen tries in their four games. Only one Five Nations side in the previous forty years had outscored them, and that was Wales, too – the 1969 vintage.

Carwyn and Doug now set about putting together the pieces of the jigsaw. There was a push from Ireland for the great Mike Gibson to be named captain, but as much as they rated Gibson, they had only one man in mind for the leadership role, the man who had played a seismic part in transforming his club, London Welsh, from a side of disparate exiles into one of European club rugby's powerhouses, a man who had now steered Wales to their greatest achievement in twenty years: Sydney John Dawes, known to his teammates as Syd.

Dawes became the first Welshman to captain the Lions. His key philosophy was the importance of the counter-attack and having fifteen ball players in his team. Carwyn and Doug knew that that was exactly the way they wanted to take on New Zealand.

John Dawes: Carwyn promised that he would ring me with the decision as to whether or not I'd be captain. I must have had two thousand phone calls that day. By midnight I was a nervous wreck. Then the phone went again. It was Doug, with some good news.

Carwyn James: The first thing I looked for in a midfield player is a person who can take and give a ball quickly in one movement. The classic example was John Dawes.

Willie John McBride: He was the most underrated player of my era.

Mervyn Davies: Syd was the single biggest influence on my career. He was my mentor and one of my dearest friends. As a centre, he never had the explosive thrust of a Ray Gravell or the all-round ball skills of a Mike Gibson, but he had the sweetest pass I have ever seen on a rugby pitch. What he lacked in pace or niftiness he compensated for with sublime timing and quickness of mind. It was amazing how Syd's hands responded to his rugby brain. He played the game with lots of guile and no panic. His philosophy was simple: move the ball, move the ball, move the ball.

Dawes was the first piece of the puzzle, but there was still work to do. At that time, the potential tourists had to make themselves available for selection and there were some notable stars of the

Five Nations Championship who were unsure whether they wanted to go on the trek – among them, Barry John and Willie John McBride.

Barry John: To be honest, I wasn't going to go to New Zealand at all. We'd won the Grand Slam but I'd been knocked out when scoring against Scotland and then I broke my nose against the French, which was put back in place on the touchline. The concussion from Murrayfield stayed with me for a long time afterwards. I was working for Midland Bank, going out on the road and meeting people. For weeks after Scotland, I was having to pull in at a lay-by for twenty minutes' kip. I knew the concussion was bad. I was really feeling it. I thought I needed the summer off to recover.

Carwyn rang me a few times, but I avoided speaking to him. In the end, he came out to see me. He spoke to my wife and asked how I was and she said she wasn't sure. He told me how much he wanted me to be part of the tour and then left me to think about it. So my wife and I had a long chat and she said, 'Look, I think you should go. If you don't, it's going to be three months of misery with you sitting here and wanting to be out there.' So I rang Carwyn. 'Okay, count me in.' If it had been anybody else but Carwyn, I wouldn't have gone.

Willie John McBride: I remember Carwyn came and talked to me because I wasn't going to go in 1971. I'd been on three Lions tours and I was working in the bank and they'd been very good to me. I'd made up my mind not to travel to New Zealand. I hadn't formally announced it, but I'd let it be known that I wasn't going to be available.

And then Carwyn phoned me and asked if we could have lunch. And I remember going along and thinking, 'Why is he having lunch with me?' After a while he said, 'Look, you've been around a long time and I want to talk to you. You've played against these guys in the Five Nations. Who are the forwards that you think we should be taking to New Zealand?' And I thought, 'Well, this is a new angle. Selectors never normally talk to me about things like this. They always just do their own thing.' I thought it was just brilliant, because as a player there are so many things that you see on the field that the average punter doesn't see.

Just little things – but important things. Guys like Mervyn Davies who are invaluable on the ground, who never lose the ball, who do the small stuff that make the big things happen. So I thought this was all great and then at the end of the meal he said, 'Have I heard a rumour that you're not available?' So I told him that I had to give my career a bit more attention. Carwyn took a big draw of his cigarette, blew the smoke up in the air and looked at me and said, 'But Willie John, I need you.' And do you know, no one had ever said that to me before. He said, 'I understand your disappointments about your previous tours – but I can assure you, this one will be different.'

After that I looked at him for a moment. Then I said, 'All right, then. I'll go.'

Carwyn, Doug and their selectors went through their player options with military precision. They had thirty names to find – sixteen forwards and fourteen backs – and they began at full-back. They picked two: Bob Hiller, the prolific goal-kicker from England and a Lion in South Africa in 1968, and the runaway favourite for the Test spot, the twenty-two-year-old medical student from Wales, JPR Williams.

JPR Williams: Unlike a lot of the guys in the Welsh team at the time, I came from a middle-class family, but I think that made me that much more determined to prove myself, to prove that I wasn't the boy with the silver spoon in his mouth. I think that's why I became so brave on the field.

If I got the ball, I wanted to attack, I wanted to run. Kicking was always a last resort for me. I was really a flanker playing full-back. I didn't like to kick the ball and I'm very glad I wasn't given much talent as a kicker because it meant I had to run.

Barry John: JPR was a great tackler, he was solid under the high ball, he made devastating bursts into the line and he had great pace, strength and positional sense. Knowing that JPR was behind me gave me the freedom to express myself on the field, because if I made a mistake I knew he would be there to cover. He was one of the toughest competitors I've ever come across, a maniac when it came to putting his body on the line. He'd do anything to win.

Four wings were picked: Gerald Davies of Wales, who was now on a golden run of six tries in his previous five Tests; David Duckham, the sidestepper from England; Alastair Biggar, the powerful runner from Scotland; and John Bevan, the twenty-year-old who had only just broken into the Welsh team and whose international record was the stuff of dreams – played four, won four.

They went with five centres – the big two being the captain, Dawes, and Mike Gibson of Ulster, a veteran of thirty-five Tests for Ireland and eight for the Lions.

Gareth Edwards: Mike Gibson was magnificent. He was an independent soul and tended to do his own thing, but what stood out was the preparation he would put in before a game. He worked so hard. When we got out on the field, his vision was astonishing, and he could sum up situations in an instant and react accordingly. He could tackle like a demon. His basic skills were immaculate.

As back-up in the midfield there was the England captain, John Spencer, and Dawes' midfield partner in the Grand Slam team, Arthur Lewis, who, like Bevan, had the perfect record as a Wales player – four Tests, four wins. Chris Wardlow of England was the fifth pick, but he fractured his jaw before the tour and Chris Rea, scorer of two tries for Scotland in the 1971 Five Nations, went instead of him.

At half-back, things were very straightforward. Barry John was the pre-eminent ten (with Gibson capable of filling in at fly-half as well as centre) and at scrum-half there was nobody to challenge Gareth Edwards. His Welsh back-up, Ray 'Chico' Hopkins, was also selected, even though he had only one cap to his name. The way Carwyn saw it, having a guy as great as Gareth as your competition, Chico had to be one of the unluckiest scrum-halves in the history of the game.

Four props were chosen: the diminutive Ian McLauchlan and the wily Sandy Carmichael from Scotland, along with Sean Lynch, the robust Irishman with just four caps under his belt, and his vastly experienced countryman, Ray McLoughlin, a former Ireland captain and a man so wise in the ways of front-row play that he wasn't just a player, he was a de facto coach, too.

John Dawes: Ray McLoughlin had the answer to every problem a pack meets on a rugby field. Ray was a great 'probability man'. To him, rugby was like a game of chess, and Ray had to work out all the options in any particular situation and then explain them to whoever was listening. When he roomed with Barry John, Barry would say that he used to go to sleep with Ray still going on and on about the game.

Ian McLauchlan: I was probably the opposite of Ray. I didn't have much of a clue about what the Lions were and I never expected to tour. On the night we played France in January 1971,

I'd gone to a restaurant with some teammates, and Norman Mair, the rugby correspondent of the *Scotsman*, was also there. Norman brought along a friend of his, a little Welshman who didn't say much and never stopped smoking. We pretty much ignored him. Eventually, I asked Norman, 'Who the hell is this pal of yours?' It was Carwyn James. After Scotland's last match of the season, a letter dropped through the letter box and it contained a tour contract. I had to promise not to write a book on the tour within the next two years, give an undertaking that I would return straight home if injured, and there were details about the supply of clothing and kit. It must have taken me five seconds to sign it. My second son was a week old when I left. Eileen has always said, 'If you get an opportunity, take it.' Even when they said they weren't going to pay me, she said, 'Ach, well, I'll just get a job.' We sold the car. I said to the bank to leave the mortgage until I got back, and we just made it happen. The bank manager said he would keep the family in funds. I picked up £150 in cash to top up my 75p-a-day expenses while on tour. I was all set.

The hookers were West Country farmer John Pullin, a hugely experienced player who had started three Tests on the previous Lions tour in South Africa, and thirty-year-old Frank Laidlaw, former captain of Scotland and a Lion in New Zealand in 1966. Behind them in the second row were more gnarled operators. Willie John was in there again after his chat with Carwyn, and so was Gordon Brown, the charismatic twenty-three-year-old from Ayrshire.

Gordon Brown: I was going away on my first-ever Lions tour. My mum packed five suitcases – I had more vests than the whole team put together. Willie John was going on his fourth Lions tour and he had one wee sports grip. He was sitting on his bed in his pyjamas, smoking his pipe, and I was in awe of him. I was trying like hell to think of something to say. Eventually the big man put me out of my misery. 'Broonie, do you fucking snore?' Now, seemingly I'm a very bad snorer, but I told him no, absolutely not. And just to make sure I didn't, I sat up all night and read a book.

The Welsh Grand Slam locks completed the group: Delme Thomas, who played for the Lions in New Zealand in 1966 before he had ever worn the red of Wales, and his junior partner, Colwyn Bay's Mike Roberts, a former football trialist with Everton who'd burst onto the rugby scene in 1971 with impeccable timing. Roberts had won every Test match he'd played in.

The back-row slots went to Ireland's Mick Hipwell and Fergus Slattery and Wales' Mervyn Davies and John Taylor. The tour bolters were both in the back row – the uncapped pair of Llanelli's Derek Quinnell, an emerging star that Carwyn would have known all about, and Oxford University and Harlequins flanker Peter Dixon, a rangy and relentless back row, but still a choice from beyond left field.

Peter Dixon: It was extraordinary. I hadn't been expecting anything like that at all. Someone stopped me in the quad at Oxford and said, 'Do you know you've been selected for the Lions?' I think I'd just been coming back from a tutorial or something. And I remember saying, 'I don't believe it. That cannot be.' But it was. I was twenty-seven.

I recall that John Reason [rugby correspondent of the *Telegraph*] had written that I was the sort of rugged, New Zealand-style forward the Lions ought to look at. I wasn't even in the frame for England at the time. I'd been through a couple of years of attending trials and getting a few letters from the

RFU saying, 'Can you be a non-travelling reserve?' but they'd all dried up by 1971. Then out of the blue I got the call-up for the Lions. The RFU made sure I didn't go away uncapped by calling me up to play against the President's XV before the Lions met in Eastbourne. They rushed me into the team, feeling a little embarrassed that the Lions had picked me before they had.

Thirteen players from Wales, six from England, six from Ireland and five from Scotland. The 1971 Lions collected their kit in London and headed immediately for Eastbourne, for training, bonding, plotting.

Doug Smith: You have to get the right spirit. I went on about determination, dedication and discipline. The first day together I stepped out of the lift and saw four Welshmen with Prince of Wales feathers on their chests. I told them I'd give them two minutes to put on the Lion pin badge instead and when they came back and went to sit together I split them up among players of other nationalities.

Gareth Edwards: There was negativity from the media. They were trying to find a chink in the armour. 'There are too many Welsh in there. Carwyn James as the coach, will he favour these Welsh guys?' And he was also involved in politics with Plaid Cymru. He was an academic and a scholar and spoke Russian, which was interesting in itself at the time. He had strong views about the Welsh language and politics, so he was a target for the news guys. And I remember thinking at the time, 'How's he going to deal with all of this?'

We went down to Eastbourne and he had a chat with us all and said, 'Look, boys, let's establish a couple of things here. I don't want cliques.' The 1966 Lions tour to New Zealand had a lot of problems with cliques apparently. He said, 'When people come down to breakfast, we don't look to sit with guys from our own country, we sit down with whoever is there.' That was basic team-spirit stuff, but Carwyn also went a little bit further, because he didn't want us to lose our national identities altogether. It's a fine line and he took it head on.

He said, 'Now, look, I've known Barry all my life, we're from the same village. And Gareth doesn't live too far away from me either. There's a lot being said about us Welsh boys and there being too many of us. It should be the most natural thing in the world for me to come down and say good morning to them in Welsh, it's just the natural welcome that we would have for each other. It's our mother tongue, but that will be the end of it. We won't be talking Welsh among the rest of you.'

The songs and the sessions started early on. The songs would be from all over the place – Irish songs, Scottish songs and if we sang any songs in Welsh the boys soon learned all the words. Mike Gibson could sing 'Sospan Fach' as well as I could by the middle of the tour. Everyone enjoyed each other's cultural background. We didn't try to banish our backgrounds in order to become a united group; we became a united group because we embraced the diversity of where we came from and who we were. And that was very much thanks to Carwyn.

Carwyn James: I told the Irish I wanted them to remain Irish, the Welsh to stay Welsh, the Scots to be Scots, and the English to be English. By their very nationality, each had something special to contribute. My own political philosophy is very simple: I believe that one must initially be passionately interested in one's own nation's destiny. This then allows one to feel intensely for the destiny of other nations. I have too much interest in the individual, whatever his nationality, to allow any form of prejudice to cloud the common good.

David Duckham: We came together and gelled very quickly. The comfort of knowing that you were surrounded by sheer class – it lifted me enormously and psychologically brought out the best in me. And it didn't matter that they were mostly Welsh. As soon as we got together we were Lions.

Gordon Brown: I still felt so young and inexperienced. We had a mock game of rugby league in London and I remember shouting to Gerald Davies for a pass – and I got it. I felt so chuffed that Gerald hadn't ignored me, that he had actually been happy enough to give me the ball. A simple thing like that worked wonders for my confidence.

JPR Williams: Carwyn was an amazing man – always dapper, thoughtful, intelligent, charismatic. He always seemed to have a cigarette in his mouth and almost as often a gin and tonic in his hand.

Barry John: The boys used to say that Carwyn was sponsored by Gordon's gin and Player's fags.

JPR Williams: He struggled terribly all his life with severe eczema. His body was covered in blotches and sores and his hands were always very rough. He'd absentmindedly scratch his hands when he was lost in thought, but otherwise you'd have never have known how much it was bothering him. He never made himself the centre of attention or anything like that – it was all about the players, all about the game.

Ray McLoughlin: He never ranted or raved, never banged his head off a wall before a game. He was a lecturer and he had a compelling style of speaking, which everyone listened to. The key thing was that he knew what he knew and he knew what he didn't know, so when it came to the forwards he really left it to Willie John and myself.

Barry John: Carwyn was a complex man. He'd survive on about four or five hours' sleep.

Willie John McBride: No sleep, but he was a great man for vision. 'What did you see? What was in your mind there?'

JPR Williams: He spent hours analysing the All Blacks – watching what little footage he could get a hold of and also poring over newspaper reports at South Africa House in London to try and glean all he could from the Springboks' series win over them in 1970.

Willie John McBride: Carwyn told us, 'The All Blacks are a difficult team to beat because teams that play against them panic when they get the ball and kick it back to them – so there's no point having it in the first place. And by doing that, they put even more pressure on themselves because they have to defend again.' That made perfect sense to us. He said, 'We're not going to kick the ball to them. We're going to run at them.' Everybody loved the sound of that.

JPR Williams: It was the London Welsh philosophy. London Welsh made up the core of the Wales side and Wales made up the core of the Lions squad, so we felt that the same philosophy could work there, too – counter-attacking and handling. We started off at training with the simple rule that a passed ball can cover the ground faster than the quickest runner. So we'd start off with guys racing against the ball as it was passed down the line – and at first the runners were beating the passes. But pretty soon after that, as we got used to playing with each other more and more, the passes were beating the runners and shortly after that the runners couldn't even get near the ball, it was going down the line so fast and so perfectly.

Delme Thomas: I was one of Carwyn's players at Llanelli. It was during his time that I first sat down to watch films of other teams playing. We'd watch these games and Carwyn would stop the film now and again to highlight a point of weakness in our opposition.

Gareth Edwards: It was funny – when we left Eastbourne, there was absolutely no expectation on us to win the series.

Mervyn Davies: Some people laughed at us for even daring to dream. The last Lions team that went to New Zealand had been massacred.

Willie John McBride: I always had faith. I looked at the backline and thought, 'If you can't win with that lot then you're not going to win anything. Surely to God we can get eight forwards who can get them the bloody ball.'

Mike Gibson: Carwyn made us work hard and he made us train hard but he always gave us a ball to play with, and the more we played with the ball the more it became an extension of our arms. With that confidence, we were free to express our ability, free to handle the ball from our own line, free to attack from any situation on the field. He would follow behind us, harassing us, shouting, 'Think! Think! Think!'

Ian McLauchlan: We concentrated a lot on scrummaging because we felt that we could get the upper hand on the All Blacks there. We concentrated on going down together as an eight and being settled immediately to eliminate any swinging of the scrum. We repeatedly had really long and solid sessions because we found that even on tour it was surprising how quickly the co-ordination and the timing could be lost.

Peter Dixon: Willie John and Ray said it would be tough in New Zealand, so in training they deliberately had people standing on your feet and holding you down at the lineout, which Colin Meads had been doing for years with impunity. Willie John would turn and say, 'Right, we've done a few lineouts here and it's going well, but you lot in opposition are letting us win the ball. So we're going to play it for real now. This is the kind of stuff we're going to come up against, so we're going to re-enact all that for real now.' And it would start with an elbow in the ribs, then knocking you out of the lineout, holding you down, standing on your feet, the whole lot. There would be three or four minutes of mayhem and anything went. And there was no referee to say, 'That's it, settle down now.' But everyone got the message that these had to be pretty robust training sessions without actually doing any real damage.

Ray McLoughlin: My view was that the one area where we could really get to them up front was to have a stronger scrum. Everyone would know, going to a scrum or lineout, what the signal was, and we would be poised and ready. We wanted our set piece to be slick and quick. Everything had to be efficient.

Mervyn Davies: We were the first breed of professionals with a small 'p' to come out of the United Kingdom and Ireland. We didn't consider the Lions tour to be a bit of a jolly.

Fergus Slattery: We'd been together for a week, training, and that was the first time that I'd met – or even seen – Carwyn. We had a team meeting the night before we left England and his talk was really simple, a two-minute address, no pounding of the desk or anything like that. At the end he just said, 'The tour starts now,' and he put his glass down with a *thunk* and the doors opened and we were gone.

CHAPTER SIX

DES CONNOR WAS A NUTTER

THE LIONS flew out of Heathrow on Friday, 7 May. They had a four-hour delay at Frankfurt, a stop to refuel in Tehran and then three more hours on the tarmac in Delhi. From there, they headed onwards to Hong Kong, caught a bus to Kowloon and a ferry across the bay to the Hilton Hotel. They were weary, but the night was young. Doug Smith told them they could do as they pleased. Three players went to bed; the rest went out on the lash, journalists in tow.

Ray McLoughlin: One of the players these days scratches his backside outside a hotel and it's all over the internet in seconds. In our day there was none of that; the press travelled with you.

Fergus Slattery: The tactic on the stopover in Hong Kong was to entertain the media lavishly. As long as you had more on them than they had on you, the rest of the tour could go with a swing.

Hong Kong was the venue for the mother and father of all

drinking sessions, an epic booze-up that saw the Lions board their flight to Brisbane the next day in a fragile state. They would play two warm-up games in Australia before kicking on for the big stuff in New Zealand, the first of them against Queensland at Ballymore. Queensland had nine current or recent Wallabies internationals in their starting line-up, but that wasn't saying a whole lot. The Wallabies weren't very good. They'd lost their previous seven Tests and thirteen of their previous fourteen, going back four and a half years. This was supposed to a relatively soft run-out, a confidence-boosting victory against a proud but limited side. Carwyn picked his team – and watched them lose 15–11.

John Spencer: We flew cattle class from Hong Kong to Brisbane and no one had got the right amount of sleep. We arrived in Brisbane and got dropped off outside the hotel and we couldn't get in. It was seven o'clock in the morning and there was nobody there. I just sat on the pavement with my bags, desperate to get inside and get some sleep. We played Queensland the next day, a two-thirty kick-off. We were shattered.

Willie John McBride: I was on the field. I wouldn't say I was playing, but I was on the field. With all the travel, we were so tired. All I wanted to do at half-time was lie down.

Gordon Brown: I wanted to lie down and die.

Gareth Edwards: We had no idea what time, day or place it was.

Jeff McLean: I was pulling beers in my dad's pub on the morning of the game. Then I got my gear together and went off to play on the wing for Queensland. There was a huge traffic jam on the way to the ground and the coppers stopped us at the gate at Ballymore. They weren't going to let our car in. Jules Guerassimoff, who was on the bench, leaned out the window and said to the policeman, 'Have you ever seen this many people riot?' The copper looked confused and said, 'No.' 'Well you will if you don't let us in – we're the players.' It's always nice when you get recognised before one of the biggest games of your life.

Lloyd Graham: I played full-back and I kicked a field goal near the touchline, just inside the Lions half. It's become a local legend, that one. It's got longer and longer by the telling, until after a while, if you'd asked someone, they'd probably have said I'd kicked it from over the creek in Finsbury Park.

Barry Honan: I was working as a teacher at Marist College at the time and they gave me the day off for the game, which was decent of them – I was captain. I was back at work the next day and a few weeks later I got a bill from the Queensland Rugby Union for three jerseys I'd swapped with the Lions.

John Taylor: We were given a toy lion by a well-wisher before leaving the UK and were instructed to give it to the first provincial side that beat us. The last words were, 'I hope you bring him home with you.' He never even made it to New Zealand.

Mick Hipwell: The lion was shoved in the corner of the clubhouse that night and no one gave a shit about it. The feeling in Brisbane was that we were just another Lions team that was going to get beaten by everyone.

John Taylor: The previous two Lions tours were fairly disastrous and the worst fears the public had for us seemed justified when Queensland beat us.

Gordon Brown: Afterwards, Doug and Carwyn did their best to try and cheer us up, but no matter what they tried – and I appreciated their efforts – I was miserable. The Aussie players didn't really help matters, to be honest. One of the Queenslanders, a prop called Dave Dunworth from the Brothers Club, had a real gloat in the clubhouse afterwards. 'Last year we kicked shit out of Scotland and you guys did nothing about it,' he said. 'We did the same today and you guys just lay down without a fight again.' I wish we'd played them again on the way home.

JPR Williams: It was a blessing in disguise. We were underrated after that, but within the party we knew we had one of the best back divisions of all time. Everybody thought we were the 1966 Lions all over again, but we knew we were nothing like them.

John Taylor: The following morning, we flew down to Sydney for the second game against New South Wales. I met Craig Ferguson, who was going to be refereeing our game and had refereed the match between Wales and Australia in Sydney in 1969. He sidled up to me all cheery and said, 'Good to see ya, John. We going to have our usual slanging match on Saturday?' 'Oh, very probably,' I said.

Barry John: New South Wales had just returned from New Zealand after a five-match tour and their manager on that tour was Craig Ferguson. Their manager was the bloody ref. At one stage he went up to Gareth and said, 'Edwards, come here, it's our ball.'

Carwyn picked his strongest team, and as the heavens opened and the pitch cut up, the Lions sneaked home in the mud, 14–12. It was another deeply flawed performance, a game that would have done nothing to strike any kind of concern into the heart of the Kiwis.

Barry John: How we managed to scramble home, I'll never know. The rain was incredible. Ours was the only match played in Sydney that day. The New South Wales rugby union hadn't insured the game because they didn't have enough money, so they had to play it. They couldn't afford to pay the punters back for their tickets otherwise.

Des Connor was the Queensland coach. He was also coach of Australia. In truth, Des Connor was a lot of things. As an international scrum-half, he had won twelve caps for Australia between 1958–59 and then emigrated to New Zealand where he won another twelve caps with the All Blacks from 1961–64. Connor played on the same team as Colin Meads. He might have later returned to the land of his birth, but he still had New Zealand very close to his heart.

By 1971 he had become one of the southern hemisphere's most respected coaches. He was not impressed by the Lions in Australia and let them have it with both barrels between the eyes. 'These Lions are hopeless; undoubtedly the worst team ever to come here,' he said.

Barry John: Des Connor was a nutter.

Gareth Edwards: We were written off before we'd even set foot in New Zealand.

David Duckham: I roomed with Mike Gibson for both matches in Australia and got on well with him. He didn't say a great deal. He was intense. You could see his legal background in the precise manner in which he always spoke. I tried to pick his brains about his experiences in New Zealand with the 1966 Lions and he was fascinating. The guys who had been there in 1966 – Mike, Willie John, Ray, Delme, Frank – they all knew what was coming our way.

Fergus Slattery: Mike was like Carwyn in many ways – very, very private. Did a lot of things on his own, not a big drinker.

Mike Gibson: I'd have a lemonade and lime. I didn't want to drink. I just didn't have any tolerance for it. I didn't want to do anything that would prejudice my game.

John Spencer: Not many people have a bad word to say about Mike Gibson, but I'm going to confess that he pissed me off. He managed to get himself onto the team selection committee and he realised very quickly that he was never going to oust Barry from the number-ten jersey, so he chose himself at centre for the Saturday side and worked on his relationship with Barry and Syd. With Syd guaranteed a starting place, that meant that all the other centres, including me, were scraping around for game time in the Tuesday and Wednesday team and were often having to play out of position. People look back now and say what a genius Mike was in the centre on that tour, and he was brilliant, but any of the other centres could have done just as well with guys like Gareth and Barry and Gerald and JPR around them. I don't want to sound sour about it, but that's what happened.

Fergus Slattery: Mike's always been a very serious guy, very private, but there's no bad side to Mike Gibson. He'd annoy you now and again because he's so fucking serious, but there's no bad in him at all, and he was just the most phenomenal player. He had great pace and was a great tackler and he knew how to position himself around the field. He was a top-class player and he had a super tour. He had a super scrum-half, a super fly-half and had these lightning-quick players outside him. John Dawes was the only player that I'd call average. That's not trying to do him down; it was more that in that backline, everyone else was a fucking superstar.

CHAPTER SEVEN

HE SQUIRMED AND WRIGGLED – COULDN'T TAKE IT ANYMORE

IVAN VODANOVICH met the Lions off the plane in Auckland and went with them to their hotel, the Intercontinental, the largest in the city. There was a reception for the arriving tourists. Doug Smith flabbergasted everyone when he predicted that the Lions would win the Test series 2–1 with one game drawn. Chris Rea said that you could hear the laughter coming all the way up from Invercargill. The local media asked Colin Meads for a response. 'The Lions are cocky,' he said, sternly.

Carwyn admitted to feeling on edge now that the boys had landed in New Zealand. The first game was days away, against a combined Counties-Thames Valley side. There was talk of disaffection in the ranks of their opponents, some chatter about the make-up of the side heavily favouring Counties over Thames Valley. Carwyn didn't much like the sound of that. He thought that any rancour would harden into united ferocity before kick-off. 'Some people are telling us that that this will be an easy game,' he said. 'But it is, for us, a moment of truth.'

Carwyn James: As soon as we arrived, we could feel the difference. We knew we were in a rugby country now.

Ian McLauchlan: I went for a walk the night we arrived and at the first corner was a travel agent with two huge windows and both were filled with profiles of the Lions – photos, ages, who you played for, everything. Two blocks further along the road it was the same again. That was a culture shock.

JPR Williams: Our training sessions were always of a high standard. If you made a mistake you had to do a few laps of shame. Lynchy had to do quite a lot of them. Everything was focused on accuracy and quality and no drill was ever the same. Keeping it inventive was one of Carwyn's great triumphs.

Defence sessions were also pretty full-blooded, and when we ran semi-opposed at the end of each training session there were usually one or two minor casualties. But it's what we needed to do to prepare for what was coming our way.

Sandy Carmichael: JPR would often take part in the forwards training to try and toughen up his body. The way he came flying into those practice rucks was terrifying for everyone.

JPR Williams: Carwyn eventually banned me from Monday training because I was injuring too many of our own players. I used to do a lot of scrummaging against the front row.

John Spencer: He was a bloody maniac. None of the Welsh lads liked to train; they'd always have bad hamstrings and have to excuse themselves – especially Barry. But JPR was different, he loved it. He was a lunatic out there.

Willie John McBride: I'd enough experience of playing New

Zealand teams to know the sort of tricks they got up to at lineouts and around the ruck, so we would always include shirt-pulling, holding back or holding down in all our practice sessions. It sometimes ended in bloodied noses, rolled ankles, the odd clash of head and so on, but it was invaluable.

Barry John: I was sharing a room with John Pullin on the first floor at the Intercontinental. We'd been out to train and it had been an awful day, so when we got back to the hotel I still felt grotty. That evening we were due to go to the High Commissioner's to be formally welcomed to New Zealand and I said to Pull, 'Look, I'm just going to go up to the room to have another shower, I still don't feel that clean.' So he headed off to the bar in the reception and I went up for a second shower. I was in the bathroom, having a wash and singing a song or two when I heard the door to our room open and someone came in who I assumed was Pull coming to get something. Eventually I got out the shower and came through and I remember thinking almost straightaway, 'Something's not right here.' Then Pull walked in and I realised what had happened. And I said, 'Pull, I've got some good and bad news. The good news is that I'm alive and well and was singing very nicely just now. The bad news is that we have fuck-all stuff left.' Whoever had broken in had taken my watch, and to this day I've never replaced it. My wife had given me a nice one which had an inscription on it and it was gone; Pull's camera was gone; all our valuables – gone. And after that we made sure we stayed higher than the first floor – the logic being that we would have more time to catch the bastard if someone tried the same thing again.

The host stadium for the first match was in the Auckland suburbs of Pukekohe, a newly built arena with a capacity of 40,000 in a town where the population was only 6,000. The Lions won 25–3,

Gareth, John Taylor and John Spencer getting the tries and Barry kicking the rest. It was a solid beginning, but not one that had the locals reaching for the panic button. The *Dominion* reported, 'The flaws were many and instead of winning by twenty-two points the Lions should have won by forty-two.' Barry John, they reported, was 'guilty of too much individualism'.

Barry John: I scored three penalties, a drop goal and two conversions, but I was pretty disappointed with my own performance. My balance wasn't what it should've been. The boys took the piss and said that my new gumshield was too heavy and was making me fall over.

Gareth Edwards: It was a bit of a tough one for some players. John Spencer hit a strange crossroads. He was forced to play on the wing and missed three or four try-scoring opportunities. We'd worked about five overlaps in the match but John had only made it to the line once.

The press slated him. I've seen great players injured on Lions tours, or out of form and left out of Test teams, and they've been dragged down by it. They've been miserable and spread that misery through the rest of the team. But not John Spencer. He laughed and joked even though his heart must have been bleeding.

John Spencer: It was difficult because I'd only played two or three games on the wing in my life and one of those was in the last minute of the Varsity Match, so I was very inexperienced, and they're very different positions to play. But I mucked in; I was captain of England and I was only twenty-three, so I said, 'Of course, I'll play wherever I'm picked.' I just wanted to get a game. And so I was picked on the wing and Carwyn wasn't always happy with my wing play but I'd say to him, 'Look, don't have a go at me, I'm doing you a favour here by playing out of position.'

Peter Dixon: Having the skipper in the centre, it's hard for the others selected as centres. And you think of Spencer and Duckham, who went out there as a centre pairing and they never played in the centre there together or again when they came back. They were both used on the wing. And they very bravely didn't turn their back and say, 'Sod it, I'm not up for this.' They put in the graft to help the team – and there's a lot of graft you have to put in on a tour like that, especially when you're a second-string guy having to run opposition lines in training for weeks on end.

John Spencer: I realised very soon after we arrived in New Zealand, and I was playing on the wing and only getting to play centre when Arthur Lewis and Chris Rea were at stand-off, that my chips were cooked as far as a Test place was concerned. But I thought the best thing I could do was get on with it, not whinge, and put my heart and soul into the Tuesday and Wednesday side and try to work through the disappointment. And that's exactly what I did. I did a fair bit of practical joking and tried my best to lift people's spirits when they were down. I just said to myself, 'You're captain of your national side, you've got to contribute positively to this.' I took a few others with me – Alastair Biggar, Bob Hiller, Frank Laidlaw. I said, 'Well, lads, it looks like we're going to be mid-weekers for the majority of this tour, so we need to help and support the other guys and make sure they win the Tests. We're Lions – we're not second-tier Lions.'

Mick Hipwell: The management set the system for each training day early on in the tour – you got up, you had your breakfast, you went down and got on the bus at nine o'clock. Carwyn and Doug met the press at twenty to nine and did a press conference with them. We all got on the bus and went to the ground and the condition was – and we were told from the start – that training in the morning was mandatory and if there was any messing or anything that we were unsatisfied with, when we got on the bus after training the names would be given and you'd be back in the afternoon for special training.

After the game in Pukekohe, some of the lads met a sea captain in Auckland and they ended up having a great time with him. He persuaded them to go and see his ship and they got back about half eight, quarter to nine in the morning, just in time for the bus. They were in a pretty bad way. Luckily I hadn't been with them, so I was fine. Training was a big laugh with these guys and we got on the bus at around half eleven, twelve, and Carwyn came on and pointed to the lads who'd been on the piss and said, 'You're back on this bus at quarter past two.' And we're all like, 'Oh dear . . .'

So the boys trained for the rest of the afternoon. They got back in at half five, drenched in sweat, totally fucked, and they went to bed and we didn't see them until the next morning. You knew where you were with Carwyn. If you fucked up or didn't train well, then he'd have you back in the afternoon – and that was it. We all understood that.

But it wasn't just about getting beasted in training; we always worked on skills. We used to do drills in the twenty-five and you had to manipulate the ball back and forward down the line before you got to the try line. And if you got the speed of the ball down the line the way he wanted, you'd then jog. But if you dropped a ball or got it wrong, you were off sprinting up and down the pitch. And in doing that he built up everyone's skill for putting the ball across the body without checking. If you dropped a ball, you paid for it, but it eventually got so good that we were able to do those drills at sprint level and the passing would be perfect. And all the players bought into it. He also hated it if you kicked the ball away – he'd climb into you if you did that, he hated the idea of giving away possession needlessly. He would do all sorts of different drills so that we learned to play and pass under pressure, and it was one of the reasons why our counter-attack got so good.

The tour party headed south to Wanganui – Colin Meads territory. At Spriggens Park, they would play another combined side – Wanganui-King Country – in what was considered a significant step up from Pukekohe. The Lions had been there before. There was a historical backdrop – some ghosts, if you will. In 1966, the Lions had come to Spriggens Park in a demoralised state. Mike Gibson was in that party. So were Frank Laidlaw, Willie John McBride, Ray McLoughlin and Delme Thomas. They'd already lost to Southland, Otago, Wellington and New Zealand twice by the time they fetched up in Wanganui and they lost there, too. It was a debacle and right at the heart of it was Pinetree.

Round here – round most places – Meads was God. He had a dark side to his game but that only added to his legend as far as his people were concerned. There was the Ken Catchpole incident in 1962, when he dragged the great Wallabies scrum-half out of a ruck by one leg and tore his groin muscles so severely that it ended his career. There was the sending off in 1967 at Murrayfield when he kicked fly-half David Chisholm. There was the time, in 1969, when he smacked Welsh hooker Jeff Young and broke his jaw after Young had the temerity to grab hold of Pinetree's shirt at a lineout.

Mervyn Davies: He epitomised the natural strength and hardness that New Zealanders like to identify with. We were in his domain now.

Ian McLauchlan: When we played King Country, I started in the front row with John Pullin and Sean Lynch. Before the game, people said Lynchy and I would be massacred. I was against a giant eighteen-stone prop who had been converted from the second row.

In the first scrum, he was launched into cloud nine like a cork out of a bottle. From then on he squirmed and wriggled and couldn't take it any more. When he dropped his hand, getting ready to punch me, I said, 'Don't even think about it, pal, or I'll put you in hospital.' In any rugby, if somebody hits you then you have to hit them back. It doesn't matter when and how you do it, but you've got to make them understand that you're not a soft mark. If you don't then they'll do it again and again and then somebody else will do it and you'll become a bloody punchbag. I came from a background where the punchbag was always on the other side. The New Zealanders believed that the Lions in previous times were all about fair play – but after that, Colin Meads said, 'These Lions don't believe in fairy tales.'

Two tries from young John Bevan and another from Mervyn Davies saw the Lions home 22–9. There wasn't a single thing Colin Meads could do about it.

The game was just a few minutes old when Meads was crunched in a tackle by Mervyn Davies and took a blow to his sternum that left him gasping for air. He played on. Later, it turned out that Meads had suffered torn cartilage of his lower rib. Somehow, he lasted the eighty minutes, but he was a diminished soul. When questioned afterwards, the thirty-five-year-old was sanguine. 'I'm just an old man trying to play rugby,' he said.

David Duckham: I'd had half my ear ripped off. I ended up in casualty, sitting next to Meads. We swapped a few words and he told me not to worry about my ear. He seemed to think it was pretty trivial. Maybe to him. I think he knew that night, though, that New Zealand were in for quite a challenge from us.

Ian McLauchlan: We were in the pub after the match having a private party. Sandy Carmichael and Dave Duckham are on the door trying to keep the gatecrashers out and they're taking some stick from the locals. 'Pommy bastards!' they're shouting. Colin Meads was with us after his trip to the hospital and he overheard what was going on. Pinetree goes to the door and looks down at the local guys, then says, 'These people are friends of mine. If you abuse them I'll take it as a personal insult . . . and you know what that means.' You've never seen a crowd disperse so quickly in your life.

The Lions kicked on for Hamilton, to play Waikato. Twenty-six thousand people squeezed into Rugby Park and watched the tourists run amok. Barry John controlled the match from start to finish, running, stepping, bamboozling. They began at such an electrifying pace that the veteran New Zealand broadcaster, Bob Irvine, told his listeners that they looked like scoring a century before lunch.

Seven tries were scored – a hat trick for the unstoppable Bevan and one each for John Dawes, Derek Quinnell, Ray McLoughlin and Barry John. In their report of what went on, the New Zealand *Sunday Times* saluted the Lions, but there was almost a desperate tone to some of what was written. They said that complacency might be their enemy. They banged on about Waikato's full-back, Butch Pickrang, and a penalty he had missed to make it 11–11 in the opening half.

Poor Butch got it in the neck for allowing the Lions off the hook. 'It appeared that if the Lions ever had to face a pressure that was more sustained than this they could crumble.' What the reporter saw, few others saw. The tourists had won 35–14. It was the most points the Lions had scored in a provincial match or a Test in New Zealand since 1959, a run of twenty-eight games.

Gareth Edwards: What I remember most from that match was the sheer science of Ray McLoughlin's scrummaging. He handled his opposite number as if he was an inanimate object to be shifted up and down like he was on a car jack. Ray just slotted the poor man into whatever cog he wanted – you could almost hear the ratchet clicking through the guy's vertebrae.

Ian McLauchlan: He told me afterwards, 'You won't believe it, but I had to hold the guy down just to have something to push against.' It showed that the New Zealanders, who had never really bothered too much about scrummaging techniques, had a weakness which we could exploit. But it looked as if it would be Ray and not me who'd be doing the exploiting in the Test matches.

Ray McLoughlin: Chico Hopkins was hilarious. He came up with a nickname for me that stuck for the entire tour –Wilder. There was a TV series at the time called the 'The Power Game'. There was this character called Wilder who was very authoritative. So there were times when there were team meetings when I would have my say about various things and there was one day when Chico stood up and said, 'Look, he's just like Wilder.' I don't know what it was that reminded him of the character, but from then on I was called Wilder.

Carwyn James was delighted with the bottom line in Hamilton but he knew the intensity had to increase. 'We're still in third gear,' he said, as the tour headed back to Auckland. Third gear wouldn't be good enough against their next opponent at Eden Park – the Maori. There was rancour in the air around the Maori and Carwyn didn't like it. For two years and more, the standard of their play had been poor and their results lamentable. It was said that Maori rugby as a concept was now on trial.

The team could have done without the intervention of one of their own – Manahi Nitama Paewai, sometimes known as Doc

Paewai, a nephew of Lui Paewai, a Maori member of the great 1924 All Blacks otherwise known as the Invincibles. The Doc had been a player, too, with Otago, New Zealand Universities, New Zealand Army, a few games for Auckland, a lot more games for Wellington and some more games for the Maori. As an administrator, he spent time on the Maori Advisory Board of the New Zealand Rugby Football Union, but come 1971 the Doc wondered about the future of his old team.

Just weeks before Carwyn's Lions turned up, Paewai called for the phasing out of Maori rugby at international level. It caused a storm of protest and the Lions coach knew that a backlash was inevitable. He looked at their team, led by Sid Going of North Auckland, and was sure of two things – their quality and their commitment. Such was their will to prove people wrong and ensure their survival, an Auckland paper advised the Lions that their tour was about to go to a fairly dark place. A crowd of 48,000 turned up to see a battle – and a battle they got.

CHAPTER EIGHT

ATHLETIC PARK – MINDBOGGLING

IF THE Lions were under any illusions about how fired up the Maori were, they were disabused pretty quickly. Only a few minutes had been played when the violence began; Sean Lynch was thumped in the face by Val Baker, a second-row bruiser out of Taranaki. Lynch left the field bloodied and dazed.

The Maori were not just playing a game of rugby, they were playing for their forefathers. After all the talk of shutting them down, and the Doc's remarkable and unwelcome contribution, their motivation was never as strong as it was that day in Eden Park, and at their helm was the epitome of Maori rugby – Waka Nathan.

Waka had been a flanker in Fred Allen's All Blacks. He'd played fourteen Tests and had won thirteen of them and drawn the other. Including non-Test touring matches, he had worn the black jersey thirty-seven times and only ever lost once. Somehow, from the blindside of the scrum, he had also managed to score twenty-three tries.

Willie John and Mike Gibson and the other survivors of the 1966 Lions knew all about Waka. He was one of the main reasons why the Lions had gone down in flames on that tour.

His playing days were over, but his coaching days had just begun. Waka was big on psychology, heaping praise on the Lions' shoulders before the game. 'No bullshit,' he told the journalist John Reason, 'this is the best touring team I have seen in this country. They could go through this country unbeaten. I would give anything to be able to play against them.'

That was the challenge laid down to his own players, who he then went to work on. He reminded them of the history of the team, that they were the original All Blacks, that they had first worn the black jersey, they had first worn the silver fern, that it was the Maori who first did the haka. As the New Zealand Natives, they played against Ireland in Dublin in 1888 – and won. The All Blacks weren't even a thing in 1888. The Maori didn't come together often, but throughout their history they'd been a force to be reckoned with.

Not lately, though. Two defeats to Tonga in 1969 and another to Fiji in 1970 had sparked the debate about their relevance and their future. Some thought they were an outdated concept, a team that needed putting out to pasture. The Lions walked straight into that. Lynch's battered face and a split mouth that needed fourteen stitches were the manifestation of Maori thunder.

Gordon Brown: Baker broke his wrist when he hit Lynchy. They both went to hospital in the same ambulance.

Barry John: Breaking the boy's wrist with his lip. Fair play.

Sean Lynch: You win a few, you lose a few.

Ian McLauchlan: They were fairly worked up, those lads.

Gordon Brown: It was an eighty-minute brawl.

Ian McLauchlan: Supposedly they'd been drinking brandy beforehand.

Barry John: One of the joys of Lions touring was that each player was adopted by a school, and the school that adopted me was Auckland Grammar. When you were in town you went along and said a few words at assembly. You spoke to the kids, got to know them a little bit. The Maori game was on a Wednesday and I wasn't playing, and I was glad because it was pissing down, so I went to the school and I was halfway through my speech when I got a tap on my shoulder to say that Syd had hurt himself and I was playing. I finished up by telling the kids that I was looking forward to facing the Maori because they played it hard and fair, the way rugby should be played. I was wrong. It was the second most dangerous game of the tour.

I was on the pitch, soaking wet, and I looked over to the touchline and saw the Auckland Grammar school uniforms and I remember thinking, 'Christ, two hours ago I was telling those kids nice things about the Maoris, and now these lunatics are trying to take my fucking head off.'

Mike Roberts: I was in the second row with Gordon Brown that day and after Lynchy went off I had to go and play tighthead. I saw Ken Going, their centre, giving John Spencer a smack in the mouth at one stage. Everyone saw it apart from the referee. Maybe he was a slow blinker. A couple of minutes later, John came flying into Going, late as you like, and completely flattened him. A beauty.

John Spencer: Ken came at me with a short arm and I had about eight stitches in my face around my lips. I went off to get stitched up and he probably thought he had done the business, but I came back on and absolutely floored him. It was what we used to call a stand-up crash tackle and I smashed him. The referee then had a word with us and said, 'Any more of that and you're both off.' But it was really just a way of saying, 'You're not going to do this to us, we're not going to run backwards, we're not going to disappear.'

Gordon Brown: We won 23–12 thanks to another try from John Bevan and the brilliance of Barry's boot. A conversion and six penalties. Lethal. We left the pitch at full-time and Willie John turned to me and said, 'Welcome to New Zealand, son. This is what it's all about.'

John Spencer: We went into the changing room and Doug Smith said, 'Just calm down, boy. Calm down. We don't want to see any of that again.' And he walked out the changing room and the rest of the guys all gathered round and Broonie lifted me off the ground and said, 'That's the stuff, Spence!'

Ian McLauchlan: You use these incidents to bind you together. Doug knew exactly what he was doing when he asked us not to talk about it with the press afterwards – don't vent your anger, let it fester, let it make you stronger, and then express it by stuffing the next side you face.

Sandy Carmichael: Ray McLoughlin worked it out one day. There were 48,000 people at the Maori game, 25,000 at Waikato, another 25,000 in Wanganui and 20,000 in Pukekohe. That was 118,000 at our first four matches.

Ray was a very analytical guy and he was beginning to get irritated because the New Zealand Rugby Union were restrictive with what they were giving us. Ray worked it out that, given the number of tickets sold and the cost of the tickets, the tour had already been paid for. So we said, 'Right, let's do something about this, let's ask for two bottles of wine on the table at every dinner instead of just one.' And that's what we got. We were delighted.

David Duckham: We worked on our fitness a lot when we were on tour, but Carwyn was ingenious. One thing we would regularly do in training was passing circles – we'd get seven or eight players in a circle with one in the middle. We all had to pass the ball to him as fast as we could, in and out of the circle, and he had to flip it out as fast as he could, trying to disguise where he was passing it. We would vary it so that you had to hit the deck after your pass if you were in the middle and then get back to your feet before the ball came back to you. It was like the *rondo* passing at Barcelona and Eddie Jones' obsession with how long his England players spend on the ground and out of the game. Carwyn was doing similar stuff forty-five years ago.

Delme Thomas: Carwyn had one pet hate – kicking the ball into the opposition's half. He didn't see any point to it. He preferred the outside-half to place a much shorter kick just over the heads of the line of defence. That would force the full-back to come forward and force the other backs to turn round and run back. He saw no point in kicking long, right into the full-back's hands. 'For goodness sake, you're playing really well and working hard to win the ball and then you kick the bloody thing away!'

He had an ability to assess when certain players needed a push and when they needed a rest. He said to me once, 'Anyone can put a saucepan full of water on the fire and boil it dry. The trick is to put the saucepan on the fire and keep it simmering for as long as possible and then bring it back to the boil again. It's no use having a player 120 per cent physically fit if his mind is tired.'

Mervyn Davies: I always felt slightly detached from the coaches' words. Clive Rowlands, my coach at Wales, was a scrum-half, John Dawes was a centre, Carwyn a fly-half. None had played number eight, none truly understood what went on in the maelstrom of the scrum. But what Carwyn did was he invited us to take personal responsibility for our role but without ever telling us what to do. He had a persuasive knack that led us to believe that his suggestions were ours, not his. One of his greatest strengths as a coach was an ability to listen.

Delme Thomas: It was no coincidence that Carwyn and Barry were such good friends. Carwyn understood him. In the changing rooms before a game, Carwyn or John Dawes would run through some moves they expected to see in the game. Barry would say, 'Yes, okay, I understand these moves. And you can call whatever move you want, but if you call a move and I can see a gap somewhere, I'm bloody going for it'. And Carwyn would stand there smiling quietly to himself, winking at some of us. It needed a mind like Carwyn's to understand a mind like Barry's. Carwyn brought the natural creativity out of him.

John Spencer: I didn't think he was the greatest coach. If you said that to JPR he'd think it was blasphemy, but I played under coaches who were better than he was. He was a great organiser and he was a great philosopher about the game but I thought he got quite a lot of it wrong. I might be on my own in that. He put me through clinics that were useless. Don't put me in clinics to try and teach me to play on the wing because I'm not going to play there after this tour. When he started to talk to the backs in Welsh I said to Gareth and Gerald and Delme and Derek Quinnell, 'Teach me some phrases because I'm going to kid Carwyn on that I can speak fluent Welsh.' And it really used to piss Carwyn off when I did it. Whenever he had a snipe at me I'd tell him where to go in Welsh – and he hated it. But I'm probably out on a limb saying that.

Fergus Slattery: After training one day, six of us forwards decided to do a bit of extra body work and when we finished we sat around and had a chat. Then, five or six of the backs came running up over a sand dune after doing an extra session on the beach. They joined us. Barry was there. After a few minutes, Barry jumps up all indignant at something somebody has said. 'How dare you suggest that I should have made that tackle! I don't tackle! Those guys over there tackle!' and he points to four of us forwards. Everyone breaks their fucking bollocks laughing because Barry John is openly telling us he that he *won't* tackle and pointing at us gorillas and saying that it's our job. Then next thing we know, a tractor with a trailer comes up the road and Barry stops it, speaks to the driver, and then hops on the trailer and disappears. Calling Barry a mad genius is a bit too strong, but he was unconventional. Different.

The Lions had come through their first four games with aplomb, but not all of New Zealand was convinced. Oh sure, their forwards looked tough and their backs looked electric, but they hadn't played a proper force yet; they hadn't met a team that could put them on their heels and ask them questions for the full eighty minutes.

The expectation was that things were about to change. Athletic Park, Wellington, was another ground that held bad memories for the 1966 survivors. Mike Gibson, Willie John McBride and Delme Thomas had all played Wellington on that Lions tour. Gibson, in particular, had had a nightmarish experience in the 20–6 defeat.

Now the Lions were going back to Athletic Park.

Carwyn had pre-selected the teams for the first six matches of the tour while still at the Lions' Eastbourne hotel, with the intention of giving every player and every combination plenty of time together in the early stages of the trip. He also knew that by game five – Wellington – he'd have a good idea of his strongest side. And that's what he went with at Athletic Park. This was not a day to experiment, this was a day to go full throttle with his made men to see what they could do.

Ray McLoughlin, John Pullin and Sandy Carmichael made up the front row, Delme Thomas and Willie John McBride were behind them and John Taylor, Fergus Slattery and Mervyn Davies were the back row. Gareth partnered Barry at half-back; Mike Gibson partnered John Dawes in the midfield. The back three had David Duckham and John Bevan on the wings, with the incomparable JPR at full-back.

The night before the game, a seventeen-year-old Wellington local, Rod Camp, was the first in the queue for tickets for the match, the line eventually stretching all the way through the suburb of Newtown to Wellington Hospital.

'Four of us slept outside the main stand that night,' recalled Camp. 'We were fuelled by some dreadful Red Band beer which tasted like cod liver oil. We were all keen as mud on rugby. We camped outside the gates at the north end of the ground until they opened at 10 a.m. The local radio station, 2ZB, asked us who was going to win. Wellington were fielding a bloody good team that day – Ian Stevens, Graham Williams, Andy Leslie, Grant Batty and John Dougan were all either All Blacks or about to be – so we said about 22–12 Wellington.'

Athletic Park was bursting at the seams when Graham Williams, the former All Blacks flanker, and Andy Leslie, a future All Blacks captain, led their team out onto the field. Wellington were one of the great provincial powerhouses of New Zealand rugby, but after just eight minutes they were all beginning to look anaemic.

Fergus Slattery: I was playing against Graham Williams, a guy who played for New Zealand about six times and who was at the end of his career. I always obstructed guys at the back of the lineout, pushed them or blocked them. It just meant our fly-half could do whatever he wanted to do and you'd get away with it once or maybe twice, but then a guy might give you a smack. About fifteen minutes into the game I obviously pissed this guy off and he just punched me and I punched him back and he punched me again and I started laughing. I thought, 'This is fucking ridiculous, I have no right to be punching this guy and he has every right to punch me because I was messing him around in the first place.' But even at that early stage, we were flying.

Gordon Brown: For weeks Carwyn had been telling the New Zealand press that we were still only in third gear. 'When we click, you'll see something,' he said. Well, we clicked.

John Pullin won a strike against the head and Gareth Edwards darted down the blindside before slipping the ball to John Bevan to score. Barry John slotted the touchline conversion. John Taylor scored a second try and two more followed before the break – from Barry after a scorching run from Duckham and from Bevan again after wondrous interplay between Gibson, Dawes and JPR. The Lions led 18–3 at half-time.

Fergus Slattery: John Bevan was the youngest player on tour and, in the best possible way, he was a simple and uncomplicated player. He had pace and he had strength. If you put him away, then bingo, he'd do the rest.

Barry John: Early in the second half, we were almost underneath our own crossbar at a scrum. Syd said to me, 'Fancy it?'

Mike Gibson was standing next to me. 'What do you mean?' he said. 'What are you going to do?'

I said, 'I'm going to chip them.'

And Mike said, 'No, no. Don't.'

I said, 'I am. If you want to come with us, it's up to you.'

And that was it. The ball came out of the scrum, I did a little dink over the top with the left foot. Mike was off like a greyhound. The ball stood up and he angled away to the left, gave it to John Bevan and he was in under the sticks for his third try. After that there was no holding Mike Gibson. When he was playing for Ireland, more often than not they were geared to losing. Everything was a dogfight and Mike rarely had the opportunity to show what he could do. That Wellington match was the making of a lot of us. But most of all, it was the making of Mike Gibson.

The Lions were roaring. Duckham and Bevan combined once again, the Englishman swerving and sidestepping past five Wellington defenders before lobbing the ball to Bevan for his fourth try. Although the final whistle was approaching, Gibson still found time and space to glide in for two more scores to make it 47–9. It was one of the biggest beatings the Lions had dished out to any team in any country, ever.

The *Dominion* newspaper didn't hold back. In the space of eighty minutes at Athletic Park they had a Damascene conversion. In a breathless report, they wrote of 45,000 in the stadium and millions more around the country being stunned by the Lions' quality. They declared Barry John, who scored another nineteen points, as the greatest ten in the world, hailed Mike Gibson, 'the conducting maestro', as the greatest back and Bevan, now with ten tries on tour, among the most exciting wings ever seen in New Zealand. It was a performance 'touched by perfection'. Their headline read, 'Onslaught crumbles capital.'

Andy Leslie: I remember early in the game John Bevan scored a try, which was disallowed because the referee, Bill Adlam, thought he was offside, but he wasn't offside, so he could have had five tries. I played 144 games for Wellington, but of all of those, the most memorable was that one against the Lions. I remember tackling Mike Gibson in one corner and then when I got back up, John Bevan had scored in the other. They were just unstoppable and the width they put on the ball was unheard of at the time. Every one of those Lions backs just shifted like the wind. I can still hear the crowd yelling out, calling for them to score fifty. And they were hollering and cheering the Lions because they were playing such great rugby.

John Dawes: It was payback for many of us Welsh players who'd been taken to the cleaners in New Zealand two years earlier, and for the likes of Mike Gibson, Willie John and Ray McLoughlin, who had suffered badly with the 1966 Lions. There was a lot of personal pride restored in that game.

Willie John McBride: A match I'll remember for as long as I live.

Graham Williams: They were the greatest team I ever played.

Bryan Williams: I was sitting at home in Auckland watching that game on TV. It was a wake-up call for everyone. The counter-attacking display that the Lions put in that day was mind-boggling. I think we realised then that we were up against a mighty team.

Andy Leslie: After the game we went up to the Grand Hotel and sat upstairs. Our coach, Frank Ryan, put a couple dozen beers in the middle of the table and said, 'Righto, boys, we're training tomorrow. We're going to sit down and we're going to change everything. This is the sort of rugby we're going to adopt.' That game was such a huge learning curve for us. At both my club – Petone – and at Wellington, we started to approach the game like the Lions. We moved the ball more and that in turn created more enjoyment and we reaped the success of it. It was a great legacy that they left us – I don't think that any side has ever learned more in a single game than we did that day. It changed us completely.

It was the freedom they played with, running the ball from all over the paddock. And we decided after that that the best area to attack from was on defence. When all the other teams were on attack, the Lions weren't thinking about defence, they were thinking about attacking and scoring tries.

John Taylor: For the first time the New Zealanders began to understand why we called Barry the King.

Barry John: That whole King thing was a bit of a laugh and I played up to it.

Ray McLoughlin: Barry reminded me of Muhammad Ali. He had the 'I'm the greatest' mantra which was a kind of game. He always used to call the forwards donkeys. Three times a week he'd come up behind me in the restaurant and would put a hand on my shoulder, and he would say, 'Remind me again, Ray, are you a loosehead donkey or a tighthead donkey?'

Chris Rea: Ray would go into a long diatribe on the art of front-row play, but Barry would always cut him down. 'Ray, just get me the ball and I'll do the rest.'

Ray McLoughlin: And he did. There was some great stuff in that game, but Wellington were weak in comparison to the side we faced in 1966. I think the various provincial matches would have given New Zealand notice that there was a lot of scoring potential in our side, but New Zealanders being New Zealanders, they would have thought that at some stage they were going to bring us back to earth.

Peter Dixon: After every game we played, it was always the same. 'Wait until you get down to Southland, they'll give you a proper doing,' and so on. 'They're going really well, they'll show you.' It was great, we loved that – it was a running joke throughout the tour. It literally happened after every game. 'Oh, you boys were okay, but you were pretty lucky to beat us in the end. Just you wait until . . .' And this would be after we put thirty points on them and scored seven tries. 'Oh, it was pretty close.' Close? In their minds you were never the better team. It was an anomaly, an off day for them. They seemed unable to see the strange run of off days suffered by almost every team we played.

Ray McLoughlin: We didn't get ahead of ourselves, but that's not to say we didn't celebrate pretty enthusiastically.

Willie John McBride: I was sitting in my bed like a good boy that night. I was quietly reading my newspaper and I could hear this commotion going on downstairs, breaking glass and all sorts of things. And I could hear Doug Smith's roaring voice: 'What are you bastards up to?' And then all these thumping feet as the boys who had been causing all the mayhem ran away to hide from him.

Doug Smith: I immediately went upstairs to Willie John and said, 'Here, what the hell are you doing?' And he's sitting in his bed with his pipe, and he said, 'Oh, nothing at all, manager, nothing at all.' And there was a rolling of the curtain and I went over and kicked it and Arthur Lewis fell out. And then a rolling in the wardrobe and I opened the door and Sean Lynch fell out.

On the field and off, there was no doubt about it – these boys could play.

CHAPTER NINE

A DAGGER IN THE HEART

THE LIONS were not short of pace, creativity and tries, but a new player who brought buckets of each of those qualities joined the party as they headed across the Canterbury plain to the holiday town of Timaru. Gerald Davies had stayed behind in Britain to finish his exams at Cambridge, and only now was the Welsh wing a member of the tour. He arrived in Timaru to find the place shrouded in fog and rain. Immediately, Carwyn put him into the team to play a Mid Canterbury, South Canterbury, North Otago select at Fraser Park.

Fergus Slattery: The New Zealanders were first class. They loved having you in their villages and cities, loved having you in their bars. The reception we got was amazing. Timaru, though, was a shithole. It was a one-horse town where the horse would have bolted if it had the chance.

John Spencer: It wasn't as good as that. It was a gold-mining town, but the gold had run out. There was tumbleweed rolling down the street. It was like a Western. And the only entertainment they put on for us was to visit the freezer works and the lamb slaughterhouse.

Compared to the greatness of the Wellington performance this was a different planet. There were players in the squad who knew now that their chances of Test rugby were all but gone – not just because their own form wasn't as good as it could be, but because the form of their rivals was stratospherically high. Bob Hiller was trying to oust JPR, John Spencer and Chris Rea were competing with John Dawes and Mike Gibson. Under the weight of the task, they struggled.

In a 25–6 win, Rea scored one of the Lions' five tries, but he wasn't impressive. The effervescent Chico Hopkins got another, David Duckham got one of his own and Gerald claimed two on his first appearance, bringing his total for Wales and the Lions to eight tries in six games. In the aftermath, Carwyn was disappointed with the performance, but when he saw how wretched both Hiller and Rea were feeling about how they had played he kept his silence.

Chris Rea: We were all hugely competitive beasts, otherwise we wouldn't have been there. But, if I'm honest, I didn't enjoy the tour all that much because I wasn't playing well.

John Spencer: Chris wasn't a great kicker of the ball and I got shovelled a load of rubbish in that game. It ruined Chris's chance of a Test place and it didn't help my chances at all either, nor guys like Alastair Biggar, who was on the wing outside. It was a tough day.

Ian McLauchlan: We had a rule where we were asked not to drink midweek, but after that match we were stuck in Timaru with nothing to do, so John Pullin, Sean Lynch, myself and Mike

Roberts went to this quiet bar and said to the guy behind the counter that we didn't want to speak to anyone. We ended up absolutely blotto. Carwyn knew everything. The next morning he said we were going to have a cavalry charge, and 'you four are going to lead it'. We had to charge six fields three times. I developed a real admiration for Lynchy that day. He was running and throwing up at the same time.

Delme Thomas: Lynchy would go to church every Sunday no matter how heavy the Saturday night had been. Then back he'd come to the hotel with a wide grin on his face: 'I've wiped the slate clean, boys. I can start again.'

The Lions got out of Timaru and kicked on for Dunedin where they would play another of the provincial heavy-hitters, Otago, at Carisbrook. The most anticipated clash was that between Ray McLoughlin, the Lions loosehead, and Keith Murdoch, the Otago tighthead. Legend abounded about Otago's man-mountain. There were pictures of him holding up one end of a car while the tyre was being changed. There were stories of his thermonuclear temper. There was endless evidence of his contempt for journalists. Murdoch was a scary individual.

Colin Meads: I remember the first time I encountered Keith Murdoch. I hadn't met him on the field but I'd sure heard a lot about him. We all had. It was in the All Black trials in 1970 and he was in Lochore's team. I was captain of the other side. I'd been playing rugby for a long, long time but I hadn't come up against this character before. In the trial, he stood behind me in the lineout and every time I went to jump he just pulled my arm away. After he'd done it a couple of times, I said to him, 'Hey, you do that again and I'll knock your head off.' He looked at me, chuckled and said, 'Have a go.'

I turned to Jazz Muller, one of my props, and said to him, 'Jazz, get this bastard,' but Jazz was having none of it. He knew all about Murdoch. 'Aw, no. Hell no, not me.' Then I turned to Jake Burns, the other prop and he said, 'You look after yourself.' I thought, 'Well, I'm a great captain aren't I? I've got myself into a position where I have to do something about it.' I decided to wait until about three minutes from full-time, knowing that when I hit him it would have to be good, because if he was as tough as they said he'd get me back before the end. I'd have to make sure he went down and didn't get up. So I waited until it was their throw-in – and I thumped him. It was a beaut. I thought I'd broken all the bones in my hand. Murdoch reeled back several yards. I'm saying to myself, 'Fall over, fall over for Christ's sake.' He didn't; he shook his head and rejoined the play. I thought, 'Oh Christ . . .' I was running around as fast as I could with Murdoch chasing me. He was stalking me. The final whistle went and, boy, the relief. Then I looked up and saw him coming straight towards me. He put his hand out. I grabbed it and shook it hard. He grinned and walked off.

The day before the game, the journalist John Reason went for lunch with Arnold Mansion, the president of the Otago Rugby Union, and as they were leaving they bumped into Murdoch in the car park.

John Reason: Arnold stopped the car and said, 'Hello, Keith,' and Keith said, 'Hi.' Then Arnold said, 'Keith, I would like you to meet John Reason.' Keith stretched out his hand and I shook it. 'John is one of the overseas pressmen with the Lions,' said Arnold. Murdoch pulled his hand away as if it had been stung. 'I don't talk to pressmen,' he grunted. 'Fuck ya!'

Greg McGee: I played number eight for Otago against the

Lions. Around the Wednesday, we had scrum practice out at Tahuna Park. While we were practising, I heard this English voice calling out to Keith. I later found out it was John Reason, the rugby writer. He obviously hadn't learnt his lesson from their first encounter. He said 'Keith, can I have a few words?' Keith turned around and said, 'You can fuck off'.

In 1971, Murdoch was just beginning to show how potent a player he could be, and with McLoughlin destroying every opponent he had come up against so far on the tour, the rugby public in New Zealand were licking their lips at the prospect of a battle that never materialised. McLoughlin hurt a shin in training and then Murdoch ruled himself out. He gave no reason. He just wasn't playing. Nobody had the nerve to ask him for an explanation.

Carwyn James: Otago was a key match. A key match.

Ian McLauchlan: Dunedin is a funny place if you're a Scotsman. Dunedin is Gaelic for Edinburgh and all the street names are the same. There's a road that climbs a hill above Carisbrook which gave an amazing view down onto the pitch and a lot of spectators used to watch from there. They called it the 'Scotsman's grandstand'. Some people tried to claim that it was called that because of all the Scottish heritage around Dunedin, but we all know it was because the spectators got to watch the games there for free.

Despite the sunshine, the field at Carisbrook was a quagmire and tore up with alarming ease. It restricted the Lions' running game and reduced the contest to an arm-wrestle. John Taylor, John Dawes and JPR scored the tries in a 21–9 win. Barry kicked twelve points to take his total to seventy-eight – a new record for a Lion in New Zealand after just five games.

Greg McGee: I was twenty years old in 1971, green as can be, but even I could see that Lions had a collective IQ that was way ahead of us. They were so much more intelligent than us. They were just too smart. Years later I found out just how smart they were, when I was coaching in Italy. It was 1976, and I realised that, having been a loose forward, I didn't know what the tighthead should do if the loosehead was boring in. So I bought that book, *The Lions Speak*, in which each one of the players from the 1971 tour detailed their role and their responsibilities. I based my whole coaching on that book.

At Otago it was all just 'get stuck in'. In one practice we'd done umpteen scrums and I asked the assistant coach, Sam Simpson, if we could do a few moves off the back of the scrum and he just looked at me. 'McGee, we've got one half-back and that's enough, you just stick your fucking head in the scrum and push.' That's what it was like, and then into this environment come the Lions, with guys like Mike Gibson and Carwyn James and Barry John.

Mike Gibson: Top-level rugby is about sacrifice and courage. If you have to fall on a ball or make a tackle, you do it. If you think about it for a moment then you're in trouble. Barry was different. He would basically say, 'I am created for better things than defensive chores. I'm going to lend something special to this game and therefore I need to direct all my energies there. I will show myself to the game in due course but not in a defensive capacity.'

I was inside centre – and he was absolutely sincere about not tackling, because when the moment came he just wasn't there. In one game, Colin Meads thundered around a ruck and I threw myself at his feet. I think he fell over me, but I was left with a lump on my forehead for the rest of the tour as a reminder. It used to make Barry smile whenever he saw it. But then he'd turn it on and you forgave him completely. At first, when you saw his tactical kicking, you might say he was lucky that so many balls he kicked landed a yard short of the line and then ran into touch, but when you saw him do it for three months, time after time after time, you realised what an exceptional talent he had. His tactical kicking was just pinpoint. He destroyed full-backs.

Barry John: My job was to catch the ball and give it, and I just told the boys to get it to me any way they could. Out there on the field was my little paradise, where I was free – it was a marvellous feeling. We didn't have many moves; it was largely instinctive, the way we played. We sorted any moves we might come up with out on the field and Carwyn, what a brilliant man he was, let us express ourselves.

Mike Gibson: One of the great rugby lessons I had was from Carwyn on that tour. His policy was if you had an opportunity, even in your own twenty-five, then don't think something will go wrong, don't think someone will drop a pass. He said, 'You're too good to think like that, you've got to assume the pass will stick, so just have a go.' It was wonderful for the ego and the confidence to hear him say things like that. I always think fear of the mistake is the most inhibiting thing for a back. Players should never be afraid to look for an opportunity. If a player has the anxiety – 'I wonder if I'll retain my place' – the answer is he'll put a kick into touch.

Greg McGee: That's what New Zealand rugby had become, only we couldn't see it. It was the 1971 Lions who started putting the dagger into the heart of that old New Zealand rugby kingdom.

They plunged the knife a little deeper when they went to Greymouth to play West Coast-Buller, another combination side that couldn't live with them, not even for a half. The Lions led 31–0 at the break. David Duckham scored five tries. He got a sixth later on. Alastair Biggar and Bob Hiller scored a seventh and an eighth. It was a rout, more a training run than a proper match. Not that the Lions were complaining, for coming next was a game where mayhem was guaranteed, a contest that even from a mile out looked like a fifth Test match. The Lions were heading for Lancaster Park. Lying in wait – Canterbury.

CHAPTER TEN

CANTERBURY – IT WAS JUST A BIT OF BIFF

WILLIE JOHN McBRIDE had crystal-clear memories of Lancaster Park, Canterbury and the 'physical hurricane' that descended on him when playing there for the Lions in 1966. There'd been talk that the local team were looking for a scalp, and McBride didn't have long to wait to find out the truth of it. Right from the kick-off, they let him have it.

'I caught the ball and was surrounded by their pack, who started punching, kicking and assaulting me because I'd had the temerity to hang on to the ball. They got hold of me and took me thirty or forty yards downfield towards my own line, the blows raining down on me as we went. The more the blows came in, the bloody sight harder I held on to the ball. There was no way I was going to let go of it for those bastards.'

It wasn't the violence of the 1966 Canterbury forwards that infuriated him the most, though. It was the inaction of his own forwards. None of them piled in to help him, not one. They all stood back and let it happen. Some laughed at the hiding McBride had taken. 'I knew then that we had no hope of winning the series. It was obvious our players weren't prepared to take the pain.'

With the Lions rampant, there was pressure on Canterbury to send them a message ahead of the first Test, which was just a week away now. And if McBride remembered every detail of the aggravation in 1966, there were two men in the other side who knew all about it as well. When the teams were named, the Lions didn't need a magnifying glass to identify the top two enforcers in the Canterbury side. There they were at tighthead prop and openside flanker – A. E. Hopkinson and A. J. Wyllie – Hoppy and Grizz.

Carwyn James discreetly removed Barry John from the fray, citing a back injury. He wasn't prepared to risk his playmaker. Mervyn Davies was rested so that he could continue his rehabilitation from a groin injury; Gordon Brown was out with a sinus infection; and John Taylor's hamstring wasn't right. Gerald Davies was under the weather, so was rested.

The remainder of the fancied Test team were selected en masse. Ray McLoughlin, John Pullin and Sandy Carmichael were in the front row, with Willie John and Delme Thomas in the second row and Fergus Slattery, Mick Hipwell and Peter Dixon behind them. Gareth partnered Mike Gibson at half-back, while Arthur Lewis and John Dawes reprised their Grand Slam-winning centre partnership. The back three saw JPR, John Bevan and David Duckham combine.

They fetched up at Lancaster Park expecting a battle. What they got was all-out war. The violence started at the first scrum. Sandy Carmichael went to work on Tane Norton, boring in on the Canterbury hooker and blocking his view of the feed. Alister Hopkinson, Carmichael's opposing prop, fired a few warning barbs the Scotsman's way, but Carmichael ignored them. So Hopkinson went to town.

Humphrey Rainey: I was the referee. The day before the game, I met up with a group of Canterbury referees at their usual Friday night gathering point at Coker's Hotel in Christchurch. They were joined by Carwyn James and Cliff Morgan. The hour would have passed pleasantly enough had it not been for conversations with several people, which, for the first time, indicated that all was not to be plain sailing the following day. The story was consistent and unsettling. 'Things' would happen in the first ten minutes, I was told, that I would not be able to see and which it was best that I did not observe. I was inclined to ignore these stories.

Jim Stewart (Canterbury coach): We thought we had a chance to beat them, and the tension was very high. It was clear in the previous games that the Lions were doing a lot of damage in the front row. Hoppy said to me, 'What am I going to do about it?' I said, 'It's in your hands, but I'm not going to have the whole game ruined by the front row,' and that was where it started getting out of control.

Fergie McCormick: They started the game in anticipation of us being a dirty pack of bastards. Sandy Carmichael was obviously going to play merry hell in the front row by slipping off Hopkinson's shoulder and blocking Tane Norton's view of the ball coming in. He did it twice and was told to stop. He didn't and, yes, he was hit.

Bryan Williams: I guess as an Aucklander who had played against Canterbury before and then many times since, I gotta tell you, they were mean hombres. Back then we didn't have television replays or TMOs or anything like that and if you played in Canterbury you knew you were going to be stomped on and you were going to be kicked and all the rest of it. People just accepted it. If you were lying near the ball, you knew that you had to move away quick or else they were going to deal with you. It's just the way it was down there. Always has been. It wasn't news to us. It was what you expected from a match involving Canterbury at home. That was the Canterbury style.

Colin Meads: I knew the Lions would be pulled up at Canterbury. They got away with murder in Wanganui, just lying all over the ball and slowing it up. Try doing that against Canterbury and you'll soon know what they think about it.

Ray McLoughlin: That's a load of bullshit. The violence in the Canterbury match had nothing to do with us killing the ball. Fergus Slattery got whacked at a lineout, Sandy was taken out in the scrum – no one was lying on the ball in those situations. Gareth got whacked in open play and that had nothing to do with our rucking.

Fergus Slattery: Canterbury just went out to kick the shit out of us.

Sandy Carmichael: It was the big game going into the first Test and Ray and I were on the pitch, so it looked like we were going to be the props in the Test side. They decided to target us. Basically, up to then, he and I had screwed to the ground anything of size and strength in New Zealand. They had forgotten about front-row play. They hadn't a clue.

Ray McLoughlin: I couldn't see any of it because I was on the other side of the scrum but I heard Sandy shouting. There's not much you can do about it when you're on the other side of the scrum. We didn't know at that stage that he had a couple of broken bones in his jaw.

Alister Hopkinson: From the first scrum, Sandy Carmichael started boring in on Tane Norton and a few fists started flying.

Sandy Carmichael: It wasn't just in the scrums, I got kicked in the head at a ruck. You can see it on film. There's a ruck and I go to ground and someone kicks me in the face.

Alister Hopkinson: There was no kicking. It's one of those things that I always said, 'If you get sent off for kicking, don't come to me for sympathy.'

Ian McLauchlan: Rugby is like boxing. You don't need to go out and fight dirty, but if somebody is going to punch you, then you've got to lay into them. If you don't, they will keep punching you. If you hit back, they won't. It's like bullies all over the world. I was on the subs' bench when Sandy came off injured. I was ready to go, but Sandy wanted to go back on. Travelling 12,000 miles to get the shit kicked out of you is not my idea of fun. Sandy never retaliated. Some saw it as a flaw in his character, others saw it as a great strength. He was a rugby player, he wasn't a boxer.

John Taylor: Canterbury treated the game as a war, the invader to be repulsed at all costs. The game was a disgrace to rugby.

Doug Smith: Bastards.

Sean Lynch: Put it this way: I was injured, and from the stands it was one of the most vicious matches I've ever seen. They were the heavy mob and you had to go for them because they were going for you.

Humphrey Rainey: Any hopes I had of an enjoyable game were dashed in the first few minutes and it took twenty minutes to restore some sanity.

Fergus Slattery: They went out with this thuggish attitude. Gareth was running across the pitch and Alex Wyllie came up behind him and punched him in the back of the neck. Gareth and somebody else went to the referee and said, 'What are you going to do?' And the ref said, 'I'm only refereeing what I can see.' It's a bit like saying, 'Good luck, lads, do whatever you want.'

Humphrey Rainey: I watched the forwards, as best you can watch sixteen men. It was obvious from the injuries to players on both sides, and the attitudes of the teams, that playing the man was of greater importance than playing the ball.

Mick Hipwell: You know, I hate knocking referees. They picked a guy for that game that was good, but he was young and he was inexperienced at that level. It took off straight away and he wasn't able to handle it. But the two teams were. I remember the referee saying that he was going to referee the game and let the brawling go. Which was a shame because we were two very good teams and it could have been a cracking game.

Gareth Edwards: Before he tried to take my head off, Grizz warned me. I'd beaten him off the base of a scrum and he said, 'Hey, scrummy, you do that again and I'll break your neck'. Ray was our pack leader and he saw it all. He went up to Grizz and caught him a real good one. I remember the blood spurting out of Wyllie's cut eye and onto my jersey. I've been quoted as saying I've only ever been scared twice playing rugby. Once was playing for Cardiff against Neath and the second was that Canterbury match.

Ray McLoughlin: Canterbury had a reputation of being harder than everyone else. New Zealanders are great ones for intimidating guys. I'd been urging everyone to show their teeth immediately in the face of the intimidation that was bound to happen. That was essential to avoid being psychologically beaten. I was leader of the pack that day. I remember a moment when I was of the view that I should just call all the players together, walk to the touch line and get Carwyn James to call the whole thing off because it was no longer a rugby match. I remember thinking that if I did that, we'd look like chickens and that would affect morale, but at the same time it was also important to put it out there that we had come to play rugby not engage in boxing matches. In the end I decided against it. In retrospect it was the right thing to do because it showed that we weren't going to be physically intimated out of a game.

David Duckham: I didn't really get involved, being stuck out on the wing, but I'd have liked to. Fergie McCormick was one of the instigators trying to wind us up. I remember the whistle had gone for a forward pass and as I ran past him he gave me a big nudge with his shoulder. I turned to him and said, 'Don't be childish,' and he just grinned back at me. It was that sort of game, really niggly, annoying, but also brutal. They were panicking. We had won so many games so well that they were seriously worried about how we were going to go in the Tests – and that was Canterbury's way of trying to help the national cause.

Ray McLoughlin: There was a melee going on and as part of it I charged in and proceeded to hit Wyllie. I was pulled by my jersey as I did so and ended up hitting the side of his head with my thumb and chipped a bone.

Fergie McCormick: The Lions tried to claim that Ray

McLoughlin's broken thumb was our fault. That's almost funny. The punch-up when that happened was started by Willie John McBride. Hamish Macdonald was walking back to a lineout and McBride hooked him. There was no doubt about it. All the players, including the Lions, knew it. That was when the big skirmish started. Two injuries resulted from it. Alex Wyllie was standing with his hands on his hips, McLoughlin went to him and hit him in the eye. It broke McLoughlin's thumb and gashed Wyllie's eye, a wound which needed stitches and which, had it been a fraction lower, would almost certainly have blinded that eye. Ray himself would hardly attribute his attack on Wyllie to retaliation.

Alister Hopkinson: Alex wasn't involved at all. He came in to have a look at what was going on. McLoughlin threw a punch, and he broke his thumb. Alex was the unlucky bystander in that one. But he still got the blame.

Gordon Brown: The Canterbury forwards were frighteningly over-motivated and seemed prepared to stoop to the slowest level of gutter thuggery. With Hopkinson, Wyllie and Penrose in the driving seat, they kicked, punched and elbowed anyone in a red jersey who came anywhere near the ball. It was a wonder that nobody was killed.

Alex Wyllie: Killed? Bloody hell! It was just a bit of biff.

Sandy Carmichael: By the time I came off the pitch, both eyes were pretty well shut, so they sat me on the bench and put ice packs on my face. Ian McLauchlan came towards me to see how I was just as I went to blow my nose, but it was blocked and because the sinus was cracked the air blew into my eye socket, which inflated like a balloon. That was the first time – and probably the last time – I ever saw fear in Ian's eyes.

Peter Dixon: The Canterbury match stands out as brutal. It was a battle all the time, primarily among the forwards. At the lineout there'd be a fight at the start of it, then the ref sorted it out; you'd have the lineout again, and then there'd be a few sly punches as you were running across the field. There was also trouble at the scrums, with their second rows throwing punches through on our props. I respect Sandy for not retaliating, but if he'd said anything to me I would have swung one in. I was not really aware he was being hit, mainly because everyone was fighting their own corner. I was determined that if anything came my way it was going back again. There are a few pictures of me trying to flatten Grizz Wyllie and vice versa. It carried on between Wyllie and myself a few years later when Canterbury were on tour in the UK.

Tane Norton: The Lions blamed us, we blamed the Lions. It was just one of those things that blew up – and they didn't back off.

Mick Hipwell: I got a few knocks, but nothing compared to everyone else. I actually thought I was going to get sent off because I belted someone right in front of the referee, but he didn't give a shit.

Willie John McBride: I don't think there was a ball on the field for the first half hour. We lost Carmichael and then we lost McLoughlin, so the two props were gone. Slattery got injured, Mick Hipwell got injured and there were others. It was bloody nonsense and the referee was a disaster. There was a premonition that there could be trouble.

Delme Thomas: That was, without doubt, the dirtiest game I ever played in.

Fergus Slattery: I was concussed after about eight or nine minutes and remained pretty out of it until about ten minutes into the second half. The openside on their team was going off at the lineout to pursue our fly-half, and I decided to try and run in his way each time he did it to buy Mike more time. I did it about five or six times and you could see that Alex Wyllie was beginning to get fucking irritated with it happening – you know, me getting in the way – so we were having a little bit of a tête-à-tête. Alister Hopkinson came up from the front of the lineout. I didn't see him, but I got this massive fucking punch in the mouth, completely blindsided. It cracked a bunch of teeth down to the root. I was down on the deck, concussed, but I played on, and after a while the concussion kind of started to drift away, so I'm able to remember all these different things that happened in that game, even though I was fucking away with it.

I can still see it in my mind right now – about five minutes later, running across the pitch, looking towards the goal posts and just seeing this huge crowd of people and thinking, 'Where the fuck am I?' I didn't have a clue. I went to Peter Dixon at the next lineout and asked, 'Where are we?' And he looked at me, all agitated, and said, 'What do you mean "where are we?" We're in bloody Canterbury!' About ten minutes later I asked him again – but he'd just been smacked and had no idea. 'I don't know where the fuck we are. Fuck off.' I only realised where I was in the final quarter of the game.

Fergie McCormick: Hoppy and Grizz got a lot of flak for that game, but fists were flying on both sides and I just think the Lions picked on the wrong guys. When Alex Wyllie was on your side, you couldn't meet a nicer bloke. But he was not a happy man to meet when he was in the other team.

Willie John McBride: It was just sheer nonsense. All sorts of stuff. Hopkinson and Wyllie were the two guys who started it. Hopkinson is dead now. There was a guy Tane Norton who was captain of the All Blacks. He was always a good friend but he wasn't proud of that stuff. There were two or three thugs on the field. They say it's part of the game and they get away with that. We knew they would target people like Gareth. I'd seen it all before. We won the battle and we won the match and we won it well and it gave me a feeling of what we had. We had guys who wouldn't lie down.

Amid all the violence, it is sometimes forgotten that a game was played and a result was posted. The Lions won 14–3, John Bevan and Arthur Lewis getting the tries.

John Dawes: The really memorable score was John Bevan's. He was confronted by three defenders near the Canterbury corner flag – and wallop, he ran through the lot of them.

Ian McLauchlan: Arthur Lewis had said to Bevan before the match, 'If you get the chance, don't try to run around them, run through them.' And on the way to the clinching try he knocked three of their guys down. It was an amazing try. Two of them converged on him and he blasted his way right through the middle of the pair of them and then through McCormick. You don't do that very often in New Zealand.

Sandy Carmichael: He was like a bowling ball going through the middle of the pins. To this day I'm in awe of that score.

Mick Hipwell: John Bevan went through Fergie McCormick and it was incredible. Just busted straight through him – and this was a seasoned All Black full-back. Then I remember the ref blowing the whistle four, five minutes early and I turned around and saw him racing for the dressing room.

John Dawes: We won the match but, in another sense, we were losers. Half an hour's havoc had robbed us of our two frontline prop forwards with all their experience and know-how. I wouldn't say that Carwyn or the rest of us were demoralised, but we were worried that we now had no depth right before the Test series.

Ray McLoughlin: On the tour, Carwyn used to talk about coaching at the conscious and the unconscious levels; at least, he talked about that up to the Canterbury match, when it took on a new meaning. He dropped it from then on.

Alex Wyllie: After the game it was going to be reported as a hard game, typical of a top New Zealand provincial side. Then Doug Smith and Carwyn James got hold of their own media and said, 'No, this is what you'll write it up as – it was dirty rugby. And if it doesn't stop, all hell will break loose.'

I think the complaints were tactical – the last guy the Lions wanted to face in the Tests was Hoppy, so they did all they could to try and make sure the All Blacks would be hit by a media storm if they selected him. The game really wasn't as bad as it was later portrayed.

Fergie McCormick: There were plenty of bruises and stitches in our dressing room, too, but we didn't set them up under bright lights for the photographers. We're not claiming to be innocents, but we'd at least like the right to impartial judgment. What we got from the press was a kangaroo court.

Mervyn Davies: The New Zealand press themselves were outraged by their countrymen's antics and dubbed it 'the game of shame', and one paper, *The Truth*, went further, writing, 'New Zealand rugby has become as grotesque as a wounded bull.'

Willie John McBride: I remember Doug Smith coming on the bus after the game and saying to me, 'We'll beat the All Blacks next week,' and half our team had gone to the hospital. I'm looking around me and saying, 'I'm needing a lot of convincing here.'

Barry John: Afterwards, we went to the post-match function, but the Canterbury boys missed it en bloc. I think they had taken some advice that it would be best not to go – which is a shame, because it was really only three or four of them who had been bastards.

Sandy Carmichael: We went to watch carriage racing at the local track that night, and I put my sunglasses on because my face didn't look too well. Some of the New Zealanders were there, sneering, 'Why are you wearing sunglasses at night?' And I said, 'So nobody else can see exactly what you've done to my face.'

Willie John McBride: I knew Hopkinson and Wyllie well and got on with them, but there was always a coldness after that game.

Sandy Carmichael: The next morning, Doug Smith came to my room and said, 'I'm terribly sorry, Sandy, but it'll take eight weeks for you to repair yourself and there's only eight weeks left – so you're going home.' And that was it.

I was sharing with David Duckham, who was one of the finest gentlemen I've ever met. He said, 'Sandy, it's up to you. We can sit in this room for another two or three hours and when you're ready to go and meet the boys I'll come with you. I'll stay with you.' So, that's what we did – and he stayed with me the whole time. When we eventually went down, we discovered that Ray McLoughlin had to be sent home as well because he had broken a scaphoid. It had been like Custer's Last Stand.

David Duckham: It's lovely to hear that Sandy remembers that. He was one of the guys I really looked up to – a big man in every sense. God, I loved him to bits. He had that great Scottish wit about him. But he was so down. They'd smashed his face in. A cynic might say that he should have retaliated, and that if he'd retaliated the damage might not have been so bad. He was a big man; he really should have looked after himself better.

Peter Dixon: What I think is even more unforgiving in some ways is that Sandy didn't say to us, 'I'm getting hit.' If he'd said he was getting hit, we'd have all piled in to help him, the second row or the flanker would have been straight in there at the next scrum. But he just took it.

Sandy Carmichael: I've never named names and I never will, and the reason is that if I tell, then the story ends. I don't want them to forget, and if I leave it this way then they can't forget. I got a phone call from New Zealand when the Lions were there in 2005 asking me about it – and that's great because they haven't been able to draw a line under it.

As All Blacks coach, Ivan Vodanovich was asked his opinion about the Battle of Lancaster Park. His reply outraged the Lions. 'I didn't see any Canterbury man punching,' he said flatly. 'I saw crude attempts from the Lions to lie on the ball in rucks while making no attempt to get free. That's why they suffered so many injuries against Canterbury, who drove into the rucks in classic formation. The same thing will happen in the first Test if the All

Blacks can't get at the ball. If the Lions persist with these tactics, Carisbrook could become another Passchendaele.'

Fergus Slattery: In the changing room afterwards, I looked at JPR's back and it was covered in these lines from studs where he'd been kicked to pieces at the bottom of a ruck. Whenever we went down on the ball, their players were always straight in there and just stood all over us. Every time. And when I say 'they', it wasn't just one guy, it was three, four, five, six guys. You were pushed out the back of the ruck with the boot and, you know what, that kind of rucking was fair. In the beginning you thought it was ridiculous, but that was one part of the game that I wouldn't complain about. I think they were right to do that because Vodanovich was correct, we *were* lying on the ball to slow it down and we *were* trying to get in the way of their players to make life difficult, and in that context, that kind of rucking is fine. That was the way they played and that was their system for sorting out guys trying to lie all over their ball. We improved a lot in that area – which tends to happen when you get the shit kicked out of you.

But it's the other stuff that was unacceptable. I think Vodanovich's comment about us lying on the ball and so on was a fair one, but the other incidents had nothing to do with that. Sandy Carmichael's face was punched to pieces in a scrum. What does that have to do with what we were doing at the ruck and the maul? What does the guy running up behind Gareth Edwards and punching him in the back of the neck have to do with us slowing their ball down?

Doug Smith was appalled that Vodanovich had used such a word as Passchendaele, but declared that the Lions wouldn't be intimidated. 'I regret the tone of his statement,' said Smith. 'We still intend to go on the field to win by playing the kind of rugby we have shown since we came to New Zealand. You cannot turn our players away from this approach. For them, that's what rugby is all about.'

Mervyn Davies: Vodanovich's rhetoric and Canterbury's punches did more to prepare us for the first Test than any training session could have done. New Zealand rugby was worried. They were resorting to the lowest form of intimidation. Jack Sullivan, chairman of the New Zealand council, deserved credit for defusing the situation when he slapped down Vodanovich by saying, 'There will be no battle at Carisbrook next Saturday.' Some perspective was needed; it was, after all, just a game. But in case it happened again, Carwyn schooled us to get our retaliation in first.

Willie John McBride: Vodanovich said afterwards that the cause of all the trouble was that Lions were killing the ball. Sure they were always saying that. When there was a ruck situation and there were guys on the ground, they would always say, 'It was their fault, not our fault.' They would always say that. They would never take the blame. He said that if it was Passchendaele they wanted, it would be Passchendaele they'd get. It was a disgraceful thing to say. A stupid thing to say. I remember when Sandy went off in that game, I took over and I said to the guys, 'Look, there are two ways this is going to go now. We either go back to the dressing room and forget about this or we stand here and fight. And I'm going to stand here and fight.' And the other guys were great, they all stood up beside me, we won the fight, we won the match and it was bloody marvellous. And that was the day we grew up.

Ray McLoughlin: It's funny, I hurt my thumb but it wasn't so bad that it stopped me playing. I played on for the rest of the match. It was a bit sore afterwards so I booked myself in at the local hospital and I didn't for one minute think it would be the end of my tour. Not for one minute. But the man told me that he had to put a big plaster of Paris thing around my thumb with this big piece of metal in there to stabilise it. He said if I didn't do that, there would be big trouble down the line with my hand. And once that thing was on my hand, that was that.

I've been asked a lot over the years whether I regret missing out on the rest of the tour and my answer is this – since then, life has been good to me. There have been the lows, but on the whole life has been good to me. I wouldn't want to take the chance of it being different. So, no, I don't have any regrets. It's part of the total package of life.

JPR Williams: There was a bit of a siege mentality afterwards and Doug Smith was very good at engendering that. The Mouse [McLauchlan] and Lynchy took over from Ray and Sandy, but there was worry among the group, and certainly amongst the management, that we might struggle without Ray and Sandy. On the Sunday after the game we had a team meeting and Carwyn said that we had to prove now that we were a team of thirty players.

Fergus Slattery: I had to stay behind in Christchurch to get dental treatment. I had this pink enamel mouthguard made that I had to keep in my mouth all the time for four weeks. A fucking nightmare.

The Lions were battered and bruised, and now the All Blacks looked forward to the Test series safe in the knowledge that they'd taken out two of the tourists' wiliest operators. Just like in 1966, Canterbury had done a job. What Vodanovich was unaware of, though, was what had been going on in the stand as the mayhem was breaking out on the field. At half-time, Carwyn had gestured to Barry John.

Barry John: I was watching from the stand and it was savage stuff. At the break, Carwyn said, 'Barry, come down and sit next to me.' And while I sat there and watched all this carnage going on, he turned to me and said quietly, 'Interesting?' And I said, 'Yes. Definitely.' Because amid all the violence we kept one eye on Fergie McCormick at full-back. I studied all aspects of his game, but mainly his positioning. I thought a lot about that afterwards. As well as the punches and the kicks I saw something else that I stored away. Carwyn saw it, too.

CHAPTER ELEVEN

LIKE THE LUFTWAFFE COMING IN

Ian McLauchlan: A lot of folk thought we were going to miss Ray McLoughlin, but I didn't rate Ray McLoughlin as highly as everybody else seemed to. He never did anything outside the scrum. He was totally immobile. It pisses me off that, after all these years, people are still saying that he was the first choice loosehead.

JPR Williams: Typical Mouse.

Fergus Slattery: Ian McLauchlan would be regarded, generally, as a bollocks. I don't regard him as a bollocks because I don't need to. I don't have any problems with him. I know how to manage him. But I would say that most players would say he's a bollocks. He's a slightly bad-natured guy. If you don't see eye-to-eye with him, you're not going to be in his camp. Call it spiteful, call it what you want, but he's not a guy I'd have on my Christmas card list.

Peter Dixon: Slatts has got the gift of the gab. Ian is dour, a typical west of Scotland man, but hilarious with it. I thought Ian was absolutely wonderful.

Mick Hipwell: I'll tell you a story. Mike Gibson got tied up early on in the tour because of the memories of the 1966 tour and he tensed up a lot. And Bob Hiller had a few problems at home and he wanted to go back to the UK. So the two of them disappeared from the tour shortly before the first Test. They disappeared on the Thursday and we weren't told that they were gone or anything; Ian McLauchlan was gone as well. Carwyn had sent them up to a lake in the mountains to go fishing. Now, there was nothing wrong with McLauchlan. He was sent off with them to help them relax – Carwyn and Doug knew that he could help them. You couldn't look at Mighty Mouse and not have a laugh. He'd have you laughing within an hour no matter what was going on in your life. And you know what – they came back on the Monday and they played the best rugby they ever played after that trip. That's great management. And fair play to the Mouse.

John Dawes: The Mouse had tremendous self-belief. It's interesting that he says that about Ray, but it doesn't surprise me. My guess is that he rated himself above both McLoughlin and Carmichael, so when he stepped into their boots he thought it was simply a case of him getting what he deserved.

Whatever the pecking order of the looseheads, the fact remained that Ray McLoughlin needed replacing. So, too, Sandy Carmichael. On the face of it, the selection committee's options to replace Carmichael were limited to just two: Barry Llewelyn, who had played all four games for Wales on the road to the Grand Slam, and the twenty-four-year-old Fran Cotton, who just broken onto the scene with England. Llewelyn made himself unavailable, so it was now down to Cotton. Everybody considered him a certainty.

Everybody except Carwyn, who bypassed him. The Lions went instead for John Dawes' London Welsh teammate, Geoff Evans, a major surprise given that Evans wasn't a prop at all – he was a lock – and on top of that, he hadn't played an international match for Wales for over a year.

As the stand-in for McLoughlin, the committee could have gone with Denzil Williams, the Welsh veteran, or John Lloyd, another Welshman, who'd been in and out of the national team since 1966, or Piggy Powell, who'd been England's loosehead throughout the 1971 season. Instead, the Cornish farmer Brian 'Stack' Stevens, with just five caps to his name, was selected.

The tour party limped their way out of Christchurch and onwards to Blenheim to play Marlborough and Nelson Bays on the Tuesday afternoon before the first Test. Bob Hiller, ever the man to lighten the mood, told the boys that, after Canterbury, he was deciding to wear a mouthguard for the first time in his rugby life. 'And if anybody can get me a crash helmet, I'll wear that, too,' he joked.

Hiller's dirt-trackers (the midweek team, now known as the T&Ws – the Tuesdays and Wednesdays) wanted to lift the spirits of the squad after the bloodbath at Canterbury. They'd done it by half-time in Blenheim. Alastair Biggar got a hat trick and there were more tries for Chris Rea and Ian McLauchlan as the Lions led 23–0 at the break, winning 31–12 in the end. They returned to the hotel to find more injury news – Mick Hipwell's damaged knee from Canterbury was more serious than everyone had thought and he looked doomed for the rest of the tour. Another one gone.

Mick Hipwell: I injured my knee away back in Australia, against New South Wales. I tackled someone on the cricket crease and my knee cracked off the hard ground and I knew that I had torn something. But as long as no one knew and I just pushed through it, it was fine. It finally gave in during the Canterbury match. Carwyn and Doug wanted to give me a few weeks to see if it would come right, but I knew it was done and that was me off home.

Word reached the Lions of Ivan Vodanovich's selection for the first Test. The New Zealand coach named six new caps in his team, a gamble that had the local press in an advanced state of apoplexy. Bruce Hunter of Otago and Ken Carrington of Auckland would make their debuts on the wings, Bob Burgess of Manawatu was selected at fly-half, Tane Norton of Canterbury was the new hooker, Peter Whiting of Auckland the new lock and Alan McNaughton of Bay of Plenty the new flanker.

There was vast experience and class as well as the rookies, of course. Fergie McCormick was full-back, Bryan Williams was in the midfield, Sid Going was at scrum-half. The pack had Jazz Muller, Ian Kirkpatrick and Colin Meads, the captain. Keith Murdoch, the wild man of Otago, was picked in the front row, but for a second time on tour, he withdrew. Richie Guy from Auckland brought the number of new caps to seven. Grizz Wyllie was on the bench, just in case the All Blacks needed a little more biff, as Fergie liked to call it.

Tane Norton: The team for the first Test was picked the night after the Canterbury game. Ron Urlich was the incumbent, but after Lancaster Park I thought, 'That's me shot,' because I spent more time sitting on my backside than I did playing that day. I was pleased as hell to get into the Test team to play the Lions for the real prize.

Bryan Williams: We were confident. We were at home and we hadn't lost a home Test series since the Springboks had toured in 1937.

Ian Kirkpatrick: Without anything ever being said, if you wore the All Blacks jersey, you didn't lose – that was it. If we lost, it wasn't a good time, I tell you. If you lost, boy, you had to pay. Losing wasn't part of it. It never crossed our minds for a second that we were going to do anything other than win the series 4–0.

Colin Meads: I don't think they should have made me captain. It was an honour, don't worry about that, but I was getting to the end of my tether. Everyone pulled out after 1970 and they picked young fellas who I only met for the first time when the Test team got together. We had a bunch of new players and I didn't know any of them. Ian Kirkpatrick would have been ideal. He was a good guy and everyone liked him.

Bryan Williams: Pinetree broke his arm in 1970 and then in 1971 he broke his ribs. No one would play rugby now with the injuries he had.

Sid Going: He felt restricted as captain. He wanted his team to get stuck in, but his leadership stopped him from leading the way in that regard.

Colin Meads: I used to be the guy that the captain would turn to if something needed sorting out and I would go and do it. But the captain can't be the one dishing out stuff like that. I'd have preferred Kirky to have been captain and then I could have concentrated on playing my own game and sorting out the Lions if they needed sorting out, if you know what I mean.

After the win in Blenheim, Doug Smith and John Dawes retired to Carwyn's room. When they arrived, Carwyn was standing by the window, his head clouded in smoke, his eyes glued to a sheet of paper. Every now and then he would scratch at his ribs or his lower back or his wrists, or rub the palms of his hands. Plagued all his life with eczema, his skin beneath his clothes was blotched red and often marked with sores and open cuts. The only visible sign of his affliction was these moments when he would absentmindedly scratch at a thickening of the skin on his hands. But just as the irritation had not distracted him when he had been playing rugby, so it did not distract him now as he pored over the team sheet with Smith and Dawes.

The side that had blitzed Wellington had been the starting point in their discussion, but thanks to Canterbury, there was no way they could put the same fifteen out again in Dunedin for the first Test. Sandy Carmichael and Ray McLoughlin were gone. Ian McLauchlan and Sean Lynch were the props now.

John Pullin was a shoo-in at hooker. Willie John was a cast-iron selection in the second row. Gordon Brown had shown impressive form, but having missed the last two games with illness, the nod went to Delme Thomas, a Lions veteran, Grand Slam winner and proven foil to McBride. The back row, though, was trouble.

Mervyn Davies had hardly played over the previous few weeks because of his groin injury; John Taylor was struggling with a hamstring; Slattery was still wearing an enamel mouthguard to fix his teeth; and Derek Quinnell had been battling like a hero when everyone else was injured, but his knee wasn't right. Peter Dixon was fit and healthy, but he was short on Test experience. Was it right to throw him into an international against New Zealand at Carisbrook when he had only played once for England in little more than a glorified friendly? Carwyn went for it – Dixon, Davies and Taylor would be his back row.

The backline picked itself, more or less. Barry and Gareth at half-back, Gibson and Dawes in the centre, JPR behind them. The only bone of contention was who should play on the wing. All three candidates were on fire: John Bevan was about to break Tony O'Reilly's record for tries scored by a Lion on a single tour; David Duckham had just scored six tries in one game; and Gerald Davies, well, he was Gerald Davies. A magician. In the end it was Dawes who made the call. He would speak to Duckham and break the news – the Englishman would be on the bench. They had to go with the Grand Slam-winning wings for this one.

John Taylor: Mervyn and I were in trouble before the first Test. He hadn't played since the match against Wellington, and I'd pulled a hamstring against West Coast-Buller and had missed the Canterbury match – which turned out to be a blessing. It meant that we had to prove our fitness at the training session before the Test and it was probably the hardest, longest, most gruelling I ever took part in. Carwyn had been criticised for selecting us because we had been unfit and I think that he was determined that if we were going to break down it would be before rather than on the day of the Test match.

Gareth Edwards: That training session was a bloody disaster. We did a relay to finish off. We had to run the length of the field, then run across and tag the next guy. And I was on the last length of the relay and I went into a pothole and tweaked a hamstring. I'd done two lengths of the field and was coming across on the third length and the field dipped down a little. I had maybe fifteen or twenty yards to go and I went into this bloody hole. I'd had hamstring trouble before so I knew exactly what it was – and it felt like my whole world had collapsed. The huge psychological effect of it. You just knew it would be weeks before it would heal properly. When I told Carwyn he said, 'Don't say a word; keep this between us. I want you to start on Saturday so nothing's changed.' And that's what we did. I went on and played for as long as I could. Carwyn didn't want anybody getting out of sorts with last-minute changes, so we kept the injury secret.

Willie John McBride: In the absence of Ray McLoughlin, I took charge of the forwards, and we concentrated on training Sean Lynch and Ian McLauchlan. Sean was thrown in at the deep end. He'd only had four caps for Ireland. He coped tremendously with the actual rugby, but he couldn't really cope with the concept of touring. He was homesick and distracted at times. Sometimes he'd go berserk.

Ray McLoughlin: I was still in New Zealand. It was only later that I went home. While the rest of the boys were in Blenheim, I went as a spy to one of the All Blacks' training sessions in Dunedin and then reported back to Carwyn. I wanted to see what kind of things the All Blacks were doing off lineouts and scrums. It was interesting to watch them run through their moves, then Carwyn and I went through it in detail, discussing what the boys should expect.

Sean Lynch: Ray drilled the Test pack hard in the build-up to the first Test and did a lot of the preparation with Willie John. These guys had been there before and knew what it was all about. Ray had great ideas, particularly about the formation of the pack, and he did a lot of the power training. He had us carrying three players on our shoulders over twenty-five yards. That sharpened you up. His vision of the game was light years ahead.

Fergus Slattery: Against a team like New Zealand, all three rows of the scrum have to be performing brilliantly if you wanted to get parity, let alone domination. Your lineout has to be good, your scrummage has to be good and your loose play has to be good. You need mobility. To be fair to Peter Dixon, he was what I would call a good player, not a great player. Mervyn Davies was a superstar player. John Taylor – I'd put him down as a good player. The second rows were rock solid. Gordon Brown, Delme Thomas, Willie John McBride – hard guys, what you really need. And in the front row our two props were our second-choice props, Sean Lynch and Ian McLauchlan, but both were very, very important, both were very, very good scrummagers. And John Pullin at hooker was a big, hard hooker. He wasn't skinny or lanky as you could sometimes get. He was the right shape to take on New Zealand.

John Spencer: Delme Thomas picked up a knock before the first Test and Carwyn decided there would be forty scrums in practice and the forwards would scrummage against the non-playing lads. But Delme had this knock, so Carwyn looked around and all the bigger non-playing backs disappeared off to the physio immediately. I was the tallest back around – not bright enough to disappear. I went into the second row with Willie John. He just tucked me under his arm and in we went for forty scrums. It was horrible. McLauchlan and Pullin kept rubbing their hips against my head, trying to give me cauliflower ears.

Willie John McBride: We were surprised by some of their selections – the young lad Bob Burgess at stand-off, picking Bryan Williams in the centre rather than the wing, and continuing to play Fergie McCormick, who was getting on at that stage. There must have been better full-backs playing in New Zealand than Fergie.

Fergie McCormick: A lot of people probably felt that I should have been another one of the guys to retire after the South Africa tour. I was thirty-one and in those days that was getting pretty long in the tooth for a full-back, but I knew what my physical condition was. I was knocked about in South Africa a bit, but beyond that, I was as fit as ever and it annoyed me that people wrote me off because of my age. All men are different physiologically and different mentally. So many sportsmen hit thirty and although physically they're as good as they were last year or the year before, there's a mental block there that says, 'Get out, old man. You're thirty and you've done your chips.' So I'd be thirty-two when the Lions came. So what? What's the difference between thirty-one and thirty-two? Fifty-two weeks. Three hundred and sixty-five days. Suddenly I've lost everything? That's just crap, isn't it? I was determined to go out there at Carisbrook and show everyone that I was still as good as ever. We were all going out there to smash the Lions.

Fergus Slattery: The maître d' at our hotel in Dunedin was talking to four of us on the eve of the First Test – Gareth, Mike Roberts, me and somebody else – and he stated New Zealand would win, so we obviously said rubbish and he was so adamant we inquired as to the best bottle of wine he had in store. Chateau Lafite 1934. So the bottle was put up as the wager.

Ian McLauchlan: Willie John had a forwards meeting. He was sitting there, his pipe in his mouth. He sat for a while and didn't say anything and then he began to speak. 'A lot of you will think you have been in hard matches, and possibly you have,' he said. 'But wait until tomorrow. It will be the hardest game of your lives. The All Blacks will hit us with everything except the kitchen sink. Maybe they will hit us with that as well. They've got to beat us. There's a whole country here that's telling them they've got to beat us. They will be out to give us a doing. Think about it. Then go to bed and have a good night's sleep.' I was ready.

Delme Thomas: When it comes to pre-match meals, every player has his own routine. I had a routine of breaking two raw eggs into a glass of sherry and downing it in one.

Gordon Brown: It looked disgusting. Fair play to him. He had arms like the Incredible Hulk.

Barry John: The team chat in the hotel had been very edgy – many guys couldn't sit still for more than a minute or two without getting up or squirming. The forwards seemed to be literally trembling with energy. As the bus neared the ground there wasn't much conversation. The coach pulled up and Chico start his chant of 'Give us an L, give us an I . . . LIONS!' That was our war cry every time we got off the bus and every time we left the changing room.

Gerald Davies: The first Test is a critical one because, in a psychological sense, it throws the gauntlet down. Instead of chasing the home team, the home team are now having to chase you. And that's a good position to be in.

Willie John McBride: Before we went out on that field, I told the forwards, 'The one thing to remember is that no matter what happens in this game, when it's over there'll be no excuses. Either we've won or we haven't. If we haven't won, we're not good enough.'

Mike Gibson: It's all very well people saying 'Good luck', but there comes a moment in the changing room when you are suddenly alone. All of the people who have been helping you are gone. You've got fifteen men standing there and that's when you feel the tension. There's an anticipatory nervousness. You feel it in your stomach. It's like sitting an exam – you go in and pick up your pen and for those first three or four lines you can hardly control your hand. And it's the same on the rugby field. You go out and they play the national anthems and there's this adrenaline flooding through you, and I used to try and stay as composed as possible, because within two minutes I knew I could be making an important decision and if I'd exploded in the changing room and beaten my head against the wall then I'd be in no fit state to make that decision properly.

So I just wanted to be left alone in the changing room, to sit and think. I would close my eyes and prepare by visualising things: 'I'm taking the kick-off. I'm fielding the kick-off. I'm making a break. I'm running right. What's happening?' And it was vivid, because if you've lived it in your mind you're more likely to deal with the situation when it happens in reality.

Willie John McBride: It had been a horrible morning, lashing with rain. There were gutters overflowing outside and they'd played five or six curtain-raisers on the field before we played, so it was all cut up. It was a horrible day. And I remember us being shown into this old sort of changing room with condensation everywhere and puddles on all the benches. Psychologically, it was a good place to be because the players were angry. I remember with about ten minutes to go, I looked up and Gerald Davies was combing his hair in the mirror and I said to John Dawes, 'Syd, can I just take the forwards for a wee minute?' because I didn't want any of them to see Gerald combing his bloody hair.

Carisbrook was mobbed, a 45,000 capacity with another 10,000 watching from Scotsman's Grandstand, the hillside overlooking the stadium. Many of them had been there since six that morning.

John Taylor: Dunedin is one of the friendliest cities in New Zealand, but Carisbrook was always a forbidding place to visit.

The ground was a hotchpotch of permanent and temporary stands. They somehow increased the capacity to 45,000 for the first Test, and if you couldn't get a ticket there was always space on the railway embankment up on the hill behind the main highway that skirted the ground. I was always too busy to notice, but trains would apparently slow down or even stop so that passengers could watch when there was a big match being played. We were playing on a glutinous surface. We were almost a stone a man lighter in the pack – Mighty Mouse weighed in at barely fifteen stone – and most of the home pundits thought that would be crucial. They thought that the All Blacks would be too powerful for us.

Ian McLauchlan: The first man I saw when we ran onto the pitch was Jazz Muller, who was my tighthead opponent. He was eighteen and a half stone. I thought, 'Christ, I've got to humph that about all afternoon.'

Barry John shaped to kick off to the left-hand side, but stepped over the ball and John Taylor banged it to the right. The All Blacks gathered – and motored. Driven on by Sid Going at scrum-half, they blasted into the Lions like there was no tomorrow. They made ground through the forwards and through big Bryan Williams thundering up in the midfield. Carisbrook screamed its approval.

Willie John McBride: I said to the forwards, 'Look, we might not have this ball for a while. They're going to run at us and run at us.' Ian Kirkpatrick caught the kick-off and it was just wave after wave. After twenty-five minutes we'd hardly touched the bloody ball. I was getting up from the ground, aches and pains everywhere, and there beside me was Sean Lynch on his hands and knees, muck everywhere, and he said, 'Jesus, we need someone to count these bastards because I've tackled about thirty of them.'

Ian McLauchlan: The first fifteen minutes were the hardest rugby I ever played. I wasn't nervous. I'd trained for that moment for years. The fact that it was physical didn't bother me. The only anxiety was born out of a desperation to succeed. It was murder because they looked so much fitter than we were. Despite all the pre-match pep talks we were still a bit in awe of them.

Mervyn Davies: I don't think I'd ever tackled so much in a game in my life. I never worked so hard in a game without touching the ball.

John Taylor: I had no more than a couple of touches.

Peter Dixon: I touched it three times. If that.

Gareth Edwards: It was like the Luftwaffe coming in. We were diving here and there, stopping this attack, stopping that attack. We were just chasing shadows. They were relentless. The first twenty minutes of that first Test match was the fastest twenty minutes I'd ever played in. They just came from everywhere.

Bryan Williams: We had attack after attack but it would come to nothing because some bugger would drop the ball. If all your best players have retired over the summer, you're coming in totally underdone. We virtually played the Lions into that game. If we'd scored early and scored again, then scored again, I don't know how things might have gone.

Barry John: Remember I was telling you about Carwyn calling me down to sit beside him at the Canterbury match and the thing we both saw and found really interesting? It was Fergie McCormick's positioning and his lack of speed on the turn.

Carwyn James: The day before the first Test, myself and Barry were playing a game of snooker and I turned to him and said, 'Look, do me one favour, I don't want to see this man playing against us in any more Tests. Can you take care of him?'

Barry John: I knew what I needed to do. It was clear as day to myself and Carwyn at Lancaster Park that I needed to kick into the space behind him. I had to get him running all over the place. And that's what I did.

Fergie McCormick: I thought, 'That little prick, he's put another one to the side.'

Barry John: Everyone expected me to launch up-and-unders, but I kicked the ball diagonally, making him turn and run. Why do what you're expected to do? To me, it was about keeping the opposition guessing. I was two-footed, so going left or right made no difference to me. It was all about waiting for the moment, and if that meant doing nothing but kick or pass for seventy-five minutes, so be it.

Fergie McCormick: He was placed under no pressure at all by our loose forwards. He could have taken time to read a book and count the laces on the ball before he kicked. He stood deep and picked his shots. Had our wingers been doing a proper covering job, as wingers are supposed to do, we wouldn't have been in so much trouble. If only the wingers had got off their arses.

Willie John McBride: Every kick that Barry put in was amazing. We won that Test by kicking it, not running it, which was one of the great ironies of the tour. McCormick had to scramble for everything, and when he got the ball in his hands he was two or three yards from the touchline, which meant he had no option but to kick from a very difficult angle – and he didn't kick well at all. It was a tremendous display of tactical thinking and then perfect execution.

Barry John: Fergie never played for New Zealand again. So that was that.

Ian McLauchlan: Jazz wasn't giving me any trouble. I burrowed in underneath him. He could have adjusted his feet to bring his great weight down on either my neck or my shoulders. You can't support eighteen and a half stone continuously for eighty minutes if a prop as heavy as that is continuously working on you. But he didn't try any of these things. He concentrated more on trying to pull down with the arm. That didn't work. He also tried turning in on Pull, which I don't think was a very good idea. Props shouldn't try to work on their own, but that's what he was doing. That made my job much easier. As far as I was concerned, the lower the scrum was the better – and that suited Pull as well. Pull was staying very cool, winning the ball every time Gareth put it in. Lynchy was muttering, which meant he was enjoying it as well. We knew we had them worried when they started throwing punches, but we gave as good as we got.

Peter Dixon: The Mouse truly anchored that scrum. He's short man, and obviously that was a strength in some ways because he was able to get underneath his opposition and lift them up and he never went backwards or got bothered if someone slapped him or whatever. Lynchy was a totally different character. You'd think, 'How does this man manage to play?' Partly because of the amounts of alcohol in him, but it also seemed to be such a struggle and a pain to him – he looked pained all the time. Yet he was exactly like Ian, going through the same sort of things, and if someone belted him, he'd just brush it off. I don't think I ever saw Lynchy hit anyone; he just seemed to take the beatings, shrug them off and carry on, and the opposition eventually realised it didn't make a blind bit of difference. Maybe all the booze anaesthetised him, I don't know. Or maybe the smell of booze on him just confused the opposition – 'How can this guy be playing when he's clearly been drinking his body weight in booze?'

Ray McLoughlin: The business about Muller being so much stronger than everybody else was an illusion. I don't think that he was that much stronger than Ian. There was a large quantity of non-productive weight in that eighteen and a half stones.

Willie John McBride: Carwyn knew that Gareth wouldn't last the game, but psychologically it was very important that he was named in the team. He wasn't on the field very long and then he came off and little Chico Hopkins from Maesteg came on and, you know, he played bloody well. People forget that.

John Pullin: Gareth was a great player, but I'll never forgive him for walking off the pitch. We had a scrum under their posts and Gareth buggers off. All he had to do was put the ball in, then either leave it to the back row or just give it to Barry to drop a goal or unleash the backline. But he disappeared and there was no one else to put the ball in. Eventually John Taylor did the job, but he didn't have a clue how to put it in. He shovelled it in and they got the ball and kicked it downfield. It was our best chance the whole game.

Gareth Edwards: I'd hoped that the hamstring would hold up, but it went again. Everybody who has had anything to do with rugby or athletics knows how tender a hamstring is. I felt a twinge early and knew that it would be pointless to play on. The injury would just get worse and worse. I would have been out for the rest of the tour.

Ian McLauchlan: It was downer that Gareth went off, but Chico came on and we never noticed the difference. He made some cheeky little breaks.

Mervyn Davies: Chico played a blinder.

Mike Gibson: He did, but Barry was the sort of player who could have played well with Harry Secombe at scrum-half.

Barry John: I said to Chico, 'Don't worry about anything else today, just hit me with the ball.' But he was a cocky little bastard and after about ten minutes it was as if he was back in Maesteg. He tried to make a break down the blindside. Kirkpatrick came round the corner and slammed him. It was like a comic strip moment because he was face down in the mud and we had to pull him up and when we did there was this Chico-shaped mark in the ground. I said, 'Shall we just go back to the original script?'

Shortly afterwards, Barry had an attempt at goal, from forty-five yards out, right on the limit of his range. In an effort to give it as much power as he could, he completely mistimed his strike and topped the ball, sending it scudding towards Jazz Muller who tried to gather it but instead fumbled it forward.

Barry John: Playing for the knock-on, I was.

Willie John McBride: And that's when we got the try, completely against the run of play.

The 1971 Lions party at Eastbourne. *Back row:* Dr Doug Smith (manager), Mike Gibson, Chris Rea, Ian McLauchlan, Fergus Slattery, Sandy Carmichael, Derek Quinnell, Mike Roberts, John Spencer, Sean Lynch, Delme Thomas, Mick Hipwell, Peter Dixon, Carwyn James (coach). *Middle row:* Arthur Lewis, Willie John McBride, Mervyn Davies, Gordon Brown, John Dawes (captain), Bob Hiller, John Bevan, Alistair Biggar, John Taylor. *Front row:* Ray McLoughlin, Ray Hopkins, John Pullin, Gareth Edwards, Barry John, Frank Laidlaw, Gerald Davies, JPR Williams, David Duckham

The 1971 All Blacks at Dunedin. *Back row:* Ken Carrington, Richie Guy, Ian Kirkpatrick, Peter Whiting, Alan Sutherland, Alex Wyllie, Bob Burgess. *Middle row:* Bob Duff (selector), Howard Joseph, Jazz Muller, Alan McNaughton, Ron Urlich, Tane Norton, Bryan Williams, Bruce Hunter, Pat Walsh (selector). *Front row:* Ernie Todd (manager), Sid Going, Wayne Cottrell, Colin Meads (captain), Fergie McCormick, Bill Davis, Ivan Vodanovich (coach)

The coaches going head-to-head in the series, Carwyn James (*left*) and Ivan Vodanovich (*right*).

Fergie McCormick unleashes the irresistible force of Bryan Williams against Transvaal in 1970. *Photosport NZ*

Carwyn begins to espouse his tactical philosophies for the tour as the party take a break in training.

our captain John 'Syd' Dawes carries his
manager, Doug Smith, during a training
un. As Mervyn Davies recalled, 'The threat
f having to carry Doug the length of the
itch for a training misdemeanour helped
ocus our collective minds.'

After the shock defeat to Queensland, the Lions get their first win on the tour against New South Wales in Sydney. Delme Thomas rises above the challenge of New South Wales' Owen Butler, watched by John Pullin (number two) and John Howard (number one). *Getty Images*

Having been crunched by Mervyn Davies, New Zealand's talisman, Colin Meads, has his ribs bandaged during King Country/Wanganui's match against the Lions in 1971.

The Lions forwards (*from left to right:* John Taylor, Mervyn Davies, Sandy Carmichael, Willie John McBride, Delme Thomas and John Pullin) win the ball at a lineout and form a protective barrier for Gareth Edwards during the Lions' demolition of Wellington at Athletic Park. *Getty Images*

Bruce Hunter can do nothing to stop John Dawes diving over to score against Otago. *Getty Images*

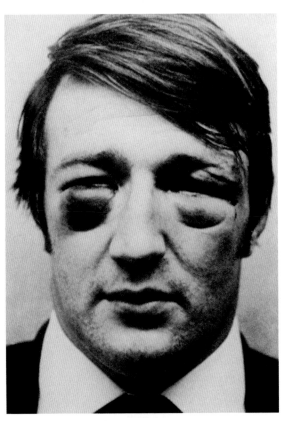

Sandy Carmichael shows the shocking damage he suffered to his face against Canterbury.
John Reason

Sandy Carmichael and Ray McLoughlin prepare to head home. *John Reason*

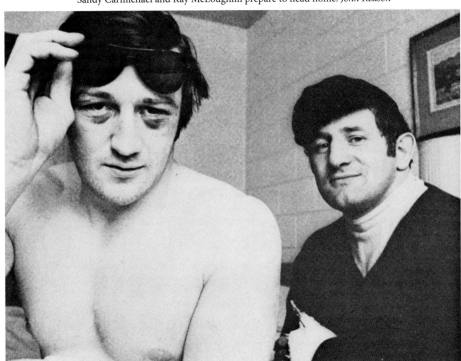

Above and right: Ray McLoughlin, compete with Gerald Davies' hat, John Reason's binoculars, his own tape recorder and a plastered thumb, spies on the All Blacks' practice before the first Test at Dunedin. Gordon Brown, meanwhile, watches the training session from the other side of the pitch. *John Reason*

Willie John McBride addresses the players during a break in play in the first Test. 'No matter what happens in this game, when it's over there'll be no excuses. Either we've won or we haven't. If we haven't won, we're not good enough.'

Barry John launches a counter-attack from deep within the Lions' territory during the first Test. *InphoPhotography*

Fergie McCormick. After an illustrious Te career, he would finish his time in an All Blac jersey having been toyed with mercilessly Barry John's near-faultless kicking display.

Colin Meads launches another wave of All Black attack during the first Test,
supported by (*from left to right*) Sid Going, Ian Kirkpatrick, Jazz Muller and Richie Guy.

The Mighty Mouse: Ian McLauchlan charges down Alan Sutherland's attempted clearance kick.
He would dive on the loose ball to score a decisive try in the first Test.

The two sides of a result. *Left:* A dejected Meads heads for the Carisbrook dressing rooms after the All Blacks' loss in the first Test. *Right:* Doug Smith and Mike Gibson burst into tears in the tunnel after the final whistle

Delme Thomas wins lineout ball against Southland. *Auckland Weekly News*

All Black prop Jazz Muller flies into a ruck with his studs raised high while playing for Taranaki against the Lions. *Auckland Weekly News*

Barry John scores against New Zealand Universities, with the crowd stunned into silence by the magic of his running and the Universities' players lying, helpless, in his wake. *Auckland Weekly News*

Bob Burgess dives over to score early in the second Test. *Auckland Weekly News*

Gareth Edwards flicks the ball back to Barry John at Lancaster Park, chased down by Sid Going and Ian Kirkpatrick. *InphoPhotography*

Gerald Davies brings down Bryan Williams before the All Blacks' wing had caught the ball, and in so doing concedes a penalty try during the second Test. *Photosport NZ*

n Kirkpatrick bursts away from a ruck on s way to the Lions try line – and into rugby ʒend. *InphoPhotography*

Former All Black great, Brian Lochore, puts a clearance kick after turning out for a 'one-o comeback match' for Wairarapa-Bush. *Aucklar Weekly News*

David Duckham bursts away to score a sensational early try against Poverty Bay/East Coast. *InphoPhotography*

Geoff Evans rumbles over to score against Auckland. *Auckland Weekly News*

Back in black: Brian Lochore alongside Colin Meads in the third Test in Wellington. *Photosport NZ*

Gareth Edwards hands off Bob Burgess on his way to creating a try for Barry John in the third Test.

Mike Gibson bursts away to score against Manawatu-Horowhenua.

Bob Hiller stretches out to score against Manawatu-Horowhenua. The Boss added three conversions and three penalty goals to his haul at Palmerston North. *Auckland Weekly News*

JPR Williams dives over for the Lions' second try against North Auckland. Ken Going and Bevan Holmes (on the ground) are powerless to stop the Lions' fullback. *Auckland Weekly News*

Alistair Biggar dives over the Bay of Plenty line as Miles Spence tries to pull him down. *Auckland Weekly News*

Gordon Brown goes down after taking a right hook from Peter Whiting at the second line-out of the fourth Test. Whiting looks ready to have another crack should Brown rise to retaliate.

While Brown is off the field receiving treatment, Wayne Cottrell bursts through to score for the All Blacks. *Getty Images*

Gerald Davies and Bryan Williams compete for a high ball during the fourth Test.

arry John slots another goal to add to his
cord-breaking points haul for a Lions tourist.

Gareth Edwards takes a quick tap penalty to break away up field in the fourth Test –
it would prove to be the spark that eventually led to Peter Dixon's try.

Peter Dixon, under a pile of bodies, crosses to score in the fourth Test.
'I like to remember it,' he said, 'as a classic eighty-yard try.' *Auckland Weekly News*

Tom Lister dives over to score for the All Blacks to keep the game on a knife-edge.

The right boot that sealed the series. 'I liked to call it the eighth wonder of the world,' recalled JPR, modestly.

he players raise their arms in joy – and
o little surprise – as JPR Williams fires
ver his monstrous drop-goal.

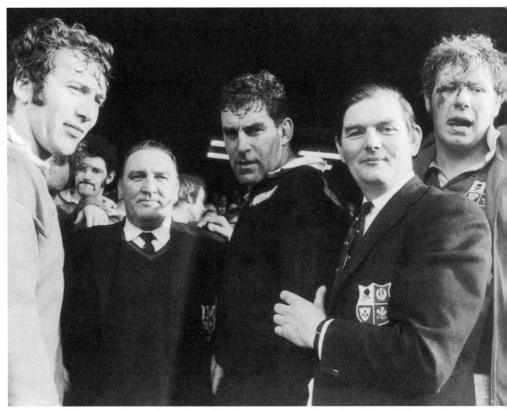

The end of the road. Colin Meads says farewell to the Test arena as a player alongside Lions' skipper John Dawes, manager Doug Smith and coach Carwyn James. Only second-row Gordon Brown would continue playing in the international game after the fourth Test in 1971.

A rugby man to the end: Colin Meads joins the Lions for a beer in their changing room after the fourth Test. Meanwhile Gareth Edwards and Gerald Davies, far left, contemplate the strange anti-climax of achieving sporting immortality.

Fergie McCormick: John Bevan crashed into the line and made it into our twenty-five, but we managed to get the ball back. I then broke a golden rule. The ball was bobbling loose and I passed to Alan Sutherland, our number eight, when I should have kicked it myself. That forced him to kick in a hurry.

Ian McLauchlan: Sutherland was standing inside his five-metre line and he took about a fortnight to wind his leg back to kick the ball and, by that time, I'd charged down his kick. The ball just bounced nicely and I popped it down for my first Test try.

Sandy Carmichael: I nearly had a heart attack when he scored.

Barry John: I missed the conversion. I missed a few that day.

Fergie McCormick: We came back at them. A couple of minutes later I had a penalty that would have settled us down, but I missed. I was never a nervous sort of player, but that day I felt jumpy. Carisbrook wasn't my favourite ground because it could get so wet and it was a bog that day. I missed a couple of vital kicks. They weren't difficult.

Despite McCormick's miss, the All Blacks kept up the pressure. JPR pulled off one try-saving tackle and Mike Gibson made another to protect the Lions' 6–3 lead. Even Barry hurled himself in front of Colin Meads on two occasions, a freakishly rare contribution in defence. It was that sort of day.

Fergie was missing kicks, but so was Barry. Not that it bothered him. Eventually, he put over a thirty-yarder to make it 9–3, a cue for another New Zealand siege and more demonic Lions defence.

Ian McLauchlan: Tackle, tackle, tackle. Knock them down, knock them down, knock them down. Please blow that bloody whistle. Eventually it came. We'd won. We were elated, but we were on our knees. Ah, that day changed my life. Before, I was Ian McLauchlan, who had taken an awful long time to persuade selectors that he wasn't too small to play for his country. Afterwards – when Doug Smith coined the phrase – I was Mighty Mouse.

Colin Meads: As a captain, I wished I'd had more experience around me. They had Willie John and Delme Thomas and, of course, Barry John, who gave Fergie a hard time. He had Fergie running all over the bloody paddock.

David Duckham: I think I only really realised what it meant after the full-time whistle when I saw Mike Gibson embracing Doug Smith in the tunnel, and both off them just broke down in floods of tears. It still sends shivers up my spine to think about it.

Mike Gibson: In terms of significant games in my career, it's the first Test in 1971 that stands out for me. The BBC was taking a radio commentary on the second half. I remember standing in a huddle – and I shouldn't have been thinking of this – but it suddenly came over me, and it was an overwhelming thing, that my parents were going to be sitting at home listening. And then afterwards it was just a feeling of sheer disbelief, because it just didn't happen. You didn't beat New Zealand – you couldn't. All my life, I had been brought up with that. You did not expect to beat New Zealand.

Willie John McBride: I came in after the game and sat down and said, 'God, did we win that game?' Because, on reflection, we all felt that for so much of the game we weren't really in it. It was the day we destroyed the myth that the All Blacks were invincible.

Colin Meads: Afterwards, it was impossible for me as captain not to think of the easy kicks at goal Fergie missed. If only . . .

Ian Kirkpatrick: Fergie got ostracised for that, but he shouldn't have been.

Sid Going: We had all the leather we needed, but we weren't organised to score tries. It wasn't all Fergie's fault. Our changing room afterwards was so quiet. We had some of the hardest men you'd meet anywhere, men like Meads, like Kirkpatrick, like so many of them. Without being over-sentimental about it, they played with pride for their country and it hurt.

Fergie McCormick: I was so disappointed after the game. I felt there was a nine out of ten chance I'd be dropped, and deep down I knew if that happened it was curtains forever. I'd have hoped that one Test wouldn't put me out, but it did. Our selectors were conned by the Lions management, who kept going on about me being the weak link in the chain. I heard later that Ivan wanted me back in the team for the fourth Test, but he was outvoted by the other selectors. So that was it. Goodbye, silver fern.

Colin Meads: When we lost, it was a national tragedy, a national disaster and you got not abused, but scorned.

Bryan Williams: Whenever an All Black team loses, the changing room is like a morgue. You've let yourselves down, you've let your family down, and you've let your country down. You take it all in and you get determined to put it right. You can expect a backlash when the All Blacks lose.

In the weeks leading up to the first Test, Doug Smith had often mentioned in press conferences that the All Blacks had a 'weak link' in their side who the Lions would look to target, but he would never reveal who this weak link was. In the wake of Fergie McCormick's humiliation, the media declared the weak link identified. 'Not so!' boomed Smith. 'He's still there!' And so the ruse continued.

Colin Meads: Oh, the bloody 'weak link'. The press were obsessed with it. That was good stuff from Doug Smith. It got to everyone. Towards the end of the tour some of the boys were looking at me as if to say, 'Perhaps it's you, Piney.' A brilliant piece of management.

Mick Hipwell: Doug could lead people. He was an extraordinary man for organising and having the energy to take on New Zealand and making speeches – and you never heard the same joke twice. I'm serious. It could be the end of the tour and he wouldn't repeat a joke and he'd never tell a joke you'd heard before in your life.

Peter Dixon: Doug wasn't called 'Bagpipes' for nothing. Just a walking ball of sound – big laugh, lots of quips, the ability to shoot you down if he needed to. A great man.

Ian McLauchlan: One supporter alone sent in eighty pounds worth of champagne. That was a lot of money and a lot of champagne in those days. Left to ourselves, we would probably have got brainless, but we went off to the official function and that kept us vaguely in order for a few hours.

Fergus Slattery: Now, remember the bet in the hotel and that bottle of Chateau Lafite 1934? The four of us sat at the table and called the maître d' over and he spent a few minutes in an emotional state, then he proceeded to open the wine and smell it and gaze at it and then we said, 'Pour it out into the four glasses.' But no, no, he had to swirl it around in the glass first. We said, 'Pour it,' and he did, reluctantly, and then we drank it, down the hatch in a oner. It was gone in seconds after thirty-seven years of care. He cried.

CHAPTER TWELVE

THEY REGARDED ME AS A SISSY

THE LIONS left the All Blacks to their post-mortem and headed for Queenstown, the resort town on the South Island where all sorts of activities were on offer for those with an adventurous spirit.

Gordon Brown: Willie John had been looking forward to it for weeks because he'd been deerstalking in Queenstown on the 1966 Lions tour and he'd failed to find anything. This time he had a top tracker-guide and he promised him a stag as long as he didn't mind a bit of climbing. Willie John would have climbed Everest without thinking about it.

Doug Smith: Willie John and Delme spent the whole day clambering up and down mountains in the rain and they didn't spot a thing. After seven hours they arrived back to find a deer about a quarter-mile from the farmhouse. They immediately dashed into one of the deer hides and got their rifles out, only to see the deer drop dead from a shot from Gordon Brown, coming down from the opposite side of the farm.

Gordon Brown: I was jumping around punching the air, screaming, 'You beauty!' Then a voice boomed out, 'Broonie, you bastard!'

Carwyn reviewed the Test match. The All Blacks had ruled the lineout. He counted the number of times Meads and Kirkpatrick had been able to peel around the back and run directly at Barry John. He wasn't sure his message was getting through to the players. He sensed a cockiness in the squad, a complacency that he now fought hard to eliminate. 'It was strange,' said John Dawes. 'We hadn't played well and we'd been incredibly lucky to win that Test, but even though we were all aware of that, we suddenly felt like world-beaters.'

The Lions headed to Invercargill to face Southland. Invercargill sits near the most southerly tip of New Zealand and their pride in their local team runs deep. Southland had beaten the Lions in 1966, so the warning lights were flashing for all those who cared to see them. Carwyn picked a strong team out of respect for their hosts. Part Test side, part midweek; a mixture of the heroes of Dunedin, the experienced dirt-trackers, a newcomer, Stack Stevens, and Fergus Slattery, whose gnashers were now deemed strong enough for him to play again.

John Polson: I played first-five for Southland. It was only my second game for them. I went to get my haircut on the morning of the game and everybody was talking about the match. I was sitting in the chair listening to them. Nobody had a clue who I was.

When we ran out onto the ground there were 20,000 people there, which was probably more overwhelming for us than anything. The main thing I remember was the speed of the game. We were an inexperienced team and quite a lot of us, especially in the backs, had only made our debuts about ten days earlier against Otago. So we were pretty green and the difference in the pace of the game between club rugby to the pace of the Lions and the type of rugby they were playing was dramatic. Barry John ran everything, but it was a bad day for running because we had a back-row forward called Ken 'Rowdy' Stewart and nobody wanted to be running at Rowdy, even Barry John.

Barry John: I got a few pastings. Their back row was after me, so I began to draw them onto me before flicking the ball wide, and we began to cut through them quite easily after that.

The Lions figured it out and won 25–3 with two tries from Alastair Biggar and one each for John Dawes, John Taylor and Mervyn Davies. The Lions made their way north to New Plymouth for their Saturday match against Taranaki. The drums were beating in New Zealand again. The locals reckoned they saw weakness against Southland and they were sure they saw some more vulnerability against Taranaki. The Lions scraped home 14–9. As the *Dominion* put it, 'In bumbling to this lucky win the Lions looked more like the lamentable combination of 1966 than the bobby-dazzlers who had devastated other New Zealand provinces.'

The Lions had been beaten on the try-count, 2–1, and the home press reckoned they'd been beaten up front also. In a withering report, the tourists were described as being 'locked in lethargy' and 'muddle-headed', while Mike Gibson, captaining the side in John Dawes' absence, 'had to take as much blame as anyone for their dismal display'.

Their conclusion: 'If they play as they did yesterday against an All Blacks side they would be most certainly thrashed.' A Taranaki official was interviewed by the press and the confidence oozed out of him. 'The crunch is coming for the Lions,' he declared. 'And when it comes, it'll be a landslide.'

Ian McLauchlan: We should have lost against Taranaki. We survived thanks largely to Bob Hiller's boot. A touch of overconfidence had spread through the squad and we were beginning to believe that anybody could be beaten without too much trouble.

The Lions flew south to Wellington to play New Zealand Universities at Athletic Park, their last game before the second Test. They'd already put in their best performance of the tour at the Park, against Wellington, and now Carwyn asked them to deliver a similar victory. He knew that, psychologically, another dominant display in this stadium would fill the place with good karma for his boys. The third Test was going to be played there. That was Carwyn. Always planning ahead.

Delme Thomas: The Kiwis didn't have much of a clue who Carwyn was before he arrived, but he aroused their curiosity once we were there. There would be a gang of reporters at each training session and sometimes, in order to confuse them, he would do something bizarre, like walking out into the training group with cricket gear or having a game of football right in the middle of a training session. He knew exactly what he was doing.

Carwyn James: I don't think the New Zealand public really knew what to make of me. I don't think they understood the quiet approach or the idea that you could have a rugby coach who was also interested in the theatre and literature and who could think of interesting ways to keep his players from getting bored with all the relentless rugby they were playing. I think they regarded me as a sissy.

Gerald Davies: So many coaches treat the team as a group, but that wasn't Carwyn's way. So when Barry, halfway through the tour, became tired of rugby training, Carwyn sent him away with Mike Gibson to kick a football around. Some people might consider that preferential treatment of a star player but, in fact, it made sense. If the man was tired of it, why not give him a break from it? What was important was his performance during the game.

Mike Gibson: Carwyn always encouraged players to play. He embedded the confidence to take risks, and if the decision was right but the play didn't work, he'd just say, 'Do it again until you get it right.' So he coached both our technique and tactics, but also gave us our decision-making skills. He gave us the tools and then empowered us to use them. That's the way you create a culture of trust and belief within the team.

Barry John: Four days before the second Test, we played New Zealand Universities at Athletic Park. The place was packed. Don't be fooled by the fact we were playing students. In New Zealand that meant past and present, with the emphasis very much on past – which meant they had Test players in their line-up. With a crowd coming out to see you on a Tuesday afternoon, you've got to put on a show, don't you?

Thirty thousand spectators came out to watch the match on a beautiful clear day in the capital. Barry capitalised on the physical domination of his forwards when banging over two penalties, but it was his next score that gobsmacked all who saw it.

Greg McGee: I was playing number eight for the Universities. I'd also played against the Lions for Otago, so I'd already had a close-up view of what they were capable of. At one point, the Lions had a scrum about fifteen to twenty yards from our line. Before the packs went down, I had a confab with the other loose forwards, Alex Matheson and Ron de Cleene, and we agreed that Barry John was going to try and drop a goal, so we decided to go at him in an arrowhead formation, which we did. They got the ball, we came at him from all points of the compass, he realised he couldn't take his drop goal, so instead he dodged the lot of us and scored under the posts. I remember lying there on my back with the other loose forwards and seeing him dot it down, and feeling very, very stupid. What he had just done, it shouldn't have been possible.

Bob Burgess: I was playing opposite Barry and he just disappeared.

Fergus Slattery: I can still see it clearly. We had a scrum right under the posts and Barry stood directly behind us, around the twenty-five yard line, and set up to take a drop kick. Chico flicked the ball to him, and as Barry goes to take the kick, the opensdie wing forward is out on top of him. Barry steps outside him, then runs and steps outside the number eight, and steps back inside the blindside wing forward, and runs in under the posts. And when he crosses the line he keeps running another four, five, six metres and then puts the ball down. And there is total silence in the ground. And when I say total silence, I mean total fucking silence. People had just seen something they'd never seen in their lives before. 'How the fuck did he do that?' And then all of a sudden a clapping started, but it was a kind of muted clapping as they all tried to get over the shock.

Barry John: Slatts is right. There was silence and I thought, 'Oh bollocks, what went wrong there? The ref's not giving it. Did Chico put the ball in crooked? Have I missed the whistle for something or other?' And I remember there was a count of three or four seconds and then there was this clapping.

162

Carwyn James: Poetry. Sheer poetry. It was certainly above the conscious level. It was flair, imagination; it was genius.

Gerald Davies: He was a very, very clever player. Looking at Barry John play indicates starkly to me the difference between today's game and the game then – he was just a ghostly figure who glided through defences.

Ray Hopkins: From the scrum, I fed him like a baby, though, didn't I? People shouldn't forget that . . .

Barry John: We won 27–6. Before the match, I knew that I only needed to score six points to equal the record of a hundred points by a tourist in New Zealand set by Gerry Brand of South Africa in 1937. I did it with two penalties, then went on to get a try, another penalty, a drop goal and three conversions. At the end of the match I had scored 115 points in eight matches. When I scored the try that gave me the record, Cliff Morgan, who was doing a commentary on the match, fell off his chair in the excitement.

The next day's press in Wellington was all about Barry. 'By jingo! The genius of King John', went the headline. Still, they picked holes in the Lions. The scoreline in Wellington had been flattering to them. The Universities side had carved them open at times. Morrie Collins, the left wing, had exposed them and had scored two tries. Sure, there was Barry's brilliance, but there were reasons to believe that the Lions were beatable.

The next day they flew to Christchurch. The second Test was upon them.

CHAPTER THIRTEEN

I WAS A FARM BOY – TOUGH

CARWYN STILL wasn't happy with Gareth Edwards' hamstring, but he picked him for the second Test nonetheless. He knew he could rely on Chico Hopkins to do a stellar job at scrum-half, but Gareth was Gareth and that was the end of it. Even at eighty per cent capacity, he was a totem of the team.

Only one change was made from Carisbrook – and it was a surprise. John Bevan, Grand Slam winger and scorer of one try against the Maori, one against Canterbury, two against Wanganui-King Country, three against Waikato and four against Wellington, was dropped to make way for David Duckham.

Gerald Davies: John had had an exceptional start, but being a youngster, he fell out of form and form for John meant scoring tries. He could have an otherwise brilliant game, but if he didn't cross the line, it made no difference what people said to him – John would feel down. After a few games like that he became impulsive and impetuous and the more that manifested itself the worse it got for him. Carwyn tried all manner of things to get him to snap out of it, but they all failed. John became dreadfully homesick and introverted and the last half of the tour was lost for him after that. That was the one great failing on the Carwyn's part.

John Spencer: Gerald's right. Carwyn didn't look after him. He could have done more to encourage him. But Duckers wasn't a bad guy to come in to replace him. Duckers was fast, he was skilful, he could defend like a flanker and he was on fire when it came to scoring tries.

Ivan Vodanovich did what everybody thought he would do – he ended the international career of Fergie McCormick. He also did something every New Zealander demanded he do – he moved Bryan Williams back to the wing, where he had made his name and where he was most dangerous. It wasn't his intention to pick Grizz Wyllie in his starting back row, but when Alan Sutherland broke a leg in a charity match, Grizz was in. Sutherland was a fine footballer, but All Blacks fans comforted themselves in the knowledge that their team now had an extra bit of Canterbury dog in the shape of the gnarled Wyllie.

Laurie Mains: I came in for Fergie. It was my debut. I never considered I'd challenge Fergie, even though he was getting on a bit. He copped all the stick for Carisbrook. I thought he was scapegoated. I was nervous when I first joined up with the squad and met Colin Meads. I thought he was the greatest player who ever pulled on boots.

Sid Going: Pinetree was a farm boy and I was a farm boy, so our time as rugby players was pretty hard going. Before a big Test, I wouldn't be going to the gym with a personal trainer, talking to my dietician or any of the stuff they do now. I'd be out digging drains, cutting tea tree, milking cows. I'd be jogging behind the tractor and in the off-season my brothers and I would be baling hay on neighbouring farms. What we did back then made you hard as well as strong. Pinetree was a farmer, so was Brian Lochore. It's part of the fabric of New Zealand rugby, guys coming from farming backgrounds. It makes you tough, so we played a tough kind of rugby.

Tough rugby, yes, but the fans demanded winning rugby now. To lose one Test to the Lions was bad enough, but to lose two would be sacrilege, an insult to all the great men who had worn the jersey before them. From as early as eight on the morning of the second Test, more than 10,000 spectators had lined the streets outside the gates to Lancaster Park, waiting for them to open at midday. By two o'clock, the ground was at capacity – 57,250. As Barry John put it, 'The New Zealanders are fighting for their rugby lives.'

The All Blacks had the same ferocity as they had in Dunedin, but this time they had accuracy and reward. It did them no harm that JPR was concussed early on after being clobbered under a garryowen from Sid Going. 'John Dawes told me to stay on and play by instinct,' said the full-back, 'but apart from that, I don't remember a thing.'

Carwyn James: He hurt himself trying to gather a ball, then he missed a tackle off the resulting scrum and Bob Burgess scored. It was unusual because JPR never missed tackles.

Colin Meads: JPR would have tackled a tank, thrown himself in front of a rhino stampede had it been for the good of the team. But he took a big knock beforehand and Bob spotted that he wasn't quite right.

Burgess and Going were quite a partnership; Sid, the seasoned All Black who lived in the real world of farming, and Bob, the long-haired university student who played life by ear. 'You couldn't get a more chalk and cheese combo if you tried,' said Bryan Williams.

Gordon Brown: JPR was in a very dazed state, but the one moment which best demonstrated the man's natural ability was the first try we scored in the second Test. He was covering back into our twenty-five on the end of an up-and-under from Sid Going. He not only caught it, but he burst away to the halfway line, gave a lovely pass to Mike Gibson, who released Gerald Davies to score.

Barry John: Gerald could have got round nearer to the posts to help my conversion. I missed it.

It was nip and tuck. A try for Bob and a try for Gerald. At the restart, Peter Dixon gathered and the All Blacks went through him like a wrecking ball. 'I had my head gashed open,' he said. That was the catalyst for New Zealand's second try, created by Ian Kirkpatrick, finished by Sid and converted by Laurie Mains.

Sid Going: The Lions were obsessed with having a full eight-man shove in the scrum and we took advantage of that because they were concentrating so much on the shove that their heads were down. Although the Lions were pushing us back, Tane Norton hooked our ball so quickly I was able to run virtually unimpeded, because their flankers had their heads down shoving.

Ian McLauchlan: We'd become obsessed by scrummaging at the expense of other parts of our game, like fringe defence. We'd pushed the All Blacks back at will in Dunedin, feeling that this was the area of our game we had to get right. We forgot that the other things don't follow on automatically. So, in the second Test, Sid Going was able to score a try himself, going down the blindside. Sid had a hand in four of the five New Zealand tries. He had the game of his life.

Gareth Edwards: Sid Going was a brilliant scrum-half. I never got to know him well because he kept himself to himself after matches, but I respected his playing qualities. He was an ideal player for the All Blacks style – a good kicker, quick passer and the famous Maori sidestep.

Colin Meads: Sid and Bob Burgess were a great combination, but the Lions were really concerned about Bryan Williams. That was obvious when Gerald Davies tackled him as he was about to receive a pass from Sid, and John Pring, the referee, awarded us a penalty try.

Bryan Williams: Sid set up lots of my tries. I loved playing with him and I loved watching him play, because he had a bag of tricks that no other half-back of the time had, not even Gareth Edwards. He went to pass to me, and had I been able to catch it, I had the momentum to get over the line. John Pring really had no choice.

Ian McLauchlan: A close decision but a fair one.

The All Blacks were on fire and the Lions were rattled. Barry kicked out on the full, the lineout became a mess, the defence became ragged. Sid Going sparked more panic when scampering down the side of a scrum, and at the next recycle, Bob Burgess went over for his second try. For all of Lancaster Park, this was more like it. They eased into a 19–6 lead.

Colin Meads: We were able to expose Barry John as a player who was inclined to panic under pressure. A brilliant player, to be sure, but not to my mind the King of the Lions, as he was popularly crowned. I'd give that title to Mike Gibson.

Peter Dixon: We went thirteen points behind, which was a lot in those days, but we were cutting them open in attack from time to time and our scrum was dominant. We'd scored a lot of late tries in the provincial matches, but then Ian Kirkpatrick scored a wonder try, running through the middle of us. It was one of the greatest tries ever scored against the Lions. He ran it in from sixty yards.

Ian Kirkpatrick: Pinetree always says he had a hand in it. He wrestled the ball out of a ruck and gave it to me. I mean, Pinetree never gave the ball to any bastard, so I was pretty lucky to get it. I can't really explain why I did what I did. I just ran, and while I was running I don't think I heard the crowd or anything – you're too involved in what you're trying to do. I had to head for the corner flag because they were coming across at me. When I scored the try and got up and the crowd was going bananas, I felt bloody embarrassed, to be honest. I was walking back, and I thought if there was a hole I could jump into I would. It was hard to explain how I felt, I just wanted to get back to halfway and get the game going again.

Gareth Edwards: He pushed me onto my backside. I got up very quickly and went after him. I prided myself that I wasn't too slow, and I thought, 'I'll get him.' I never gained a yard on him. Not only myself but a few other guys faster than me chased him to the line.

JPR Williams: I tried to tackle him and he swatted me away like I was a fly.

Bob Burgess: I was trying to keep up with him and yelling, 'Pass it, I'm here!' And he just kept going. Greedy bastard.

David Duckham: I would have caught him but I was shoved out of the way by Ken Carrington. You can see it on the film.

Gareth Edwards: I always admired the way he played. He was a great flanker and that was one of the best tries I've seen scored by a flanker. Even though it hurt, it was great to have witnessed it – maybe not at the time, but on reflection.

Ian Kirkpatrick: Even now, I get people coming up to me to say they were there that day. Going by the numbers who say it, there must have been a hundred thousand people at Lancaster Park.

At 22–6, it wasn't just the victory that was secured, it was the All Blacks' reputation. Gerald scored a consolation try and Barry a consolation drop goal later, but it was still 22–12 when the last whistle went – and 22–12 was a hell of a score. The New Zealand press had a field day. Weeks of swallowing hard on Lions superiority was now at an end. They'd been beaten at last and grand conclusions were drawn from the loss.

The *Dominion* reported, 'In the All Blacks convincing win over the Lions in the second rugby Test at Lancaster Park on Saturday there emerged an operative word. The word was confidence, or to be more precise, over-confidence. There is sufficient evidence to suggest that the Lions went into this Test with their heads somewhere in the realms of Cloud Nine.'

It had been 'a lashing' and now 'more of the headaches seem to be shifting towards the Lions', the paper concluded. This was the return of 'New Zealand rugby prestige' and Ian Kirkpatrick bestrode it like a 'magnificent stag'. Sid Going was immediately declared the best number nine in the world. It was written that the Lions just about rescued their pride in the end, thereby avoiding the biggest thrashing by a touring side since France in 1931.

Gareth Edwards: I was struggling. I survived the whole game, but I was playing on one leg and I was up against Sid Going and Kirkpatrick in full flow. We came off the field and went into the dressing room and without having to say much we all looked around and said, 'We can win this series. I've seen more today and I'm convinced we can win.'

Mervyn Davies: It didn't wash at first with me, but then I started believing.

David Duckham: Willie John was a real father figure to many of us, and he said a few choice words. The self-belief in the room was still huge and I remember buying into that feeling so much. It was something that I'd never experienced with England, that total self-belief.

Mick Hipwell: Do you know, everyone had a task to do, even when we weren't playing – Gareth Edwards, John Dawes, everyone. When I wasn't playing, I sat in the stands and I kept a record of every time there was a ruck, who had the ball and so on, and what happened in the play that followed. So it might be ruck number three after a scrum and we would have the ball, or the opposition would, and I'd tell Carwyn whether we did or didn't make ground after the ruck, and the same for the opposition. And by doing that kind of thing, Carwyn was collecting a whole load of statistics on each game. And the second Test is a good example of that, because it was going wrong but Carwyn picked up on the areas where they were beating us and started to correct it, which is why we were coming through stronger at the end.

We were already taking control of the game, which we then took forward with us afterwards.

Ian McLauchlan: It was the crossroads of the tour. I was just one of many players who felt that we had played better at Christchurch than we had in Dunedin. The general consensus was that we'd been a wee bit lucky in the first Test and not got the breaks in the second. That defeat knocked the complacency out of us. It stopped a downhill slide in attitude which had become apparent. If we were to lose a Test, this was the one. It gave us time to come back and try and win the series. No one doubted we could still do it.

In the post-match debrief, Carwyn voiced his disappointment about his back row's defence: 'We knew a year ago that if we were going to beat New Zealand, we would have to stop Sid Going and Ian Kirkpatrick. Today, we didn't. We lost the game up the narrow side. They scored four tries there through our bad defence.'

It was a theme that Carwyn would agonise over before the third Test, and one that would make him put his players through agonies on the training field. The following day, the Lions were bussed to Christchurch airport and flown up to Whangarei for a few days' rest – or so they thought.

Ian McLauchlan: We flew up to Whangarei in an old Fokker Friendship, right through a tropical storm at 200 feet. We got stuck into the grog at the hotel and Stack Stevens threw a pint of beer right over this guy in a white suit. Carwyn saw it all and came over to us.

Carwyn James: I warned them that training the next day would be hard.

Ian Mclauchlan: And by Christ it was.

Gordon Brown: We trained non-stop for two and a half hours in the mud and rain. When Carwyn finally blew his whistle, I'd no energy to walk the short distance to the dressing room. I crawled.

With the tour only halfway through, the Lions were suddenly on their knees.

CHAPTER FOURTEEN

UP THE MOUNTAIN, DEAD BOAR ROUND MY NECK

WHEN THE All Blacks trials had taken place at Palmerston North, a tall, rangy figure could be seen watching from the stands. It must have been a strange experience for this recently retired All Blacks legend to look on from the wings. He was no longer the figurehead at the heart of his country's national game. Instead, he was simply Brian Lochore, a farmer from Wairarapa.

'I had a good crack at it,' he said of his Test career, which spanned seven years and twenty-five caps, nineteen of them ending in victory. Lochore had been one of the gang of 1970 – the warhorses who retired after the bruising series defeat to South Africa. He left the rugby field, returned to the land and dedicated himself to it just as intensely as he had the black jersey. 'I'm not a modern person,' he said at the time. 'I wish we were still ploughing with horses, I wish we were still manual farmers. It may be that pre-high-tech age in which I was brought up produced that last generation of genuine "old-fashioned" farmers which made the All Blacks naturally hard, fit men.

'Shearing is a challenge. You learn a lot about yourself. You are pitting yourself against yourself from day to day. I came to love shearing for the challenge and for the exhaustion at the end of the day. If you don't believe utter exhaustion can bring with it an almost overwhelming sense of fulfilment, of something approaching euphoria, you haven't sheared, you haven't played Test rugby – you haven't lived.'

Lochore's plan was to spectate when the Lions came to play his local side, Wairarapa-Bush, the week after the second Test, but when injuries befell the team the SOS went out and Lochore couldn't resist responding to it. He was thirty years old. No spring chicken, but no dead duck either.

Brian Lochore: Just before that game, Wairarapa-Bush lost Ian Turley to injury and they were worried that, without him, they were going to get demolished in the lineout. So a distress call came my way and I decided that I'd help them out and pull on the boots one last time.

Rain poured down and an icy southerly whipped over the field in Masterton. A crowd of around 12,000 braved the conditions and they saw the Lions return to something approaching their best form. Chris Rea set up Barry John for the first try, then Rea set up Alastair Biggar for the second. Barry scored the third, John Spencer dusted himself down after some unhappy games and got the fourth, Gareth the fifth and Biggar got his second and the sixth in all to complete the victory

Brian Lochore: I came in and did my bit. We lost fairly heavily, but I was happy with my contribution and enjoyed what I thought was my final game of rugby. It was a nice way to go out. I'd played the Lions back in 1959 and again in 1966, so it felt like things had come full circle to play them one last time.

The Lions moved north-east to Hawke's Bay, a team that seemed to take their inspiration from Canterbury. There was fighting talk in the preamble, all sorts of stuff about how the Lions shouldn't expect to breeze in and out of town without a serious examination of their mettle. Blair Furlong was their fly-half, a player of vast experience who had toured with the All Blacks on the ill-fated trek to South Africa in 1970.

Blair Furlong: We'd had a pretty ordinary year playing inter-provincial matches, and some of us were in the twilight of our careers. I said to the guys, 'Should we do what the South Africans do and try and beat them up to make it easy for the All Blacks?'

Barry John: In the first minute, someone came through a ruck with his boot flying and it missed Gareth's head by about a millionth of an inch.

Gareth Edwards: Their prop, Hilton Meech, came through and tried to, shall we say, rip my shorts off – and whatever else was in there – with his boot. As I swung my shoulders, he landed on the floor and I swung my boot at him and just missed his head. I'm glad I missed him, but at the time that wasn't the way I was thinking.

Blair Furlong: Hilton Meech was on all fours. There's a photo around somewhere of Gareth Edwards trying to take his head off.

Gareth Edwards: We were in a war zone and we had to survive. John Pullin had to leave the field because he'd been punched in the eye.

Ian McLauchlan: Hawke's Bay was my Canterbury – the worst I experienced on any tour. Neil Thimbleby was my opposite man and after a couple of minutes he just hit me in the eye. 'That's one for wee Mickey Mouse,' he said. I got my own back in the next scrum, but it's not a game I wish to remember all that much.

David Duckham: That was the day when Barry sat on the ball.

Fergus Slattery: Barry was getting mauled badly by one of these grizzly Hawke's Bay wing forwards and he was fucking raging. I didn't know that was going on at the time, but I was standing at the end of the lineout, in or around the ten-yard line, and I could see him roaring at Gareth. He was screaming, and it wasn't just a bit of the usual shouting that happens during a rugby match, he was really annoyed, and Gareth is like an altar boy, just standing there looking back at him, and kind of saying, 'Yes, okay.' But they were speaking in Welsh, so I couldn't understand what they were saying. But I realised, 'Right, there's something going on here.'

Barry John: Obviously as a fly-half you can't go in and mix it like the forwards can, but there's more than one way to skin a cat.

Fergus Slattery: We win the lineout and Gareth throws a fucking huge pass out to Barry, who had obviously told him that he was going to stand an extra five or six yards further back. So this massive pass goes back to Barry and Barry puts the ball down on the ground and sits on it. One of the Hawke's Bay flankers has torn off the back of the lineout and sees Barry sitting on the ball and he stops and then he turns around and looks at the referee and the guy turns around again to see Barry sitting on the ball breaking his bollocks laughing at him. And, of course, your man then goes fucking ballistic and he comes screaming for Barry alongside the other two back-row guys. Barry picks up the ball and runs back towards our line and kicks the ball out of the ground. Then he turned around and looked at the lads chasing him. He doesn't say 'Fuck you', but the look he gave them said 'Fuck you'. He was just extraordinary. Some balls on him.

Barry John: When I sat on the ball this big chant went up around the ground – 'Kill! Kill! Kill!' So I thought, 'Righto, better get rid of this.' I stood up and realised that I wasn't actually in my twenty-five at all, but a couple of yards outside it. So I went back into my twenty-five and then slammed it into touch. I was pilloried by everyone afterwards, including the British press. They were all calling for me to be dropped after that one. And they were right, you know. Even though the Hawke's Bay guys were bastards on the day, you've got to show respect. But for me, it was a way of saying, 'Fuck off. We don't play rugby like that.'

Ian McLauchlan: I asked him afterwards why he did it and he said it was his way of humiliating them, of proving that the game was never meant to be played the way the New Zealanders were playing it that afternoon.

Gordon Brown: The crowd was of the same gutter standard as the Christchurch crowd. They obviously felt pressurised into living up to the disgraceful demands of the terraces.

Bob Hiller: You had the Hawke's Bay guys slugging away, trying to make the game grim and horrible, and then you had Gerald out on the wing, clean as a whistle, playing rugby from another planet.

Gareth Edwards: They were trying to outmuscle us, and yet Gerald showed the beauty of rugby with some classic running. He scored one try from underneath our own posts. We did that a couple of times.

Gerald Davies: I got a second try very quickly after getting the first. Mike chipped over the top and I sprinted onto it. There were strong-arm tactics employed against us that day, but we were playing the game the way that Carwyn wanted us to play – run, attack, use all that you have. For all their physicality, what came through in the end was our ability to play rugby and attack from all corners of the field. The moves for three of the four tries started from our own half; they were all counter-attacking plays. Then I got my third. Gareth flung a huge pass out to me on the left wing and I beat the defence with speed and footwork.

Fergus Slattery: Gerald did several pieces of magic – one where he ran at his winger, stepped inside him and then stepped around him, and the Hawke's Bay full-back then ran straight into the Hawke's Bay winger and Gerald just kept going to score under the posts. Not only had he scored a great try but he made the two Hawke's Bay guys look like complete pricks.

John Taylor: Having sidestepped, swerved and out-sprinted every opposition on the wing for the three tries, Gerald moved into the centre and split the defence open for his fourth. He had this incredible ability to sidestep at full pace.

David Duckham: Breathtaking. Absolutely the best things you've ever seen.

Blair Furlong: He ended up sidestepping and beating everybody without a hand touched on him.

John Taylor: What makes a good winger? At one end of the scale we had Gerald Davies, as neat and nimble as Nijinsky, and at the other end we had John Bevan, who preferred the shortest route between two points even if there were people in the way.

We had David Duckham and they had Bryan Williams. They were world class, but Gerald stood out above the rest. His genius never stopped surprising me.

Barry John: In the dressing room afterwards I threw my boots at the wall and asked Carwyn, 'What's this tour coming to? If this is rugby, let's go home.' I could sense the management wondering whether I'd lost it. They even suggested giving me a little holiday in the build-up to the third Test. At least the Hawke's Bay coach, Kel Tremain, gave me a laugh. He was asked about Gerald's four tries and whether he would love to have him in his own side. Tremain replied, 'I'm not sure I'd want him – I don't think he knows what he's doing.' Fucking hilarious.

Gerald Davies: My father was a great admirer of the All Blacks, and he could never imagine anyone beating them. His greatest hero was George Nepia, the legendary full-back. My father had watched him play against Llanelli at Stradey Park. One of the nicest things was that on the tour in 1971 I got to meet George Nepia at Hawke's Bay, and had a photograph taken that I was able to take back to show my father.

Fergus Slattery: We had some craic, though. Do you remember Bill McKay? Great Irish and Lions forward of the 1940s and 1950s. A hard man who emigrated to New Zealand. We were in Napier, I think. He introduced himself, then said, 'Do you fancy hunting tomorrow?'

I said, 'How do you mean, hunting?'

'Wild boar'.

I said, 'God, that would be great'.

He said, 'I'll pick you up in the morning at six'.

To my surprise, Ian McLauchlan said he'd come with me. We got into this jeep and drove over hills and across this river and drove halfway up a mountain and then we stopped and we had to get out. There were Maoris there. They put a rifle over my shoulder and up on a horse I got. We edged along the mountain on these horses and if you fell off you were dead. We got to the top and Rua, the head Maori, says, 'Right, now we go hunting.'

McLauchlan went off silently and sat on a rock. He said, 'I'm having none of this shit.'

I had my rugby boots on me. We were climbing down the mountain into this ravine. We had a pack of dogs with us and the dogs caught a boar. I stuck the ol' knife in and rammed it down and that was the end of the boar. I thought, 'Jesus, look at me, I'm king of the mountains!' Then Rua takes the knife and cuts the boar down the middle and the guts flop out in a big ball. And the smell! Then he ties the two back legs together and he says, 'You kill, you carry.' He threw it over my neck.

We have to go back up the mountain with this dead boar on me. Eventually we get back up to the top and here's McLauchlan sitting on his little rock, breaking his bollocks laughing. The day comes to an end. Back on the horses, back across the mountain and we got to one of the stations, or villages, on this farm and they were having this party. I looked at McLauchlan at one stage and he has one of the rifles with the telescopic lens and there's a little possum on a tree and he shot this possum. It was about two feet away from the front of the barrel. He shot a possum off a branch. I said, 'You prop forward you! You hard bastard! You murderer!' The worst part was on the Friday on the front page of the *New Zealand Herald* there's McLauchlan dressed up in a chef's outfit with a big white hat on top of his head and a great big knife and he's standing beside the boar I killed. I said, 'McLauchlan, you shit!'

The Lions moved north along the coastline from Napier to Gisborne to face Poverty Bay, a team with not just one Kirkpatrick in the back row, but two. Ian and David were leaders, the heart of a doughty side and heroes to a passionate home crowd that was recorded at 15,000 but which made the noise of twice that number.

The Lions were scratchy from the off and had to battle to get their 15–9 win. Gareth and David Duckham got the tries, with some critical points coming from the boot of Bob Hiller, dead-eye kicker, razor-sharp wit and one half of a wisecracking double act with Chico Hopkins.

Gareth Edwards: Bob was preparing to take a shot at goal and was taking his time to dig a large platform for the ball. A guy in the crowd shouted out, 'Do you want a shovel, Hiller?' Bob turned around and said, 'Gimme your mouth, that's big enough.' Then he boomed over the goal. I used to think that Bob was aloof, an Oxford graduate with a lot of arrogance. When I got to know him I realised how wrong I was. Like John Spencer and others who produced the bright side of their personalities when doomed to be a mid-weeker on tour, he was exceptional. He had a dazzling relationship with Chico. Two more opposing backgrounds you'd struggle to find.

Mervyn Davies: They might have been as different as coal dust and cut glass, but they kept us permanently amused. It is a testament to their attitude as tourists that they remained so good-humoured. Both were trying to shift immovable objects in Gareth and JPR, but they never let their understudy status impact on their commitment to the wider cause.

The third Test was just a week away, but first the Lions had to get past Auckland, another provincial powerhouse packed with international players. Bryan Williams was in the team; so, too, Ken Carrington and Peter Whiting, all focused on making a mark and driving home the psychological advantage they'd won when levelling the series. A capacity crowd of 55,000 squeezed into Eden Park.

Carwyn picked JPR, Duckham and Gerald Davies as his back three; the two Johns, Dawes and Spencer, were in the midfield; and Gareth played alongside Barry at half-back. Save for Mike Gibson, they were Test-match strong behind the scrum. Up front, it was a bit different. Carwyn didn't go full metal jacket in the pack, partly because of niggling injuries, partly because he wanted some of his heaviest hitters rested for the third Test.

Ian McLauchlan, John Pullin and Mike Roberts, the converted lock, were the front row; Geoff Evans and Gordon Brown were the second row, with Roger Arneil (Mick Hipwell's replacement on tour); Fergus Slattery and Mervyn Davies behind them.

Mike Roberts had a heart as big as a bucket but he was walking a tightrope at prop. One day his technical deficiencies were going to be exposed – and Auckland was the day. He was lifted off his feet at a few scrums and for almost the first time on tour the Lions scrum was sent into reverse.

The trickledown of a beaten scrum was serious: the Lions back row had no time on the ball; the half-backs were hustled and harried; the flying machines out wide lived off morsels. Spencer had a rough day in the centre, spilling ball and struggling to live with the All Black Carrington. For the England captain it was the cherry on top of what had been a murderously difficult tour.

Barry tried to force his flamboyance on the game, but the longer it went on, the more obvious it became how important Mike Gibson was to Barry. Without the Irishman to run lines, communicate, offer an additional attacking and kicking option and sweep up any errors made by his fly-half, Barry's play floundered on his own ambition.

The Lions scored two tries and Barry landed thirteen critical points with the boot. They won 19–12. It hadn't been sensational, but it was enough.

John Taylor: Geoff Evans scored a fine try.

Mike Roberts: God, he talked about that one for ages.

John Dawes: We were lucky to win that Auckland match. It was a tight old game. Geoff and I scored tries, but Auckland scored three and it was only thanks to Barry's kicking that we were able to edge it.

Carwyn took his players on a short flight to Whangarei and then on a bus to Waitangi for a few days of rest ahead of the big push in Wellington on Saturday. He used his time to plot and plan, identifying where the second Test was won, who made it happen and what the Lions had to do to make sure it didn't happen again. He knew who he needed to focus on. He took out a notebook, flipped the lid off his pen and wrote down a single name on the first blank page: *Sid Going*.

CHAPTER FIFTEEN

JPR SAVED MY LIFE

ALMOST AS soon as they arrived in the Bay of Islands, a storm blew in off the Tasman. Great squalls battered the windows of the Lions' hotel, which stood right on the water's edge. It was almost as if the weather gods were warning them of what lay ahead in the third Test. The series now hinged on it.

Carwyn got Doug Smith, John Dawes and Willie John McBride into a room and kicked the door shut. The debate about selection was long and occasionally fraught. Not over the backs – they picked themselves – but the forwards. Sean Lynch or Stack Stevens at tighthead; Gordon Brown, Geoff Evans or Delme Thomas as McBride's second-row partner; Peter Dixon or Derek Quinnell at blindside; John Taylor, Fergus Slattery or Rodger Arneil at openside.

In the end, Lynch survived, but Thomas, Dixon and Taylor perished in favour of Brown, Quinnell and Slattery. Quinnell's elevation was the most significant, given that he was still uncapped at any level. He was picked at blindside with a specific mission in mind. The New Zealanders had scored all four of their tries down the same channel in the second Test, and Sid Going was the architect of most of their good work. It was Quinnell's job to neutralise him.

Barry John: We were massively in need of a break, being three quarters of the way through the tour at this stage. We were in danger of becoming overwhelmingly fatigued. We needed to get away from rugby and any talk about rugby. While we were taking it easy, Carwyn was thinking hard. He knew that the prime threat would come from Sid Going. Sid had been given too much room in the second Test.

Peter Dixon: I went on that tour as a number eight and had hardly played any blindside at all up until then. I think you could count the number of games I played on the blindside on one hand. The big thing was that John Taylor said that he wanted the flankers to play left and right, which is what they must have done for London Welsh and Wales. So if you go to the Test matches, the first two Tests we played left and right flankers, and John always wanted to play on the right. I think it was a critical mistake of management.

The back row came in for a lot of criticism after the second Test, and I have to say that I was bloody scared stiff every time I found myself on the openside. It was the wrong side for me. I had no idea what lines to run. But having said that, all the tries were scored down JT's side.

I went to Carwyn after the second Test and said, 'This is bloody ridiculous, our lines of running are useless and you've just got to have a dedicated openside and blindside.' On defence, if I was on the openside, I never knew who I was to tackle – the fly-half, the scrum-half, who? Carwyn took that on board and changed it – but ended up dropping me anyway.

Gareth Edwards: We were well beaten in that second Test and came off the field despondent. But in the dressing room, Carwyn didn't allow us to dwell on it. We'd just lumped in from a 22–12 defeat and the first thing the coach says is we are going to win the series. He'd realised that we had to nullify the back row and Sid Going. They were the main instigators. Sid was very good at getting over the gain line, so we had to find a way of stopping that. Carwyn, much to everyone's surprise, brought in Derek Quinnell to do it. He told him, 'I don't care what you do, but Going is not to cross that gain line.' That was DQ's job.

Barry John: Chico had to play as Sid Going in training and he took a hell of a hammering from Derek.

Derek Quinnell: We did scrum after scrum after scrum and initially he was beating me, but after three or four days of constant training I started to get him and he got a bit of a battering in the end. He wanted to know why Gareth wasn't doing it.

Colin Meads: Word reached us that Chico Hopkins had a hell of a time in training, acting as Sid Going, getting trampled on by the forwards.

Barry John: Carwyn schooled us individually and collectively on how we should play in the third Test. He was perfectly calm, but he must have been bursting to grab each one of us by the scruff of the neck and scream at us to do well. This was our chance to make history.

John Taylor: When the team for the third Test was announced, Pete Dixon and I had both been dropped after the failure of the back row in Christchurch, and DQ and Slatts were selected to replace us. It was a great moment for DQ. Although he had continuously struggled with a knee injury, fluid appearing every time he played, he was lean and fit, much lighter in fact than at any other time in his career and extremely mobile. I was, naturally, disappointed.

John Dawes: That's a masterly understatement. For a couple of days, JT wasn't friends with anyone.

John Taylor: The night before we left Waitangi, there was a sensational 'South Sea' party, complete with very beautiful local women. The Test team were not allowed to go, but the rest of us could. The next day, Fergus went down with a virus and I was back in the Test team. So I got to go to the party and I was playing in the Test. Result.

Fergus Slattery: I fucked up. A group of guys were having a piss-up and we were swimming in a hotel pool, an outdoor pool, up at the top of the North Island, and it was cold and I got the flu. I told Mike Roberts that I was bolloxed and that I was off to bed and said, 'You better tell Carwyn and Doug.' So Mike went off and told them. I was lying in bed feeling shite and nothing was happening, no one came to check on me, so eventually I called down to reception and asked them to get me a doctor. So the doctor came and gave me some medication. This is something like the Wednesday before the third Test.

On the Thursday, John Dawes, Carwyn and Doug come in and see me and I tell them, 'Look I think I'm bolloxed, but I need to go for a run and see how I'm feeling.' And they said, 'Fine, go for a run and let us know.' So on the Friday I get into a tracksuit and go out to a pitch at a nearby school and go for a run. And when I got back I cried off. I was completely on my own on the run and I could have come back and told them I was fine, but I had to admit that I was bolloxed and couldn't play. It was the one time that I got really annoyed with the management. In the first instance, no one came to check on me medically – and Doug Smith was a doctor. I had to go and sort it out myself. And then in the second instance I felt there was such a lack of responsibility to the side – I could have gone on to play in that match and come off after only twenty minutes or something, totally bolloxed. Carwyn was famed for his attention to detail, so it was weird that none of the three of them could be arsed to come out and watch me go for this run to judge for themselves whether I was fit to play or not. It is the one slight I have against them from the tour. I don't want to blame Carwyn directly for that, because I don't know what went on with their discussions, so I'd rather blame all three of them for not handling the situation as well as they should have.

Gordon Brown: When we arrived at the hotel up in Waitangi, the room pairings were read out. I was in with Willie John. Normally the two locks playing in the next game shared a room, so I was pretty excited. When the team was announced and I was confirmed as his partner to lock the scrum I told him I was delighted. I wasn't exactly looking for him to say, 'Well done, Broonie, you deserved it. You've been playing really well,' but I hoped that he might open up and offer me some hint of encouragement. All he said was, 'I know who I wanted for the team.' So I was there with no idea whether he had voted for me or Delme – although I suspected that he had wanted Delme. If his reply was designed to act as a spur to me to prove my selection was justified, then it succeeded. I trained like a beast during the build-up to the Test.

Willie John McBride: Broonie – I loved the man. He was an immense player, but he could be pretty lax on the training ground. Sometimes you had to give him a real verbal kicking to get him going because, at heart, he was a lazy bugger. But when you got him fit and fired up, he was tremendous. You just had to give him that nudge now and again.

Down in Wellington, Ivan Vodanovich was having issues. Although the All Blacks had dominated much of the second Test, the Lions had come back at them in the second half and the All Blacks' scrum had struggled throughout the match. Keith Murdoch was drafted in to bolster the front row but then, just as he had done before, he withdrew without explanation. Another, even bigger calamity hit Vodanovich when Bryan Williams limped out of contention quickly followed by second row Peter Whiting. There were also doubts about Colin Meads and Ian Kirkpatrick. Vodanovich tried to keep a lid on it, but he was a worried man.

Brian Lochore: The day before the third Test, Bob Duff, the assistant All Blacks coach, called me in a panic. Peter Whiting was out injured and there were doubts over the fitness of both Piney and Kirky. 'We need you,' he said. And what was I supposed to say to that? I packed up my gear and had to leave a note for my wife because she wasn't home. The note said, 'Gone to Wellington, playing Test tomorrow, will ring later.' Then I drove to Masterton to catch a train to Wellington.

Colin Meads: The decision to ask Brian to come out of retirement was a lot more complex than most people realised. A lot of New Zealanders were up in arms that we hadn't promoted a young player, but the problem wasn't just Peter Whiting's back spasm – I'd damaged my ankle and Kirky had fallen off a horse and done his ribs. So Ivan was concerned that there would be a leadership vacuum if Kirky and I didn't make the team or had to come off injured. There was good logic in bringing Brian back in. He was an All Blacks great and had been a tremendous captain. He was still playing a bit and farming was keeping him fit and strong. It was a gamble, but it was a calculated one.

Brian Lochore: They were in a very deep hole. I wasn't prepared to go to my deathbed knowing that I turned down my country in a moment of need.

JPR Williams: When we saw that they were bringing back Brian Lochore we knew they were getting a bit desperate.

Laurie Mains: What bewildered me about our build-up wasn't Brian coming back, it was the fitness work we did, rather than teamwork. Ivan insisted on all this fitness work two and three days before we played. We sloshed around with mud over our ankles for two hours on the Thursday.

Ian Kirkpatrick: I didn't really want to be there. I'd played for Poverty Bay against the Lions in a midweek game and I'd popped my rib cartilage and then I was on a young horse down at my brother's and it bucked me off. I caught my ribs on the saddle and reinjured myself. I actually rang Vodanovich on the Monday – we didn't assemble until Wednesday – and he told me to go to the doctor. My doctor was away so I went to Bill McKay, the Irishman who was a Lion in 1950. He was the worst bugger I could have gone to because he told me there was nothing wrong. I knew there was something wrong.

I had an injection before training. I'm sitting on the table and some guy races in and says, 'You'd better hurry, the rest of them are out on the field' and this needle is stuck halfway in my ribs and I'm jumping up to get out there.

Saturday, 31 July dawned bright and clear. A steady breeze – gentle by Wellington standards – blew in from the north. Carwyn and John Dawes made a trip out to Athletic Park to inspect the ground that morning and were pleased to find the pitch was in a good condition, despite the rain showers that had blanketed the city for the previous two days.

With the sun shining and the wind blowing, the turf was drying out nicely. They discussed their tactics for the kick-off. If Dawes won the toss, he would elect to play with the sun and the wind to the Lions' backs. They wanted to go out and attack the All Blacks from the get-go, wanted to dominate the Test in a manner that they had failed to do in the first two games of the series. It was going to be all or nothing – the start had to be fast, it had to be furious, and they had to establish an early lead. Now was the time to be bold.

As they left Athletic Park, they saw the queues building outside the gates. More than 20,000 were there already.

Barry John: It's not the best fun waiting around in the hotel the morning of a match. A lot of guys could barely string two sentences together. You were confined to your rooms because the foyer and public areas of the hotel were packed with fans. You just sit there thinking about the game, wondering if you're going to be good enough. People would say I always looked relaxed, but that wasn't the case – not always. I was nervous before that Test.

When the bus pulled up at the players' entrance at the ground, the entire team were singing 'Take Me Home, Country Roads'. Then we piled out and made our way through the crowds to get to the changing room – and suddenly we were alone as a team, just the fifteen players and the reserves, Doug and Carwyn. The time for talking and planning had passed. It was the moment for action, to put up or shut up. Any self-doubt I had during the morning disappeared and I remember looking around at Willie John, Broonie, Merv the Swerve, JT, Pulls, big DQ. I looked at

Gareth and Gerald, JPR, Mike Gibson, Dave Duckham, and I thought, 'This is the greatest place to be in the world.'

Mervyn Davies: Barry played rugby on a different plane from anyone else I ever saw. He was on a superior wavelength. We were all in the changing room thumping the wall and he was there in such a relaxed state you'd think he was going out for a stroll. He was so laid-back he'd say, 'Don't worry, boys, it's only a game. Just give me the ball and I'll win it for you. It's only the All Blacks. How many points do you want me to score today?' He had a tremendous influence on all of us because he had such confidence.

Barry John: I remember feeling before the match that everything I had done before in rugby would count for nothing if we didn't win. It was going to be the most important match I was ever to play in. I felt we were better than the All Blacks and that we should win – and in the process, we could revolutionise rugby thinking.

Gordon Brown: The ground was good. There wasn't much wind, the pitch was firm and the sun was shining. The dressing room was basic and stark. I started getting ready when Barry suddenly let out a great yell: 'I've left my boots in the hotel.'

Barry John: It didn't help.

Gordon Brown: We all began to panic because it had taken us half an hour to get to the ground, and with the increased traffic as the kick-off approached there was no way the boots could be picked up and brought back before the kick-off in forty-five minutes. Barry calmly went and found a police motorcyclist and sent him off to the hotel at top speed to pick up his boots.

As the kick-off drew nearer and nearer, Syd was building his team talk to a climax and yet virtually the only thing on our minds was, 'When will those bloody boots get here?'

Barry was so unconcerned. Before every game, he would sit in the corner of the changing room with his eyes closed in apparent meditation, almost as if he was saying to himself, 'The team talk is for the other lads. Now, what am I going to do today?' During the whole tour, I can't recall Syd referring even once to Barry during team talks.

So there we all were, having this team talk, and Barry was sitting there in his socks, apparently half asleep in the corner, when the door burst open and the policeman crashed in, frantically waving the boots. 'I've got them, Mr John!' Barry took them and thanked him, then said, 'You haven't polished them!'

JPR Williams: The game was only five minutes in when the All Blacks put a high ball up on Barry with their whole pack charging at him. I could see what would happen if he took the ball. I was two or three stone heavier so I came forward and took over. As I caught the ball and turned my back I felt a thud in my arse where two of the New Zealand forwards had come in with their knees. It was four days before I could sit down again. But Barry could well have been off the field for good if he had taken that ball.

Barry John: JPR acted as my bodyguard. He took the blows that were meant for me.

Carwyn James: Early on, Willie John beat his man at the lineout and the ball went out to the backs. Barry shaped to kick but then moved it to Gerald Davies, who beat his man on the outside. He chipped ahead and the ball was taken by Bruce Hunter, and John Taylor cut him down with a wonderful tackle.

John Taylor: That's all Carwyn used to say to me: 'JT, get there, get there, get there and keep the lifeblood of the moves going.'

Gareth Edwards: JT was there like a hundred-metre sprinter and knocked somebody down, then knocked somebody else down, then somebody else got knocked down, the ball got turned over.

Gordon Brown: Willie John and I creamed the ruck and the ball was laid back to Gareth like a wee egg.

Carwyn James: Gareth to Barry. Drop goal. Three points.

Barry John: When I was playing, I always looked for an early opportunity to drop a goal. If I got it there were several bonuses – a lift for my side, a boost to my own confidence and, quite often, it was unsettling for the opposition.

Carwyn James: A few minutes later we were back down in their territory again. We threw to the back of the lineout near their line and it just bobbled free on the ground. Mervyn Davies was quickly onto it and our forwards poured into the ruck. John Pullin popped the ball to Gareth who went down the blindside and passed to Gerald to score.

Gareth Edwards: He squeezed in at the corner like a little squirrel.

Colin Meads: When I think of the brilliance of that Lions team I always think first of Gerald Davies scoring that try from a near impossible position. Ken Carrington was a very good, aggressive tackler but Gerald was able to beat him on a sixpence. I still don't know how he scored – there was no room.

Gerald Davies: Barry converted from the touchline.

The New Zealand *Sunday Times*: A hurricane start for the Lions.

Barry John: Gareth came out of the blocks in that game. He was something else. They couldn't handle him.

Mike Gibson: I'd single out Barry John and Gareth Edwards as the best I played with and against. Gareth had an immensely strong upper body, if something of an unusual frame. He had long legs and this squat torso. He was a funny shape, but there was nothing he couldn't do.

Mervyn Davies: There were so many attributes that set Gareth apart from us mere mortals: his instinctive ability, the way he could read the game, his strength, his low centre of gravity, his speed off the mark, his aura of invincibility. He wasn't tall, but he was strong, and he could have been a runner, a gymnast, a footballer – so we were all thankful that he chose rugby.

He had to be a scrum-half because he needed total immersion in the game. Anywhere else in the backline would have held little interest for him because it would have involved periods of inactivity. He was quite dictatorial too, bossing his pack about where he expected the ball to be delivered from the scrum. The quick ball is 'channel one' ball, which is hooked to the blindside flanker's feet, but Gareth insisted it came out between my feet or preferably at the feet of the openside flanker. And what Gareth wanted, Gareth got. We operated according to a simple rule: we were the ball winners; he was the ball user. And he used it superbly. He was always thinking about the game, looking for ways to flummox the opposition. We might spin it wide four or five times, then, when the defence had spread out to block us, we would sit on it or go down the blindside. Gareth never allowed the opposition the luxury of settling or second-guessing us. He made them work hard both physically and mentally.

Gordon Brown: It was Gareth's brilliance that set up the next try. He burst around the back of a lineout and handed off Bob Burgess with such force that Burgess was lifted off the ground. As he drew the full-back, Barry materialised at his shoulder to take a pass and ghost over at the posts.

Gareth Edwards: Unfortunately for Bob Burgess, he was in the way and I handed him off, and then Barry was just by my side to take a short ball and score a crucial try. And when it happens like that against a side like the All Blacks, you wonder when they're going to come back, where the whiplash is going to come from.

Bob Burgess: There's that famous photo of Gareth pushing me in the face. I don't really remember much of that game because I got knocked out.

Barry John: I rated Bob Burgess as one of the most interesting characters in New Zealand rugby. He was different – and it wasn't just his long hair. Bob was a thoughtful man with an outlook on rugby and life in general that was much broader than most of the men in New Zealand rugby at the time. In 1970 he made himself unavailable for the All Blacks tour of South Africa. He was uncapped and would definitely have been chosen for the tour had he wanted to go. He put his principles first – he didn't want to play in a country that promoted apartheid. In rugby-mad New Zealand, his decision to pass up the chance of becoming an All Black was considered by many to be madness and his stand was frowned on in some circles.

I identified with Bob in a number of ways – we had similar attitudes on and off the field. The way he played rugby told you a lot about his character. He wasn't rash and he analysed situations. The great pity was that he was only able to show his great talent sporadically, as he did in the second Test, but that wasn't necessarily his fault. It was simply that he and Sid Going didn't click regularly because they weren't really compatible as a half-back combination. They both wanted to be the senior partner and you just can't have that. I'd have found playing outside Sid frustrating. Sid usually wanted a bite of the cherry before getting the ball out to his fly-half. The key to the third Test was unleashing Derek Quinnell on Sid, to make sure he couldn't boss the game as he liked to.

Gareth Edwards: We were 13–0 ahead after twenty minutes. Half-time came. I said something about all the people at home switching on to listen in to the match; Dawesy picked up on that and continued with the same thread. And I think we all bought into the thought of what our families and friends were doing at three o'clock in the morning back home. It was a huge moment for us all to imagine them waking up and tuning in to hear that we were 13–0 up. 'Can you imagine?' I said. And we took strength from that.

Colin Meads: We played poorly. At first five-eighth, Burgess kicked and kicked and kicked. First, that was contrary to our tactics, and secondly, he kicked really badly. JPR Williams was able to turn our bad kicking into good attacking possession for the Lions all afternoon. The Wellington coach Bill Freeman had a saying which put our fault that day into a nutshell: 'If you kick, kick to land, not to hand.' JPR had a bloody field day.

Willie John McBride: The one thing I would say about the forwards is that we never beat them, but we equalled them. And we got enough ball to prove that we were better than they were. John Pullin was a farmer and my background was all farming. So there was that strong mental, physical stuff in the team, but there was also Quinnell, who was a roughhouse, a hard guy who never stood back.

Gareth Edwards: Sid was always running into DQ. The more Sid got frustrated, the more he tried to do and the better DQ played.

Colin Meads: They really had us taped when they denied us any ball at the back of the lineout. In the past, All Blacks teams had scored dozens upon dozens of tries working the tap-down from the back of the lineout and then driving in on the ball carrier. When Mervyn Davies stopped us getting that clean lineout possession, one of our big attacking weapons was nullified.

John Dawes: I rated Mervyn as the second most important Lion after Barry. He wasn't afraid of hard, dirty and thankless work. What did he do in the Tests? Tackle, tackle, tackle.

Sid Going: At first I felt the recall of Lochore was probably the right thing, but once the Test started I knew it was a mistake. We didn't have enough height in the lineout to win the ball we needed.

Mervyn Davies: Big Gordon Brown bossed Lochore.

Gordon Brown: Dominated him all day.

Sid Going: The Lions weren't as good as most people give them credit for. Our forwards did too much running around and not enough driving. There was too much individualism. There was a vast difference between being a New Zealand half-back in 1971 and being a New Zealand half-back in 1967. In '67, the forwards were there to control, to give you what we used to call 'plate ball'. By '71 the pack had loosened up. I was never certain where the ball was going to pop up from. We'd gone right away from the tight core who controlled the game to a load of individuals who all seemed like frustrated loose forwards.

Carwyn James: I could see it was annoying Going, the way the forwards were playing, but some it paid off for them. Colin Meads pulled off a magician's act when he carried the ball up towards our line and slipped the ball out of the tackle. Laurie Mains went over for a try just after.

Athletic Park went berserk at the prospect of a New Zealand fightback. Even when Mains missed his conversion, the place was going crazy. The All Blacks now had a period of dominance. John Taylor got done for offside and Meads pointed to the posts. 'Bang it over,' he told Mains. For some reason, unknown even to the man himself, Mains attempted to drop-kick the penalty instead of teeing it up. The ball never got close. Sid Going was enraged, not just at a second missed kick, but by Derek Quinnell living in his face.

Sid Going: It was a Test I'd like to forget – and it was one of the few occasions when Gareth Edwards had the better of me. The Lions had a plan to stop me running, but they didn't need one because our forwards failed to get any control. With the game wearing on, and the Lions ahead, someone shouted, 'Come on, Sid, you know what to do.' From the next ruck I took two steps and was slammed. Probably Quinnell again.

Jazz Muller: Then Bob Burgess was knocked out. John Taylor hit him with a massive tackle and on his way to the floor his head smashed off my hip. I thought he'd broken his neck.

Barry John: I screamed for a stretcher.

JPR Williams: I rushed up and pulled out his mouthguard so that he couldn't swallow his tongue.

Bob Burgess: JPR Williams probably saved my life. He was a med student and he realised I was gagging, swallowing my tongue and he did whatever it was that was necessary to stop me from choking.

Sid Going: Nothing went right. We had a chance to score later on and a dog ran onto the pitch and tripped up our winger.

Bryan Williams: I was watching at home. When a dog denies you a possible try you know you've had a rough day.

When the final whistle sounded, the Lions were ahead 13–3. Athletic Park emptied in virtual silence, the only noise coming from the jubilant Lions. They were 2–1 up in the series with one Test to come at Eden Park in Auckland. For the first time in history, they had the All Blacks where they wanted them.

The Kiwi press lauded the tourists while firing some volleys at their own boys: 'In the backs, the All Blacks were schoolboys by comparison to the swift and intelligent Lions. If Barry John is the King then this could be taken as his coronation. He continued to make Athletic Park a rich and productive part of his kingdom.'

Vivian Jenkins, the Wales and Lions full-back of the 1930s turned journalist, waxed lyrical in his victory cable for the London *Sunday Times*. 'Glory Be! The day – the unforgettable, almost unbelievable day – has dawned at last. Mark well the date. It marks a turning point in Britain's rugby story.' After so many long years covering the Lions in New Zealand, he could be forgiven, perhaps, for rejoicing. His colleague, J. B. G. Thomas, was even quicker into print, the *Western Mail* match report appearing on the Cardiff streets by 6 a.m. – barely an hour after the end of the match. The 2–1 lead in the series meant that the Lions couldn't lose – a significant result in itself – but it also marked the first time that the Lions had won two Test matches against the All Blacks in a single series. The question that now loomed was whether the Lions could win the series outright in the fourth Test, or whether the All Blacks would fight back to draw it level at two apiece.

Sid Going: I took a lot of the criticism for the loss.

Bryan Williams: And Brian Lochore.

Ian McLauchlan: Bringing back Lochore was a mistake.

Gareth Edwards: It was like putting a thumb into a wall when the water was gushing out.

Bryan Williams: The worst thing about it is that Brian came back in as a lock – and he wasn't a lock. He was a number eight. It was a symptom of the woolly thinking that was surrounding selection at the time. He'd been retired for a year, playing a bit of club rugby, and was a legendary number eight and captain of the All Blacks and they bring him back as a lock. That's not going to work.

JPR Williams: Guys like Lochore were getting well past their best at that stage. Colin Meads was a fantastic player and a fantastic man, but he was in the twilight of his career by then and your legs just don't have the same spring in them as they once did.

Brian Lochore: I don't regret coming back. A lot of people have asked me why I did it, because it ruined my reputation in many ways. Some people think I shouldn't have been there, but I didn't ask to be there. I was there, I gave what I had to give and I have no regrets. I wasn't worried about my reputation. I was worried about my country.

Barry John: It was terrible, some of the stuff that came out about Brian Lochore after that match. Some New Zealand officials at a post-match function kept saying, 'Well, of course, we knew Lochore was always overrated, he never was much bloody good'. Marvellous, isn't it? To say that of a man like Brian. A great man, a really great man.

Sid Going: It set up the fourth Test as something pretty damn huge. New Zealand hadn't lost a series at home since 1937. No pressure.

Barry John: We weren't worried about the fourth one just yet.

David Duckham: There was a bit of a party.

JPR Williams: It's not often you go 2–1 ahead in a series in New Zealand.

Willie John McBride: Precisely never.

John Dawes: We gave it plenty that night.

Gerald Davies: Drink was taken, it's true.

John Spencer: Lynchy could be unpredictable when he was on the piss. Willie John and I had to tie him to his bed to keep him out of trouble.

CHAPTER SIXTEEN

RUMBLE IN THE BAY

WHEN THE boys hit Palmerston North for their twenty-first game in New Zealand, they were still on the lash. At the team hotel the beers were slow in coming, what with everyone rooting around for currency to buy the next round, so Barry John took over, opened a tab in the Lions' name and the booze started flowing more freely after that.

By the end of the night the bill had reach eye-popping proportions, but the team management gulped hard and paid up – no point in upsetting the lads now that the tour's finishing line was beginning to come into view.

Carwyn had a detailed training session for the following morning, not overly rigorous but technical and important. Once he saw the state of his players he abandoned his plan and went easy. He knew that if he flogged them he might have a rebellion on his hands, so he sent them on a gentle run and knocked it on the head after that. 'It showed his ability to gauge a mood,' said John Taylor. 'The boys loved him for that.'

Willie John McBride was made captain for the match against Manawatu-Horowhenua. On his fourth Lions tour, this was his first time leading the team out. And it was a rout. Having scored eleven tries in his first six games, John Bevan had scored only one in the previous six weeks. Injury had restricted him to four games, but most of it was caused by the mid-tour melancholy that he found so difficult to shift.

Bevan found himself, again, scoring four tries. 'His depression lifted,' reported the *Dominion*. 'He was once again the pacy, aggressive try-scorer who, if he couldn't run around his opponents, ran through them.'

The four brought his tally to sixteen, just one short of the Lions record of seventeen set by Ireland's Tony O'Reilly in 1959. Bob Hiller, John Spencer, Arthur Lewis and Mike Gibson added more tries in a 39–6 win. Willie John was carried off the field on the shoulders of his teammates while John Dawes lauded him to the waiting press. 'A great man, a great forward and a great Lion,' he said.

There were just three more games to go on the tour: North Auckland in Whangarei on 7 August; Bay of Plenty in Tauranga three days later; and the final Test in Eden Park four days after that.

It wasn't a coincidence that the last Saturday match before the fourth Test was against North Auckland, for this was a provincial team with a serious amount of class and enough forward power to trouble the Lions and send them into their last week in the country in a bruised state, both physically and mentally.

They didn't have just one Going in the team, but three. Ken was full-back, Brian was fly-half and Sid, psyched to the gills after the third Test, was alongside him at scrum-half. The pack was led by the All Black Richie Guy, and if the rest of them weren't names of international renown, they were the hardest of boys.

The Lions made the kind of start that suggested another easy day, but that's not what happened. JPR hit a beautiful line and shipped it on to David Duckham who, in the tightest of spaces, beat one man and then another and then swerved around the covering winger before diving over in the corner. Barry knocked the conversion between the posts. Easy.

David Duckham: Only three minutes had been played. I kind of jinked my way over.

Gordon Brown: It was a kind of swerve-cum-sidestep. Unbelievable.

David Duckham: I put the ball down and I thought, 'How did I get away with that?'

The Goings got motoring after that early blow. They owned the ball, prodded and probed at the Lions defence, ran at them at angles, handled brilliantly, cleared out the rucks with venom. Duckham and JPR pulled off try-saving tackles in the midst of the siege.

Ken Going: Our specialty with Northland and North Auckland was the Going 'triple scissors'. It would go something like this: if you had a decent blindside off a set piece, we'd feign to attack to the openside, but then Sid would fire a reverse pass to Brian going blind. I'd then run an angle off the wing, going back infield, and Brian would switch it to me, then I'd switch it back to Sid who would be running back towards the blindside. The secret was to hide the ball from the players, and probably only four players knew where it was going – me, Sid, Brian and Joe Morgan, our second-five. It was all about how the pass landed in Brian's hands. That would determine if he would give it to me and, if he did, I would have a split-second decision to give it to Sid or just smash it. I knew, ninety-eight per cent of the time, if I got it to Sid it would be a score. As kids we used to play all the time, with Jeanette, our older sister, as well. She was the fourth player, so we could play two-on-two.

Sid Going: We called it the Special – and it came off. We befuddled the Lions defence, got Ken into space, and even though he was brought down just before the line, Richie Guy followed up and scored. Ken then put over the conversion to make it 5–5. We felt pretty good after that.

The Lions were concerned at the break. No provincial match had been like this one, no opposition had played with the ambition that North Auckland were playing with. They were in a game now. They needed to find something. Barry John stepped up. He accelerated downfield, through a scrambling defence and got his pass away to JPR, who ran on to score.

Late in the second half, the Lions still led 8–5, but North Auckland had a scrum. Sid called the Special again. And it worked again. Sid got it to Brian, who darted towards the blindside wing, Ken came back on the angle from full-back and received the ball from Brian, before slipping it to Sid, who slashed back out towards the blindside again and into a gaping hole. Only JPR Williams stood in his way.

Sid Going: When I saw Williams ahead of me, I looked to my right for Brian. Usually he would be racing up in support, but there was a Lion – a loose forward I think – blocking my pass to him. What I tried to do was bump JPR back.

Gordon Brown: JPR exploded him.

Sid Going: Usually, so close to the goal line, I would always manage to bump the full-back off and scramble over the line, but JPR, being the great tackler that he was, stopped me dead in my tracks. I reckon I was no more than a metre from the goal line – but the chance was lost.

Carwyn James: It looked a certain score and a probably a match-winner. For all his brilliance in attack, it was his defence that won that game for us. That was the irrepressible John Williams.

There was time for one more act. The Lions won a scrum just in front of the North Auckland posts, Barry slipped back for the drop goal and, as the ball came to him, half of North Auckland descended upon him. He shaped to kick, but at the very last second he changed his mind and stepped the onrushing defence before flicking the ball out to JPR, who put Bevan over for his seventeenth, and record-equalling, try of the tour.

David Duckham: It finished 11–5 and it was the hardest game outside the Tests.

Ted Griffin, the North Auckland coach, was distraught after the match, his players having come so close to toppling the Lions. 'I don't care to be beaten, to hell with it,' he said. 'I get grumpy and sour when anyone licks my team and right now I am grumpy and sour with the Lions. There should have been a free kick against Williams, there should have been . . .' He began to stumble over his words. 'We did this . . . we shouldn't have done that . . .' But then he gave up the ghost. 'I'm grumpy and sour and I don't like being beaten. But I'll tell you something – this is the best Lions team there ever was.'

Carwyn James: On the following Wednesday, preparing for the final Test, to my surprise and delight the backs were running moves that replicated the Going brothers' double-scissors ploy. Soon the double was a triple, then a quadruple, and then, inspired by a desire to show off in front of a large crowd, we worked out seven successive scissors all executed at top speed within forty yards or less of the goal line.

The Lions were in Tauranga now, a harbourside town on the North Island. They were there to play Bay of Plenty in their penultimate game of a three-month odyssey.

There was a record crowd of 23,000, including an eleven-year-old boy called Vern Cotter, who would go on to become one of the world's most respected coaches. Ron Bryers was in charge of Bay of Plenty and he threw all sorts of experience at the Lions. In their history, only sixteen players had represented the province more than a hundred times, and Bryers had six of them on the field that day.

There was Greg Rowlands, the fly-half, with 161 appearances; Dinny Mohi, the tighthead prop, on 156; Eddie Stokes, the outside centre, on 129; Alan McNaughton, the lock, on 122; Graeme Moore, the right wing, on 114; and Jim Maniapoto, the blindside flanker, on 105. Maniapoto had been in the Bay team that drew with the Lions in 1966.

Graeme Moore: I'd never seen the ground looking like it before. We put up temporary stands and made it into this incredible amphitheatre. For the full eighty minutes you felt like you were surrounded by your mates. It's spine-tingling even now to think about it.

Carwyn James: Although we had the Test on the Saturday, everybody was keen to play. We went with Gareth Edwards, Barry John and Mike Gibson, but we left John Dawes out

RUMBLE IN THE BAY

because he'd played sixteen matches on tour at that stage and he needed a rest. Bay of Plenty had a lot of time to prepare for us. They took us on at our own game.

Graeme Moore: The Lions forwards had been dominating the All Blacks during the Test series, but at one stage our pack drove them back nearly thirty metres. Up to then we may have thought we were out of our league.

Ronnie Walker: Oh man. I was the hooker, and our captain and I couldn't believe it. I was right in the middle of that maul and at one stage I thought, 'Hell – what's wrong? I better have a look and see what's happening!' I just couldn't believe we were going forward so fast. I don't know what gear we were in but it must have been near the top. It was just awesome. The crowd was going absolutely crazy.

Bruce Trask: I was full-back and we were trailing 17–8. Alastair Biggar and Mike Gibson had scored their tries and Bob Hiller had kicked a lot of points, but we were still hanging in there. Then I scored. I remember catching the ball on the twenty-five on the left-hand side, almost on the touchline, and running across the field and scoring five metres to the right of the right-hand upright with about five guys on top of me. Those sorts of gallops made you tired. I was puffing and panting over the conversion and I should never have taken it. I should have left it to somebody else and gone away to catch my breath. I hit and missed.

We won a penalty a few minutes later and I was still gasping, so I threw the ball to Graeme Moore, but he missed as well. I probably should have had a go at that one, but I was pretty busted. The game had been going at about a hundred miles an hour.

Graeme Moore: We scored again not long after. Ron Walker scurried over in the corner. It was 17–14 now. The place was going mental. I missed the conversion. God, we missed some kicks that day. We had our chance.

Carwyn James: Barry dropped a goal at the end to take it to 20–14. It was a scary thing.

Graeme Moore: It was one hell of an experience to go toe-to-toe with them like that. Not many sides on that tour managed to play as well as we did against them.

John Taylor: We kicked our goals and they didn't and that was difference – and it was Bob Hiller doing the kicking. For the second tour running he'd scored over a hundred points without playing in a Test match.

Doug Smith: Bob Hiller – one of the greatest tourists I have ever known.

The provincial fixture list was now complete. With the exception of Queensland in the very first match of the tour, they had gone unbeaten against every provincial opposition they had come up against and smashed just about every Lions record in sight. There was now just one game left, one game that would mark them down as a team that gallantly drew a series in New Zealand or the team that became immortal through victory. They headed back to Auckland in search of history.

CHAPTER SEVENTEEN

THE EIGHTH WONDER OF THE WORLD

Colin Meads: Going into that final Test, I felt strongly that New Zealand were going to win. It was hugely disappointing that we couldn't win the damn series at that stage, but to draw it would have been a consolation. To lose it would have been a disaster. There was a lot of talk about the last time we'd lost a series at home – 1937. Nobody wanted to go there.

Sid Going: Our backline was different again from the other Tests, with Wayne Cottrell, Phil Gard and Mick Duncan outside me. We had no hope of developing teamwork to beat the Lions in virtually one training session. Phil Gard looked a useful footballer playing for North Otago, but he and I were complete strangers. He was making his debut in the final Test of a major series.

Ian Kirkpatrick: It was do or die. Desperation stuff. There was a lot of heat on Ivan Vodanovich. He had the weight of the world on his shoulders.

Bryan Williams: The pressure coming into that game was huge. It was massive. Just massive. And coming on the back of 1970, the idea of losing a second consecutive series – at home and against a side that had never beaten us in a series – was unthinkable to most of New Zealand. The press were everywhere. Every person in the street would try to stop you to talk about the game and the significance of the result. The whole bloody country was up in arms about it. Virtually every page of every paper, every radio programme, everything was about that last game and the fact that we had to win. We just had to. There wasn't an alternative.

It was an extraordinary time. For a young fella like me who had idolised the All Blacks and had been so proud of their record, to be part of the team that lost in 1970 and then to be facing a loss in 1971, that wasn't a nice situation to be in. When you're confronted with that sort of thing you either stand up or you go home.

The Lions arrived in Auckland and immediately put Derek Quinnell through a fitness test. He'd been going about with a swollen knee since his devastating performance in the third Test and Carwyn feared the worst. It took him just five minutes of the session to break down, his knee packing in the first time he tried to change direction. Peter Dixon came in and so the Lions team was set: JPR, Gerald, Dawes and Gibson, Duckham, Barry and Gareth. Up front – McLauchlan, Pullin and Lynch, McBride and Brown, Taylor, Dixon and Mervyn.

Peter Dixon: I was called in and Carwyn said, 'Peter, Derek's dropped out, can you play in this last Test match?' And I said, 'Yes, as long as I'm playing on the blindside and not this left-and-right business.' And he said, 'That's fine, don't worry about that. All I want to know is can you deal with Sid Going? You have to be the one that keeps him under control.' I just smiled and said,

'That's fine, I can deal with him.' I spoke to Mervyn about it and said that any time we had a remote sense of a blindside at a scrum, I'd come up and off that side just in case Sid decided to try go that way. I said to Mervyn, 'I'm going to go for him every time, whether he's got the ball or not. If he turns the ball inside, that's your man – but I've got Sid.'

Ian McLauchlan: The problem with any last Test is that everyone has one foot on the plane. You suddenly realise how much you've missed your wife and children. If you're not the best organised person – and I'm not always – then you remember that you should take home a few presents. But that's not all. The last match of the tour becomes a bit of a reunion of all the people you've met along the way. They turn up, they take you out shopping, they buy you a drink. That all has the effect of taking your mind off the business at hand.

There was a disturbance in the hotel on Friday night. Some New Zealand guy managed to get up to our corridor in the middle of the night and started banging on our doors. When he was halfway along the corridor, two doors opened and Willie John and Delme Thomas emerged. He had a serious problem on his hands now. He hurtled towards the fire escape, jumped down the last flight of stairs and was gone.

JPR Williams: Throughout the tour I'd stay out late after training with Barry and Bob Hiller, collecting the balls as they did goal-kicking practice. I'd stand under the posts, catch the balls and kick them back. Whenever they finished, they'd say, 'Right, you've gotta do some drop goals now.' So we'd slot some drop goals to finish off.

We were on our way to the fourth Test and there was a funny feeling because everyone was very, very nervous but they were also really looking forward to going home. So I stood up and said, 'It's okay, guys, you can all relax. I'm going to drop a goal today and it's going to win us the match.' Everyone just fell about laughing and that cut the ice. They all knew that I never kicked the ball – and I certainly didn't kick drop goals.

Gareth Edwards: Good little joke that from JPR. Bob Hiller was beside himself.

Eden Park was stuffed to the rafters: 56,000 inside, and it could have been double that had they had the room. John Pring, the referee, blew his whistle and the intensity was there right from the first second. There was a bust-up, then another. Two sets of forwards going at it and neither of them of a mind to take a backwards step.

John Taylor: In the first ten minutes, Kirkpatrick sent one at me. He missed and hit Mervyn. I threw one back and missed and hit Wyllie, which left Wyllie and me standing there glowering at each other while Mervyn and Kirkpatrick went away and sorted it out by themselves.

Gordon Brown: At the second lineout, Jazz Muller grabbed hold of me by the throat and Peter Whiting punched me in the eye, splitting the skin open like a melon being knifed. It was premeditated, otherwise Muller wouldn't have turned round to grab me. I had to go off and have the wound bound and protected.

Colin Meads: There's always been criticism that New Zealand forwards cheat, but those Lions got away with bloody murder, especially in the lineouts. There was obstruction, elbows flying, pulling down, all sorts of stuff designed to nullify Peter Whiting's superiority. It was that sort of thing that led to the incident involving Whiting and Gordon Brown.

Gordon Brown: Whiting had been taking some stick from some New Zealand journalists who didn't think he could look after himself. That was probably what was behind it.

Colin Meads: That was really just what Willie John had been dealing out to Peter Whiting, who was young and in his first Test series. I had said to the ref, 'If you don't stop it, I will . . .' Well, Whiting decided that he'd stop it himself.

Mervyn Davies: Cool heads were needed in a match like that, but New Zealand lost it completely. A team that resorts to violence is a team on its last legs.

Peter Whiting: I felt that the Lions had psyched out the New Zealand press and they were on my back a lot building up to that Test. I believed in looking after myself and Brown was jumping across the line. He was obstructing me. I couldn't get a chance to go for the ball because he was playing illegally – so I had to sort it out.

Gordon Brown: Some years later, my phone rang at home and a voice shouted at me, 'This is Peter Whiting, the bugger that split your eye open in New Zealand. I'm touring Scotland and I'll be at your home in six hours' time. Get the beer on ice and the beds made up.' He arrived and made himself completely at home. I cooked some big steaks and the beer took a belting.

Just a few minutes after the altercation at the lineout, a scrum went down at the All Blacks' end of the field, and it broke up moments later with both front rows furiously swinging punches. The threat of violence in the Tests had bubbled under the surface since Canterbury, but never materialised. In this, the most pressurised of environments, it crashed through the surface.

John Pring: I refereed all the matches in the series and I'd been waiting for something like that to happen, but we'd managed to keep a lid on it until then. Jazz Muller and Ian McLauchlan were the ones really going for it and I was worried that the game was going to get completely out of hand. Luckily Colin Meads and Willie John McBride spoke with their forwards and things settled down.

Peter Dixon: Yeah, it kicked off; each side was trying to show that they were there for real and weren't going to back down. We were each trying to establish our physical dominance, to try and scare the opposition. And if both teams are doing it and neither are going to back down, you're going to get some pretty tasty punches thrown.

Ian McLauchlan: Jazz Muller was a big man who hadn't had it his way in the scrums in the Test series. He may have remembered what the Canterbury lads had done to us and wanted to see if that would help – but I'm not Sandy Carmichael. You start something with me, I'm going to finish it. Jazz Muller thought he was scary. He should have been on tour with Scotland in Argentina in 1969. Then he'd know scary. After 1969, everything else in my career was kids' stuff.

Ten minutes had gone on the clock when New Zealand made their first statement. Bryan Williams fired a howitzer of a punt down into the Lions' twenty-five, and as the players scrambled after it JPR had no choice but to carry the ball dead, and Pring awarded New Zealand a scrum five metres out. With Gordon Brown still away getting treatment, the Lions were forced to pack down without a number eight.

Sid Going picked up at the base, drew John Taylor and passed to Grizz Wyllie. The All Blacks number eight dummied inside then switched the ball outside him to Phil Gard who got a pass away to Wayne Cottrell. The fly-half accelerated into the gap and over the line.

David Duckham: I don't know how they did it. I remember this sick feeling in my stomach. I was thinking, 'God, we're going to lose this game.' It was the most horrible feeling I've ever felt at any time on a rugby field. I was thinking, 'What are we going to do? How are we going to get out of this?' I was starting to panic. The noise from the crowd was deafening. Then Laurie Mains put over a penalty and we were 8–0 down.

Doug Smith: They looked unstoppable. We were in real trouble out there.

John Dawes: I got the boys together and said that the rest of the half had to be played down in All Blacks territory. We had to stop them scoring any more points. We could come back from 8–0, but 11–0 or 13–0 was a different prospect.

Sid Going: I never really rated Dawes, if I'm honest.

John Taylor: The chance of glory seemed to be slipping away. It seemed even more remote when Barry, having already scored 172 points, missed a penalty from fifteen yards.

While the rest of his teammates were struggling to impose themselves, one man stood firm. The Mouse was tearing it up in the scrum against Jazz Muller. When the All Blacks had field possession and the put-in close to the Lions try-line, McLauchlan did a number on Jazz and won a penalty that lifted the pressure. It was a huge moment. Gareth tapped and went. He dashed over the halfway line and then fizzed a pass out to Gerald, who chipped ahead into the New Zealand twenty-five. The Lions won a penalty and Barry put it over – 8–3 now. His points, for sure, but Mouse wasn't slow in reminding fellas about his role in it all.

Jazz Muller: I loved playing for the All Blacks; it was the ultimate. I used to sleep in my kit the night before a game. You wear it for as long as you can – because when you're finished, you're finished. And that game turned out to be my last. Propping against McLauchlan and the rest of them saw the end of my Test career. I wish I'd never played against those Lions. We couldn't handle them in the scrum. They had us stuffed.

Ian Kirkpatrick: Scrummaging in New Zealand changed in 1971 when the Lions came. We had been content with winning our own ball, while they brought that culture of wanting to put pressure on our put-in.

Sid Going: McLauchlan not only unsettled our guys with his scrummaging, he was an absolute menace around the field. Always in the way – and never penalised.

Barry John: For the first twenty minutes, the New Zealanders played as if they'd drunk an energy potion. They were fast and strong and threatened to mow us down. I thought we were going to be stuffed. I had visions of a thirty-pointer. But after a while I saw that their rugby lacked imagination. After twelve minutes they were eight points up, but I got a penalty and knew in my bones that we'd weathered the danger point. And in the last seconds of the half we scored a try, which I converted to draw us level. The ball went halfway down the lineout, Gareth collected and went off like a rocket. He was stopped, but Pete Dixon picked up and fell over the line.

Peter Dixon: I like to remember it as a classic eighty-yard try.

Bryan Williams: Oh, the pressure was bloody immense then, mate, I can tell you. The momentum swings and people make mistakes and suddenly the other team's got the upper hand.

Barry John: I was told to keep the All Blacks pinned back. In the second half we had the wind in our favour and in the first minute I put in a sixty-metre punt that bobbled and rolled between Carrington and Mains and dribbled into touch inside the All Blacks' twenty-five.

John Pullin: It wasn't luck that the ball bounced five metres from the line and rolled into touch, it was skill, and once the opposition has to turn and go back it makes all the difference.

Peter Dixon: Jazz Muller lost the head and stamped on my back at a ruck a few minutes later. Barry nudged over the penalty to put us ahead. We knew they'd come gunning for us after that.

Bryan Williams: We put them under a lot of heat and eventually they broke. I threw into a lineout and Mervyn Davies just failed to steal the ball. It fell to Tom Lister and he dived through a gap to score. That tied it up at 11–11. Laurie Mains missed the conversion. We could have done with the points.

David Duckham: Things were still so tight, but then out of nowhere we took the lead. Colin Meads had hold of me and I hurled this pass towards Barry. I just remember thinking, 'Thank God for that,' when he caught it, but Barry was set upon immediately and he flicked it on to JPR, who had come into the line. JPR shaped for a drop goal. It was surreal. JPR never went for a drop goal in his life.

Bryan Williams: I was back near the posts and I just saw this bloody thing let loose from JPR.

Peter Dixon: Everyone stopped when he hit it. It was like putting a film into slow motion, even before he takes the kick, everyone realises he's going to have a go and everything just came to a stop. But it's a hell of a long way out. When he hit it everyone turned to watch it fly through the air. And it was just turning end over end and there was no noise, the whole place was silent, no one was moving, the crowd didn't make a noise, everyone was just watching this ball fly through the air.

Bryan Williams: It just kept on coming and coming.

David Duckham: It was a monster.

Bryan Williams: And it soared through the posts. And I remember thinking, 'Uh-oh, we're in trouble now.'

Ian Kirkpatrick: Fifty-five yards, I think. Words failed me.

Peter Dixon: We were all going berserk.

Fergus Slattery: If you'd said in the changing room before the match that we would be depending on JPR to drop us a goal to win the series everyone would have choked to death with laughter.

JPR Williams: I like to call it the eighth wonder of the world.

David Duckham: Ask JPR about the gesture.

JPR Williams: I turned to all the reserves in the stand, my arms raised – 'There, told you so.'

David Duckham: He was signalling to Bob Hiller because Bob had said, 'Japes, you can only be a complete full-back if you can drop a goal.' He was telling Bob Hiller, 'See, I'm the complete full-back now.'

Bryan Williams: The Lions had been full of adventurous, open running and they tore the provincial sides to pieces playing that kind of rugby. They didn't adopt that style in the Tests, though. Other than the third Test, it was all very close-to-the-chest stuff. We didn't expect that kicking game from them at all. Their open running game had been so successful and had been so brilliant to watch that it was a huge surprise to us that they didn't continue with that style in the Tests.

Gordon Brown: I took a bloody battering in that game. Jazz Muller had mumbled some sort of warning to me in a ruck, and not long after he kicked a great gaping chunk out of my right leg just below the knee. What a bastard.

JPR Williams: I'd been watching Muller all afternoon. Right from the start he was throwing cheap shots and that final one was a shocker on Broonie. So there was a moment late on where he got the ball popped to him down the wing and you could see his eyes light up when he saw me ahead of him. He thought he was going to run over the top of me. That was never going to happen.

Jazz Muller: It felt like I'd been hit by a car.

It was a moment that summed up the defiance of the Lions defence. For all their possession, the New Zealanders failed to make decent headway and were continually pinned back in their own half. Finally, the All Blacks managed to work their way forward. They won a penalty and Mains lobbed it over to level it at 14–14.

Bryan Williams: It was only sheer grit and determination that kept New Zealand in the series, because we weren't bristling with individuals of outstanding calibre. Man for man, those Lions backs were infinitely superior and I found it incredible that, with such talent and with the amount of ball the forwards supplied them with, it went to the wire.

Sid Going: If we had had the confidence in the backs we would have gone for a try, but we settled for a penalty. A draw was going to do nothing to save the bloody series. With backs who understood each other's play – like our backs at North Auckland – we might have rescued things in the final ten minutes, but the chances we created were useless, sad to say, to the 1971 All Blacks.

Gareth Edwards: Barry missed a kick he would normally get with his eyes closed. The All Blacks missed a couple of kicks and there was a drop goal that went whizzing past the posts. There were a lot of opportunities that were never capitalised on. I had a drop-goal attempt and it was a shocker.

David Duckham: Time was running out.

Willie John McBride: There wasn't going to be a winner. Everybody was out on their feet.

Gerald Davies: John Pring blew the whistle.

Barry John: Game over. Match drawn. Series won.

Sid Going: I still think they were lucky to win it.

Carwyn James: It was a strange feeling at the end. It was a big disappointment that we didn't win the game. We should have done. We gained the psychological advantage of coming back from 8–0 down to 11–8 ahead. We desperately wanted to win 3–1 instead of 2–1.

Colin Meads: Carwyn James was a clever man. He got the referee he wanted in John Pring and he got him for every Test. How did we allow that to happen? The one referee we didn't want was John Pring, and we got him four Tests running. Jack Sullivan, our chairman of selectors, assured me after the third Test that Pring wouldn't do the fourth, but there he was. Carwyn James had him wrapped around his finger.

Sid Going: Barry John was brilliant, I have to admit it. A lot of people said Gareth Edwards made him, but Barry read each game so well – and he kicked the goals too. He stood deep and kept out of trouble. It was said he didn't tackle, but he didn't really have to. Our loose forwards never touched him throughout the series.

Ian Kirkpatrick: It wasn't great being an All Black around that time. It gets to you a bit.

Colin Meads: I became a disciple of Fred Allen's running game on the 1967 tour and wanted to persevere with that in 1971, but we didn't have the players. You should always play to your strengths.

Bryan Williams: It could have been two all. They're regarded as one of the great teams, but they only barely won that series.

If the changing room had been a morgue after the first Test, it wasn't quite like that after the fourth. I think we all realised that we had been beaten by a team that was going to go down in history not only as the first Lions team to win a series in New Zealand, but also as a team of stars, guys who would go down in legend as some of the best players of all time.

Sid Going: That's not what I was thinking.

Ian McLauchlan: I never thought anybody could approach Gareth Edwards, but when I played against Sid Going I thought, 'This is a player.' Props used to run at him and he used to turn them upside down. He was an incredible talent and so, so strong – farmer strong. A brute. He had a will to win that was incredible.

Gareth Edwards: I sat down with Gerald in the dressing room and we were absolutely knackered. There was a real sense of anti-climax. I didn't know what we were meant to feel. Gerald had always said he'd never got the match ball after a game, so when the final whistle went I ran to the touchline and got the ball from the ball boy. Gerald couldn't believe it. He sat there with the match ball in his hands and he said, 'We've just won the series.' We both looked at each other and said, 'So what?' There was an elation, but there was also a let-down, because it was all over.

Mike Gibson: That was exactly the same feeling I had. It was strange, strange.

Gareth Edwards: We were all so emotionally and physically drained. It had been three and a half months.

Peter Dixon: I felt the same. After all those weeks of winning and having had such an incredible time, the whole thing seemed to come to an end in such an underwhelming way with the draw. But then a little while later you begin to realise what you've done. And for the guys who had been on previous tours, it clearly meant a lot to them.

Willie John McBride: It probably meant more to me than anybody else because I'd been on three tours and lost all of them, and for the first time ever in New Zealand we had won. It meant a hell of a lot.

David Duckham: For a good few minutes we just sat there, totally exhausted. Carwyn came around and said, 'Well done, Duckers. You didn't get the chance to attack much today, but my God, you played your part in defence. I just want you to know that your part in this tour has been enormous.' I remember him saying that as if it were yesterday. It's always stayed with me.

Then Colin Meads came into the changing room for a beer. He came in and smiled and said, 'Well, you beat us fair and square.' And he and Willie John hugged. And although he didn't announce it, we knew that was the last time that we'd see Colin Meads on the field wearing an All Blacks jersey. There was something poignant about being there when such a giant of the game had played his last.

Colin Meads: I was captain, and in hindsight it probably wasn't such a great move. I was honoured to get the job but when you're captain there's things you can't do. You've got to be the leader rather than the enforcer. I had a role as a fixer previously. I was the one able to talk to the opposition and tell them, 'I wouldn't do that again if I were you.' When they make you captain, that's largely taken away from you. I enjoyed captaining King Country because they were country boys. They were followers. In the

All Blacks, you've got to be more astute and you've got to be able to give guidance and I wasn't that sort. I was better off as a lieutenant. I came in with Wilson Whineray and he was a born leader. He was a natural. It was easy for him, not just on the field, but off the field, too. He was an orator, a good and clever guy, whereas I only became captain because of my seniority. I'd been there so long they just gave me the job.

Laurie Mains: The guy I felt most for was Colin Meads. He'd been in so many great teams and contributed so mightily to the All Blacks, for that to happen was sad.

Fergie McCormick: Colin Meads regarded the All Black jersey as pure gold. He could do so many things so much better than anyone else in a match that he stood alone as the greatest player I've ever known. He deserved to go out on a high, not out on the back of two consecutive Test series defeats. But, still, he's untouchable. The greatest ever.

Bryan Williams: That Lions team transformed New Zealand rugby. That counter-attacking style they brought to our shores was a complete revelation. That's the real legacy of that tour for us and that's why I'm always going to be happy to talk about it and about those great players and about a great coach like Carwyn James.

Mervyn Davies: Nothing gave me quite the same buzz as being the bloke who played number eight when we beat the All Blacks.

Mike Gibson: I often think about the individual sports, about people who win the men's singles at Wimbledon or the Open Championship at golf, and there is nobody at that winning moment who can understand how the person feels. As Lions we had thirty people sharing the moment – and all of them understood.

CHAPTER EIGHTEEN

THE KING ABDICATES

THE WALES that Barry John returned to was not the same Wales that he'd left almost four months before. His life had changed in New Zealand, even though he didn't realise it at the time. None of the boys had a proper grasp on how big the tour was back home, none of them were aware of the media attention they were getting and how their heroics had captured not just the imaginations of rugby fans, but of people from all walks of life. Four nations were in thrall to the developing drama down under.

Barry found the transition difficult to handle. He was a superstar, but a reluctant one. For a man who craved the limelight while he was out on the pitch with the number ten on his back, he was the opposite when it came to real life. He didn't want to stand out; he wanted to blend in.

Barry played in three matches in the Five Nations of 1972 – three wins, against England at Twickenham and Scotland and France in Cardiff. The championship was uncompleted because the Welsh Rugby Union, and their counterparts in Scotland, refused to allow their teams to travel to play Ireland in Dublin on account of the escalating Troubles. Wales would have been short-priced favourites to complete another Grand Slam had that game gone ahead.

In a career that was forged on his brilliant unpredictability, Barry John then performed his most bewildering manoeuvre of all – he retired. He'd played twenty-five times for Wales and in five Tests for the Lions. He was twenty-seven years old and he'd had enough.

Barry John: In New Zealand, I'd been given the tag of the King. My face was everywhere. It was never something I was comfortable with and the players used to take the piss out of me over it. When I walked into the dressing room, they'd stand up and bow. It was all a laugh, but I didn't know what was going on in Wales. I thought I was going to leave all that behind me once we took off from Auckland airport.

Gerald Davies: There was no real way of knowing what was happening in the UK or Ireland. No mobile phones, no internet, no access to our newspapers, our radio, our television. If you wanted to make a phone call home you had to book it a day in advance.

Barry John: I got off the plane at one of the refuelling stops on the way home and I was on the cover of the *New York Times*. I didn't think they'd even heard of rugby in the United States.

Gerald Davies: When we landed in Heathrow, I remember looking at the thousands of people there to see us and thinking that this is what it must have been like when the Beatles arrived.

Barry John: A busload of Welsh fans from Maesteg turned up on the runway about twenty yards from our plane. God knows how they got there. In order to get away from all the bustle and noise, I had to do an interview with Kate Adie in the ladies' toilets. We were asked to attend functions at Buckingham Palace and Downing Street. Sacks of letters were delivered to my house and everywhere I went people wanted to talk to me. Every day I was asked to go to some event or other and, of course, I went. Over the next nine months I don't think I averaged one meal a week at home. There was always something to go to. I started to get bored of myself. People were paying hundreds of pounds for me to go to these events and I was telling the same stories four times a week. It was so bloody repetitive. When I opened a bank in North Wales for Forward Trust, a woman curtsied as I approached her. Everything got out of control. My job was going on the road selling finance, but I'd make an appointment and the whole town would turn up. I started staying in the office with effectively nothing to do, and getting paid for doing nothing seemed wrong.

I've always been someone who would rather sit in the corner of a room, listening and observing, than hold court in the middle of it. I just wanted to play rugby and I felt that all the attention was impacting on my form. I didn't want to stop playing, I just felt I had to, if only to be fair to myself. The regret, which I still have, was not in ending my career, but feeling that I had no option but to end it. I felt I had at least a couple more years at the top, but only if I could be me, and the celebrity thing was getting in the way of that.

Gareth Edwards: Exhaustion will have played its part as well. Barry nearly didn't go on the tour because he'd been so battered on the 1968 Lions tour and again in the 1971 Five Nations, so you then add three months of solid rugby on top of that and the toll it takes on your body is immense. I remember it took me around nine months to a year just to recover from that tour. My mind had just been blown by the whole experience.

David Duckham: Coming back in 1971 took a lot of adjusting to, not just in your career on the field, but in your general life. After being away for three and a half months, it was very hard to get back to a regular routine. We were like rock stars. We were celebrities all around the country, it was extraordinary. Unreal. Today we would have had an open-top bus tour, but we had enough going on without that. For a while, I didn't want to know the game. I tuned out. It was too much.

Barry John: I played my last game for Wales against France at the Arms Park in March 1972 and I played my last game of rugby of any kind a few months later. It was a charity match in Cardiff between an invitational Barry John XV and a side selected by Carwyn James. Only a handful of very close confidants knew that it was my final match. Gareth was one of them. I loved playing rugby, but the circus that surrounded me had just spiralled out of control. I had to fulfil three different roles at the time – the breadwinner who worked to pay the mortgage, the international rugby player who had to be at his sharpest mentally and physically and then the role of a supposed superstar required to attend functions at the poshest London hotels next to people like George Best, Tom Jones and even the Prime Minister, Edward Heath. One of those roles is pressure enough, but put the three together and you have an impossible situation.

At the end of the game I took one last look around the stadium before walking off slowly. Physically, I was leaving the pitch for the last time, but mentally the spark had gone from me months earlier. When I reached the dressing room I took off my boots, kissed them, put them down on the floor and thought quietly to myself, 'Well, this is it, Barry.' It suddenly dawned on me that I'd never wear them again.

Clive Rowlands: I was the Wales coach and I didn't know he was going to retire. The next international game was Wales against the All Blacks in 1972 and I'm convinced that they were terrified of facing Barry again. They must have had parties everywhere when they heard the news.

JPR Williams: Barry was still at the peak of his powers, so we were all incredibly shocked. Gareth went to see him to try and persuade him to keep playing, but his mind was made up. He couldn't make any money in those days either directly or indirectly as a player and he felt that the time had come where he needed to start making more money. By retiring, he could write newspaper columns, he could do fashion shoots, he could commercialise himself in a way that he couldn't if he kept playing. But it was a huge decision for him to make. And I think that it's one that he still regrets to this day. The thing about any sport is that you have a shelf life and you can't buy back those years. He could have had five great years after that – but it wasn't to be.

Gareth Edwards: He finished and Gerald and I went on another six, seven years. He would never admit it at the time, but years later I said to him, 'You do miss it, don't you?' He said, 'Yes.'

Mervyn Davies: He was rugby's first superstar, and living life under such intense scrutiny obviously didn't appeal to him.

Fergus Slattery: Barry John was a guy you would never really have got to know very well. He never stayed around. If he was with you, he'd be with you for two or three minutes and then he'd be gone and would be with somebody else and then somebody else and then somebody else. I knew him, but I didn't know him as well as I got to know Gareth Edwards or Gerald Davies or John Dawes or Mervyn Davies or JPR Williams. JPR is a guy who would come and stay in my house in Dublin. The Welsh guys, most of them I got to know pretty well, but Barry never stayed in the one spot for longer than a few seconds so I never got to know him.

David Duckham: My experience was much the same. I can't say I got to know Barry well – probably for the very same reason as Slatts. I don't think he really wanted anyone to get that close to him. Gareth was probably as close as anyone to him. BJ's problem was that he wanted to be all things to all men, especially at all the social events we went to. He would have wanted to speak to everyone, and so no one ever got to sit with him for a long time. He was the big star on that tour and so people always wanted to meet him and have photos taken with him and have him sign things and that took a lot of pressure off the rest of us, so we all appreciated him doing it.

Gareth Edwards: Barry was too young to retire at twenty-seven. He was only going to become a better player, not worse. I don't think he gave his talent full expression. He'll argue that he did, but I believe he could have gone even higher. I missed him when he went. It was sad.

Barry John: Do I regret it? Of course I have regrets – big regrets – and I've probably thought about them most days since then. Any top sportsman will tell you that you should carry on playing until the moment your body tells you that you can't do it any more. But at the time I really felt that it was the decision I had to make. I have to be honest and admit that it took me fully three years to come terms with the fact I wouldn't ever be out on that Arms Park pitch again.

Willie John McBride: Barry hit the high time and he never came down from it, you know? And that's sad. Then he thought he would retire early and that was a stupid thing to do – and he's regretted that for the rest of his life. And then Phil Bennett came in and Phil was just as important as he had been – and Barry was forgotten about almost. I don't think he ever really got over that. Phil Bennett was a great team man. I loved Phil, I still do. He's just a great person. But they called Barry 'the King' and the trouble was, Barry believed it. You hear all these great things said about you, but you've just got to let it go over the top of your head. Ah, it's terrible. The fame Barry had was unprecedented for a rugby player and he didn't have the ability to handle it. It's a shame. Sad in many, many ways. But he'll always be remembered for what he could do on the pitch. At his best he was magical. Absolutely magical.

CHAPTER NINETEEN

THERE IS A GREAT LONELINESS UPON ME

FOURTEEN MONTHS after Carwyn James led the Lions to victory against the All Blacks, he was tasked with the job of doing it all over again – not with the might of four nations in his dressing room, or even with the might of one nation, but with his beloved Llanelli. The All Blacks were on their way to Britain and Ireland on a journey of redemption, and an early fixture took them to Stradey Park. Carwyn Country.

It was 31 October 1972 and Carwyn had Delme Thomas as his captain, Derek Quinnell in his second row and Chico Hopkins at scrum-half. Only six of his starting fifteen had played international rugby: the great Delme, who'd been on the Test scene since 1966; Barry Llewellyn, the prop, who had played for Wales twelve times; the emerging genius Phil Bennett, who only had five caps to his name at that point; Roy Bergiers, the centre, who had three caps; Chico with one cap for Wales and one for the Lions; and Quinnell, who still had only played for his country in one Test match.

Carwyn had the burgeoning brilliance of J. J. Williams and Ray Gravell in his backline, but six of the team he put out to face the All Blacks ended their careers without a cap. The Kiwis might not have known too many of the Llanelli boys, but they knew Carwyn and they knew what he was capable of.

They fielded a strong side at Stradey: Bryan Williams and Bob Burgess were in the backline; Joe Karam, the goal-kicking points machine, was at full-back; and the twenty-year-old Bruce Robertson, who went on to win thirty-four caps, was in the midfield. Ian Kirkpatrick captained the team, and Peter Whiting and Alan Sutherland were in the pack with him, as was Ron Urlich, the experienced hooker from Auckland, and the much talked about Andy Haden, a supreme second row out of Wanganui who had just turned twenty-two years of age. Many years later, the *New Zealand Herald* picked its top 100 All Blacks in history; three of the side that started against Carwyn's Scarlets – Kirkpatrick, Williams and Haden – were in the top fifteen, Robertson was eighteenth and Whiting was thirty-fourth.

More than any of those guys, though, there was another man in their team who dominated the headlines, a menacing character with the number one on his back, a desperado prop from Otago who'd been named to play against the Lions on three occasions in the summer of 1971, but who had pulled out for mysterious reasons.

Keith Murdoch wasted no time in bringing his own brand of mayhem to Stradey. The game was only minutes old when he climbed into a ruck feet-first and stamped on Derek Quinnell's head. Later, he threw a punch that knocked Gareth Jenkins, the Scarlets openside flanker, unconscious. Later still, he saw Roy 'Shunto' Thomas, the Llanelli hooker, on the floor and drove his boot downwards into his face, then he booted Barry Llewellyn up the arse so forcefully that Llewellyn's shorts were covered in blood by game's end.

Llanelli stood up to it all and won 9–3, one of the most famous victories in Welsh rugby history and one of the sport's biggest upsets. 'I felt so pleased for Carwyn because he'd proved a point,' said Delme Thomas. 'He'd achieved it home and away, he'd done it with the Lions, and though he had never got the chance of doing it with Wales, he did it with a side that shouldn't have been as strong as Wales.' As J. J. Williams put it, 'He brought fifteen club boys together and they beat the might of the All Blacks.'

The All Blacks went on to beat Wales, Scotland and England on that tour and they drew with Ireland in Dublin. In their twenty-eighth game, on 27 January 1973, they faced the Barbarians at Cardiff Arms Park, and Carwyn was once again called upon to plot their downfall. It was a reunion of the squad of 1971. JPR was at full-back, David Duckham and John Bevan were on the wings, and John Dawes and Mike Gibson were in the midfield.

With Barry John in retirement, Phil Bennett was at ten and Gareth Edwards was the scrum-half. In the pack, Carwyn had some old friends: Ray McLoughlin, John Pullin and Sandy Carmichael, the front row that was broken up after the Battle of Lancaster Park, came together; Willie John McBride was in the second row; Fergus Slattery and Derek Quinnell were in the back row.

It was one of the most glorious games in history and it produced the sport's most famous try, an epic team score that Gareth Edwards finished off in the corner to the delirium of the Arms Park and the joy of all the millions who continue to watch it all these years later. The Barbarians won a classic Test, 23–11. Carwyn had done it again.

Carwyn led Llanelli to Welsh Cup triumphs in 1973, 1974, 1975 and 1976, and yet despite being hailed worldwide as arguably the shrewdest coach in the game, he was never given the chance to coach his country, the hierarchy at the Welsh Rugby Union feeling he was too much of a maverick and free-thinker for their liking.

In 1974, when Clive Rowlands exited and Wales were in need of a new head coach, Carwyn wrote a letter to the WRU and set out the terms that would have to be met if he was to take the job. His provisos were ambitious and in many ways revolutionary – and were rejected outright by the board. Ray Williams defended the decision, saying, 'He imposed conditions that were totally unacceptable. If he had been appointed on the terms that he had demanded it would have been against the constitution of the union because he really wanted to be the manager, supremo, call it what you will. He wanted to be the sole coach and the sole selector and the committee didn't have the powers to give him that, so his application was immediately ruled out of court. It was really he himself who caused this so-called rejection.'

The gig went instead to Carwyn's captain in New Zealand, John Dawes, who in his five seasons in charge won two Grand Slams and two Triple Crowns, winning seventeen of his twenty Five Nations matches as head coach.

When he got rejected by the WRU, Carwyn became BBC Wales' rugby correspondent. He began writing for the *Guardian* and the *Western Mail* and also enjoyed stints as a match commentator and analyst. In 1977, he shook up Welsh rugby when he decided to leave the country and move to Italy, where he coached Rovigo for three years. He changed their style of play, preached the thinking man's mantra anew and made them national champions in 1979. The trophy was handed over by Pope John Paul II.

Nothing could match his experiences of 1971, though. 'In Carwyn's life,' wrote his biographer and close friend, Alun Richardson, 'it was as if the heights scaled were so great that from the crowning moment there could only be a descent. There is no doubt that 1971 was a peak which affected his whole life, changed his mode of living, perhaps because he had lived it so intensely, he, the dreamer who had realised his dreams, particularly as he was never again in a position to achieve them on so grand a scale. But whatever may be said by way of regret at so short a life, he had no regrets himself and regarded his part in the success of others throughout his life as his chief source of satisfaction.'

He was a man that everyone knew, yet also one that very few really did know. Carwyn belonged in another era – with the way he thought about rugby and the way he lived his life.

While not openly gay, his sexuality was known to those he was closest to. Keeping it secret was a heavy burden. Unable to rejoice in the full colour of his character and forced to publicly repress so fundamental a part of his being ultimately led to sadness, regret, isolation and depression.

Clem Thomas, his captain from schoolboy days, recalled how Carwyn 'had no wife or children to confide in. He was in many ways a man in torment. He was private and lonely and found refuge in his own and his beloved country's passion for the game of rugby.'

His sister Gwen spoke of Carwyn for a documentary in 1993. 'Lots of things in Wales are kept quiet. Nobody knows anything about them, but it would be far better if things are not bottled up. It would give more people a chance to live their life as they would like to. Of course, they say life is what you make it, but not with everybody.'

The rugby broadcaster and commentator Huw Llewelyn Davies delved into the taboo subject of homosexuality in Wales in the 1970s. 'Carwyn couldn't lead the life in Cefneithin that he did later because the constrictions of that small community would have been a problem for him. There were some things that would never have been accepted in his home community, things that would be frowned on.'

Gareth Edwards: You could say some of us were naive at the time, or whatever you want to call it, but he was carrying a burden that today wouldn't be a problem in the same way. We were aware that people would say certain things. Not everyday conversation, but people would hint at it now and again or make veiled comments. But nobody assumed anything back then and nobody spoke about it openly.

Mick Hipwell: You'd hear the rumours over the years. He was very badly beaten up in Cardiff one time. A couple of guys did him in. I want you to be careful how you portray him because he was the best person I ever met in my life. You took Carwyn the way you got him and he was a marvellous man – a friend, a gentleman and a rugby genius. I'd have died for him.

Gareth Edwards: How would I describe Carwyn? He was a great man-manager. He was very, very astute. He could bring people together, he could say the right thing at the right time. He wasn't a big talker, he didn't shout. He would make a logical point and gave us the confidence to do things.

Gerald Davies: He was the philosopher king. He was deep thinking, quiet, persuasive, cajoling and he could bring the best out of the players. And like a good teacher, he could draw the answer out of his pupils so it was as if the pupil had come up with it himself, but really the answer had been teased out of him through the teacher's guidance. He was like that as a coach – he teased good performances out of people. I don't think I ever heard him tell a player off or be critical of them. He was very kind, gentle, persuasive, and that was his style – and in that respect he was unique.

Mick Hipwell: He just had that X factor. He could organise a group of people to do exactly what he wanted them to do. He was there to assess each person's capacity. And he then gave you a task that was within your capacity. And when you have someone that understands you like that and believes in you like that, it gets an extra something out of you, you know? And we were able to achieve what he was looking for.

Fergus Slattery: At the time we had no sense – well, certainly I didn't have any sense – of what a tortured soul Carwyn was. He was very private, very low-key, very unobtrusive. You'd never really have got to know him, but he had a presence. He was very much in control. When he spoke to you as a team or a group or as an individual, it was always very clear what he was saying. There were no complications. It was always straightforward instructions and he always came across as a pleasant guy, but authoritative.

Ray McLoughlin: I used to invite Carwyn over to Dublin every other year for the Ireland-Wales match as my guest after that 1971 tour. I got to know him very well. He was a very sophisticated, gentle and enlightened man.

Mick Hipwell: I don't know from what point on I knew that he was gay; I don't think we ever talked about it during the Lions tour. It made no difference to me or to anyone else who may have been aware of it on the tour – it was certainly never a talking point among the players. It was just a non-event.

David Duckham: I'm going to try and answer this without the benefit of hindsight. I always thought there was something . . . that there was a lot about Carwyn that we didn't know. An intense man. He got on with Mike Gibson and Ray McLoughlin very well because they were both intense in that way as well. I can imagine those three having long conversations into the night about rugby and life and the ways of the world.

I always thought there was another side to Carwyn, but at the time it would never have occurred to me, not in a thousand years, that his sexuality was the issue. Being naive as I was, I had no inkling at all that he had that kind of secret to bear. It's very, very sad that he wasn't ever able to publicly reveal all about himself and live the way he wanted to live. He'd have been able to do that today, wouldn't he? If he had been born thirty or forty years later, his life would have been very different. And he would still be regarded up there with the likes of Ian McGeechan as one of the greatest coaches of all time. I think he will be anyway, but it breaks your heart to think about that loneliness he must have suffered. And of course the way it all ended.

In 1983, Carwyn travelled to Amsterdam, and it was there that he met his end, his body found in the bathroom of his room in the Kras Nabolsky Hotel on 10 January. The official record stated that he had suffered a heart attack while shaving, and as he had fallen he had hit his head on the edge of the bath, a blow that had killed him. He was fifty-three and had died alone.

Cliff Morgan, his great rival during their rugby days, was among James' small circle of friends. For many years they had talked relentlessly about rugby, had sung together, drunk together, worked together as broadcasters.

As Morgan related to David Foot in the *Guardian* in 2001, 'Rugby is a gregarious game and I think, on reflection, it gave him some relief from his loneliness. Once in a moment of some confidence, he suddenly said to me, "There is a great loneliness upon me, you know." I was struck by his use of words.'

Years later, Mark Reason, the son of the legendary rugby writer John Reason who had toured with the Lions in 1971 and who became a close friend of Carwyn's, told a story in print. 'Once upon a time I lived in a family home where many of Britain's rugby greats often came to stay. This was thrilling for a teenage boy mad on sport. One of my favourite guests was Carwyn James. I was probably seventeen when Carwyn and I were sitting in the front room of the Reason family house in London watching the snooker world championships on the television.

'Carwyn, nervous about a forthcoming flight to South Africa, had had a few drinks. We were riffing about Welsh snooker player Terry Griffiths, another Llanelli boy, when Carwyn suddenly leant over me and pressed his mouth on mine. It was a shocking moment. But here was a desperately lonely man, with a drink too many inside him because of a fear of flying, who did an impulsive thing that would torture him for days and weeks to come. I pushed him off and left the room. Carwyn was alone again. The man was a mass of anxiety, of yellow nicotine fingers and red eczema blotches. Carwyn hid in a closet all of his life because rugby seethed with homophobia. Carwyn would never coach Wales, despite a brilliance that Graham Henry still pays tribute to, because he was "a faggot", "a gay boy" and a dozen far more offensive terms.

'He was also one of the kindest, most self-deprecating men I have ever met. He was interested in people and thought deeply. He had a gentle voice, the same lyrical lilt of Richard Burton and Anthony Hopkins that seems to flow from the soft water of Southern Wales. He is one of the true giants of the game of rugby and I am proud to say that, despite what happened on that evening, he remained a close friend of our family.

'But just four years later Carwyn was dead. I heard the shocking news on the radio of the Cambridge student house I was living in. The details were vague, but oh so painfully predictable. Carwyn, who had fallen in and out of alcoholism, died in a hotel room in Amsterdam. It was seedy and so unnecessary.'

David Duckham: We had a memorial service for him in Wales and all the tour party were there. I remember the minute's silence we had and then the drinks later to toast him. It was a very, very sad day. We all had huge respect for him as a coach and he was a wonderful, kind and intelligent human being. I think we were all glad that we'd been able to play a part in establishing his legacy.

Ian McLauchlan: What I shall always remember about Carwyn is his gentleness. In New Zealand he was dealing with a fairly rough bunch of blokes but he never had to raise his voice. Our success was entirely due to him.

Barry John: He got a tremendous respect from everybody – doctors, dentists, fitters, turners, miners – total respect, and that's an incredible achievement. Players were prepared to go out there and get hurt for him.

In life, as in death, Carwyn James was an enigma. As Alun Richardson wrote, 'You could not be with Carwyn for long without realising the contradictions in his nature, but that was not all. There were parts of his nature which were mysterious for there was a remote part of himself which he kept quite separate, a retreat from which the often brash turmoil of the rugby world was barred and in which he thought his own private thoughts.'

It is a tragedy that Carwyn lived in a time and a place where he felt unable to truly be himself. It is his great triumph that, despite a life lived under repression, he led a team of disparate rugby players, shoved together with little preparation time, across the toughest rugby terrain on the planet and achieved a level of success not seen by a touring team in New Zealand before or since. He changed British and Irish rugby. He changed New Zealand rugby. And he will be remembered forever as one of the greatest minds the game has ever known.

CHAPTER TWENTY

NO BUGGER WANTS TO KNOW YOU

IVAN VODANOVICH knew what was coming. He'd been in charge for ten Tests and he had only won four of them. He had taken the All Blacks to South Africa and had been humbled. He'd hosted the Lions and had been humbled again. He'd won just forty per cent of his games as coach and that was never going to be good enough to hold on to his position. The next time the All Blacks came together for a Test was against Australia in Wellington, almost a year to the day after the Lions had clinched the series. Bob Duff, an international lock from the 1950s, had already replaced Vodanovich as national team coach.

Colin Meads finally hung up his boots after the fourth Test against the Lions. His had been an epic journey that had spanned three decades, from 1957 to 1971. In the aftermath of the fourth Test, Meads congratulated the Lions as he bowed out. 'You've gone around the country unbeaten and you've won the series,' he said. 'This is a great achievement. It will probably never be equalled.' It was a statement which, to date, has remained as accurate as Doug Smith's prediction on the result of the Test series.

Meads won fifty-five caps for New Zealand, and throughout his fourteen years in the jersey he was a folk hero, a symbol of everything that was good about the All Blacks. He was inspirational to play with and intimidating to play against. He was a leader and an enforcer, a humble sheep farmer and one of the most unrelenting rugby players the game has ever known.

After the third Test in Wellington, Brian Lochore retired for a second, and last, time. He had been Fred Allen's captain during the golden era, an All Black who had won fifteen Tests in a row between 1965 and 1969. He was a colossus in every sense. A fine rugby player and a wonderful leader of men. His career petered out under Vodanovich. Having become used to winning, he lost four out of his last five Tests in the black jersey, his final appearance being that ill-fated call to arms in Athletic Park against the rampant Lions.

When his playing career ended Lochore turned to coaching and administration. He became an All Blacks selector in 1983 and coached his country from 1985 to 1987, a period of success that culminated with New Zealand winning the inaugural World Cup. For his service as a player, a captain and a coach he goes down as one of the most important characters in the New Zealand rugby story.

Throughout the Test series, Ian McLauchlan had Jazz Muller for company in the battle of the front row. The Taranaki Tank, as Muller was known, was a fearsome sight, with a twenty-inch neck and a height and weight advantage that gave the impression of a mismatch with Mighty Mouse.

It never panned out that way. McLauchlan's superior technique was too much for Muller, who gave up rugby almost immediately after the Lions tour. For more than twenty years he lived as a virtual recluse in his hometown of Eltham in Taranaki. Without a telephone or television, he switched off the outside world for the longest time.

In 2000 he granted an interview to a New Zealand journalist. 'You get one crack at it [playing for the All Blacks] and when you're finished no bugger wants to know you,' he said. Not a lot has been heard from the Tank in the years since.

Bryan 'Beegee' Williams went on to become an All Blacks legend, playing thirty-eight Tests up until his last on the Grand Slam tour of Britain and Ireland in 1978. Including non-Tests, he wore the New Zealand jersey 113 times and scored sixty-six tries.

His involvement in the game never let up, even after retirement. He achieved coaching success in club rugby, with Ponsonby, the great All Blacks player factory in his native Auckland. He then went to the country of his father's birth – Samoa – and sparked a golden era.

'I had it in my heart – I wanted to go and work and help Samoa, the home of my heritage, my dad's birth,' he said. 'I've got absolutely no regrets about that. Even now, people say you might've become an All Blacks coach, but so what. I was happy with Samoa for those next ten years.'

Williams was Western Samoa's technical director at the 1991 World Cup, where they pulled off a massive shock when beating Wales at Cardiff Arms Park. He was technical director for a second time at the 1995 World Cup and then took over as coach for the 1999 World Cup. At that tournament, Samoa beat Wales once again in a classic game at the Millennium Stadium. Beegee was now a giant in two countries.

He returned to New Zealand rugby years later and in 2011 was elected president of the New Zealand Rugby Football

Union. 'The experiences I've had and the things I've learned, the places I've been and the friends I've made have been awesome,' he reflected at the time. 'I thank my lucky stars that I'd been able to experience it. I'm eternally grateful.'

Fred Allen knew what he was doing when he named twenty-one-year-old Ian Kirkpatrick in his team to play France at Colombes in November 1967. The flanker's class was obvious before the Test and was more obvious still after it, when he scored a try in a 21–15 victory.

Kirkpatrick's legend really started to grow in his next Test, in June 1968, when he came off the bench – he was the first All Black to be used as a substitute – against Australia in Sydney and scored a hat trick. From that day onwards, Kirkpatrick became a mainstay of the side. Between June 1968 and his final Test, against the Lions in August 1977, he didn't miss a single game for the All Blacks.

Tall, athletic and a devastating runner he won thirty-nine caps, nine of them as captain, and scored an incredible total of sixteen tries, which stood as a New Zealand record until the wing Stu Wilson beat it in 1983. In all, he played 289 first-class games and scored 115 tries – a bewilderingly high number for a flanker in any era.

His most memorable of the lot was that famous fifty-five-metre surge in the second Test against the Lions in Christchurch in 1971. Kirkpatrick will forever be remembered as one of the game's greatest back-row forwards.

When he was nineteen, Sid Going was on the cusp of All Blacks recognition. He was an obvious star in the making, the coming man at scrum-half. It was at that time, reported the website of the Church of Jesus Christ of Latter-Day Saints, that Sid felt a calling. 'He would forgo rugby to serve a mission,' it was written.

'Some called him "crazy". Others called him "foolish". They protested that his opportunity in rugby might never come again.

'For Sid it was not what he was leaving behind, it was the opportunity and responsibility ahead. He had a priesthood duty to offer two years of his life to declare the reality of the Lord Jesus Christ and His restored gospel. Nothing – not even a chance to play on the national team with all the acclaim it would bring – would deter him from that duty. He was called by a prophet of God to serve in the Western Canada mission.'

Sid gave himself to the Lord, but he kept a little back for rugby. He made his debut in 1967 and stayed in the team for ten years, winning twenty-nine caps and making eighty-six appearances including non-cap games. He was a hugely influential scrum-half, distinctive with his side-whiskers and his speed and strength and elusiveness. He was clever and combative. Along with his brothers, Ken and Brian, he created the famous Going triple scissors move, which they were still using late into their careers.

His battle with Gareth Edwards was a sub-plot in the Lions story, a head to head between two magnificent players. Sid acknowledged the ability of the Lions but he never went overboard with his praise. He just wasn't the type. He retired from Test rugby at the age of thirty-three.

Alex 'Grizz' Wyllie, the hard man of Canterbury, stayed in the New Zealand team for two more seasons, winning the last of his eleven caps in 1973 at the age of twenty-nine. He continued to play for his province until 1979, cementing his legend at Lancaster Park. He played more than 200 games for Canterbury and was captain more than one hundred times. He led the side that beat a touring England in 1973, then did the same when the Scots and the Irish arrived in 1975 and 1976.

Grizz is remembered not just as a ferocious player but also as a successful coach. It was under his regime that Canterbury held the Ranfurly Shield for three years. Not only that, it was on Grizz's watch that Canterbury beat the Lions in 1983 and Australia in 1986. He was assistant All Blacks coach when they won the World Cup in 1987 and was head coach from 1988 to 1991. Of those who have overseen the All Blacks for three Tests or more, only Fred Allen and Steve Hansen have a better win percentage than Grizz Wyllie.

In 1996, he became head coach of the Argentina national team, taking them to a historic high of a World Cup quarter-final following a famous victory over Ireland in Lens in 1999. Grizz, the ultimate Kiwi, became an icon of Pumas rugby.

Wyllie's partner in the frontline battle on that infamous day at Lancaster Park was Alister Hopkinson, a prop forward who had nine caps and thirty-five appearances for the All Blacks before the Lions arrived. That he was never given an opportunity to add to those numbers was a source of confusion and anger among those who valued his toughness. In a period when New Zealand struggled, there were many calls for Hopkinson's return to the fold, but he never got the chance.

Like Grizz, Hoppy went into coaching. He, too, coached Canterbury. When the touring Irish played at Lancaster Park in the summer of 1992, Hopkinson's team hammered them by twenty-five points. Hopkinson fought cancer in the years that followed and passed away in January 1999 at the age of fifty-seven.

Keith Murdoch never played against the Lions in the end. In fact, he only ever played three Tests for the All Blacks, and yet remains one of the most compelling and mysterious characters the game has ever produced. The Otago prop toured Britain with the All Blacks in 1972–73. It was supposed to be a time when he kicked on and became a regular in the side, but it was actually the end of him.

Murdoch was a target of the British press from the moment he arrived, the tabloids mocking him for going missing on the Lions tour in 1971. He was like a suspect device in the early games, a ticking bomb ready to go off. His wild behaviour in the storied defeat to Llanelli at Stradey Park was an indication of his mental state, but it was when he lost the plot on the night New Zealand beat Wales in Cardiff that things took an awful turn.

He assaulted a hotel security guard that night and was sent home from the tour in disgrace. To this day, many of his fellow All Blacks – Kirkpatrick among them – feel remorse that they didn't do enough to stand up for him when the All Blacks management got heavy. Murdoch never did reach New Zealand. He got off the plane at a refuelling stop in Darwin and never got back on again. He disappeared into self-imposed exile in the outback, where he remained unfound for nearly twenty years.

It wasn't until the journalist Margot McRae tracked him down in 1990 that anybody knew where he was or what he now looked like. Given his total hatred for the media, McRae was a brave woman. Murdoch appeared to have mellowed, but wouldn't do an interview on camera. He spoke briefly about the incident in Cardiff and said he would talk some more to McRae the day after. She waited for him at the appointed venue. He never showed up.

The All Blacks were a team in decline in 1971. Change was needed, and if the New Zealanders didn't realise it before that Lions tour, they realised it afterwards. Before the season was out, progressive provincial unions such as Wellington and Counties Manukau had taken on board the lessons dealt out by the Lions and began to adopt their methods. They placed a much greater emphasis on ambitious back play and on counter-attacking from loose kicking and turnovers.

More focus was placed on finding robust scrummaging props, having been so humiliated up front. Technical details, such as using the instep to kick goals, as Barry John did, were also taken on board. By the end of 1971, Wellington, who had been routed by the Lions, were the country's most attractive attacking side.

The most significant change, however, was in coaching. The real legacy of the 1971 Lions is really the legacy of Carwyn James. The clarity of his coaching philosophy and his careful man-management were all recognised and glorified in New Zealand. The All Blacks were taken back to school, Carwyn their teacher.

They proved quite brilliant students. It wasn't long before the All Blacks were once again setting the standard; no side has won a Test series in New Zealand since the 1971 Lions. With the advent of the World Cup, New Zealand won the first tournament in 1987, then won it again in 2011 and retained it in 2015. Since 1971, the Lions have been back to tour New Zealand four times and have lost four times. They've played fourteen Tests and New Zealand have won twelve of them. When the Kiwis said that they don't ever expect to the see the likes of the 1971 Lions on their shores ever again, it was a nod to the genius of that team, but also to the changed world in which we now live. Barry John was the King back then. But rugby's royal family doesn't wear red any more; it wears black.

CHAPTER TWENTY-ONE

THE IMMORTALS

CARWYN'S CONFIDANT in New Zealand, Doug Smith, passed away on 22 September 1998 at the age of seventy-three. On his death, one of his players on tour, his fellow Scot, Chris Rea, wrote of Doug and his partnership with Carwyn, 'It was the fusion of two different characters which ignited the torch. James, academic and introverted, with Smith, forthright and boisterously self-confident.

'Doug was in charge of organisation and discipline and he discharged the latter with a well-considered balance between a light touch and, when the occasion demanded it, heavy censure. When Sean Lynch, the loosest of Irish cannons, had, with the aid of a fire hose, transformed the first floor of the team hotel into something resembling the set of Titanic, the only thing which saved him from deportation was the fact that the Lions had lost both Test props in the infamous battle of Canterbury earlier in the tour. But Lynch, a contrite soul in the cold light of day, was left in no doubt as to who was boss.

'A quarter of a century ago the Lions management team

consisted of two men – the honorary manager and the honorary coach. The physiotherapists, dieticians, shrinks and surgeons who are part of the travelling circus nowadays would not have been tolerated. Smith treated many of the injuries himself and the vision of his hypodermic needle which looked and felt like a screwdriver aimed at my groin haunts me still. His methods did, however, have a miraculously healing effect on some of his patients.

'Doug Smith was big enough to subordinate his extrovert tendencies to the needs of the team. He worked unstintingly to give his coach and his players the best possible conditions in which to do their jobs. When (two years before his death) he attended the twenty-fifth reunion celebrations of the 1971 Lions, he was a very ill man. It was a monumental effort for him, but it was a measure of his popularity and the affection in which he was held by the players that every man jack came to pay their respects to the man described by Willie John McBride as the finest of all Lions managers.'

Doug retains the honour of being the greatest soothsayer in Lions history. His prediction of a 2–1 victory has gone down in legend. That wasn't the only mind game he pulled that summer. 'Doug said at the beginning of the tour that there were two fatal flaws in New Zealand rugby that we would exploit,' said Ian McLauchlan. 'In every interview he did he was asked what the flaws were and he always said he'd reveal them just before he mounted the plane to go home. So as we got ready to leave he was asked again about the flaws and he said, "There aren't any – New Zealand rugby is in great shape. We're just in better shape." That was it. He had played them all along.'

The fourth Test in Auckland was John Dawes' final game on the international stage. He was thirty-one years old, had helped revolutionise London Welsh, had captained Wales to a Grand

Slam and had led the Lions to a historic series win in New Zealand. Had he never done another thing in the game he would have gone down in the rugby annals, but, of course, he did a lot more.

He became Wales coach in 1974 and stayed in the role throughout the golden era until he left in 1979. He'd added two more Grand Slams to his CV by then. In 1977, when the Lions returned to New Zealand, there was only one man really in the frame to assume the mantle that Carwyn held the last time they were there – John Dawes. Alas, the Lions couldn't repeat the trick and went down 3–1 in the series. He describes the 1971 tour as the highlight of his career.

Dawes lived by the mantra of expansive rugby from his first days. He joined London Welsh in 1963 and the club was a shambles. In 1965 he became captain and held the position for a record six seasons. He set about changing the culture. His work had a seismic impact not just on London Welsh, or indeed Wales, but on the Lions.

'I wanted us to be able run teams off the park,' he said. 'The perceived thinking at the time – as it has often been throughout the history of the game – was that you needed your forwards to be huge. I didn't care about having eight huge blokes lumbering around the field, I only wanted guys who were footballers.'

He helped nurture some of the very best at London Welsh – JPR Williams, Gerald Davies, Mervyn Davies, John Taylor and Geoff Evans. 'You don't need to be a good captain or indeed a good player to be a good coach, nor do you have to be a good coach to be a good captain,' said Gerald, 'but in those halcyon days of the London Welsh era in the mid 1960s and early 1970s, John did both jobs. He had a broad vision of how the game should be played. He was a great passer of the ball. It was a delight to play on the wing outside the man.'

Willie John McBride calls Dawes the most underrated player of his generation. JPR tells a story about him, not just as a player, but as a man. 'Coming into the last Test, everyone was really looking forward to going home. My mentality was slightly different because, as a medical student at the time, I'd planned to stay out and do my medical elective in Auckland, so I wasn't in quite the same frame of mind as everyone else. The tour came to an end and I had to wave everyone off as they went home, which was a hard experience. I came back in November. I'd no idea just how big a deal the whole thing was back home because the New Zealand public tried to dampen it down a bit afterwards. When I arrived in Wales I was absolutely gobsmacked by the publicity surrounding the tour and all the dinners that were going on.

'What was very special about that group of players – and John Dawes in particular – was that there were a huge number of functions organised for us, but Dawesey said that they had to be postponed until I was back from my elective and we could all go to them as a team. He wasn't going to have me left out from it all, which was a wonderful thing for him to do.'

When the tour was over and the *Dominion* newspaper wrote of the victorious Lions, they singled out JPR Williams as one of the giants of the summer. 'Seldom had a full-back as brilliant as this twenty-two-year-old medical student toured New Zealand. As he had been on the Welsh tour in 1969, he was serenity personified as he went in to take high kicks. But there was now more to his game. He ran into the backline with judgment and invariably with penetration and as the tour developed he showed a remarkable flair for launching counter-attacks. A natural athlete who once won the Junior Wimbledon tennis title, he was one of the glamour players.'

The *Dominion* said that JPR was the greatest visiting full-back since Gerry Brand of South Africa in 1937. 'His bravery under all conditions was of Victoria Cross standard. Yes, John Williams' name will live forever in the memory.'

JPR's extraordinary international career spanned 1969–81 and took in Triple Crowns, Grand Slams and the two most successful Lions tours of all time – New Zealand in 1971 and South Africa in 1974. He won fifty-five caps for Wales and eight caps for the Lions and won seventy-one per cent of the Tests he played in. There are so many images from his time in the red jersey, but that booming drop goal in the fourth Test in Auckland, and the looks of amazement on the faces of his teammates, takes some beating.

Bob Hiller was in JPR's shadow in New Zealand, just as he had been in the shadow of the captain, Tom Kiernan, on the previous Lions tour in 1968. As a consequence, he never got to play in a Test, but he was still a prolific points scorer and a majestic tourist. It was a testament to his quality that he still managed to score more than one hundred points in the summer of 1971. Hiller only played two more Tests for England after New Zealand, bringing his total to nineteen. He retired at twenty-nine and dedicated himself to a career in education.

After he scored four blistering tries against Hawke's Bay, the local press called Gerald Davies the 'prince among wingers'. After scoring three more tries in the Test series, bringing his total in New Zealand to ten, the New Zealand rugby public voted him the world's most exciting wing. It wasn't just the tries he scored and created, it was his pace and the ease with which he could change direction off either foot at top speed that marked him out as special.

Davies turned down an invitation to tour South Africa with the Lions in 1974 on account of the apartheid regime in the country. It's a decision, he says, that he has never once regretted. Thirty-five years later, in 2009, he was chosen to manage the Lions in South Africa. He won forty-six caps for Wales, scoring twenty tries. He played his last Tests in Australia in 1978 and even at the age of thirty-three he was lethal, touching down in both games against the Wallabies. Davies is remembered as one of the most thrilling players in rugby history.

David Duckham, the blond centre-cum-wing, was never the quickest player, but he made up for a lack of gas with a rugby intelligence and a sidestep to die for, an integral part of his game that he learned as a young man watching his rugby hero, Peter Jackson, playing for his local team, Coventry. 'Put a sidestep and a dummy together properly and you really are in business,' he said. It was a principle he played by throughout his time in the Test arena.

He emerged on the scene when English rugby was in a hole. Of his thirty-six caps for England between 1969 and 1976, he won only eleven of them, but his class made him an obvious pick for Carwyn's Lions. In the game against West Coast-Buller, he tore up the record books when scoring six tries. In all, he scored eleven tries on tour, a try count only bettered by John Bevan.

'David was always very intense and aggressive in his play, although always such a gent off the field,' said Gareth Edwards. 'I sometimes thought he was a bit too intense before big games. He would stand in the corner of the changing room, fists clenched, psyching himself up. I wanted to tell him to relax because that was when he played his best rugby – and at his best he was world class. But early on in a tour you didn't know guys well enough to say that kind of thing – it was only later that you could do that, by which time he had started to relax into the environment. He played some outstanding rugby.'

John Bevan, the kid from the Rhonnda, was the youngest in the Lions squad, but what an explosive beginning he had to the tour, scoring ten tries in his first four games. He was immensely powerful, a finisher of high quality. At one point on tour he looked certain to break Tony O'Reilly's all-time Lions try-scoring record – seventeen scores established in New Zealand in 1959 – but Bevan also finished on seventeen. A mid-tour slump checked his progress, but he came back strong towards the end, when he scored four tries against Manawatu-Horowhenua.

His fellow Lions will always remember him for the battering ram try he scored amid the violence of Canterbury, and he scored a similar one in that unforgettable Barbarians game against the All Blacks at the Arms Park in 1973, brushing off the wing Bryan Williams, the centre Ian Hurst and the full-back Joe Karam to score in the corner.

Later that year, after just ten caps for Wales, in which he scored five tries, Bevan was lost to rugby union, transferring instead to Warrington in rugby league. He played more than 300 games for Warrington and scored more than 200 tries. He won seventeen caps for Wales and another six for Great Britain, scoring ten more tries. In 1974, he won the Challenge Cup final and was later inducted into the Warrington Wolves Hall of Fame. To his last day on the rugby field he remained a try-scoring machine.

After an early injury, things didn't look good in New Zealand for the Scottish winger, Alastair Biggar, but he recovered to have a fine tour. With Gerald Davies, David Duckham and John Bevan as his rivals for a Test spot on the wing, he was up against impossible odds, but Biggar still scored nine tries in his ten games, a return that showed the depth in quality the Lions possessed.

Biggar came from farming stock but his career was spent in the City of London as a foreign exchange broker. A quick and powerful winger who could also do a turn at centre, he played his rugby for London Scottish. After the Lions tour he played just two more Tests for his country, a hamstring injury putting paid to his career at the young age of twenty-five. Sadly, Biggar passed away in February 2016 after a battle with cancer.

Mike Gibson, the Northern Ireland solicitor, was always different. He was never one of the boys, never a man to head for the pub and party like so many of his teammates in 1971. He was a hard person to get to know, but what was obvious was his class and his dedication to his sport. Long before the idea of professionalism was even a concept in the British and Irish game, Gibson lived his life like a finely tuned athlete. He wasn't getting paid a penny, of course, but he was training and thinking like a full-timer, even back then.

He was at the peak of his considerable powers in 1971. It was his third Lions tour and he went on two more after it. He and his fellow Ulsterman, Willie John McBride, are the only players in history to have been selected for five Lions tours.

Gibson carried Irish rugby on his back for many years. Playing ten or twelve, he was the beacon of hope, a player who could run, pass and step, who could read a game like no other. He was the complete player. Through a difficult era, Gibson was world class, from his debut in 1964 to his last days in the green jersey, a historic series win in Australia, fifteen years later. He won sixty-nine caps for Ireland and twelve for the Lions and will be remembered as one of the finest players the game has ever seen.

John Spencer was twenty-three years old and England captain when he went to New Zealand. He had an exacting time down there. He'd earned his place in the squad by playing centre, but found John Dawes and Mike Gibson blocking his route. Carwyn James shifted him to the wing, but there wasn't much opportunity for him there either. He got off to an error-ridden start in his first game against Thames Valley and it was a battle from there on.

Spencer doesn't eulogise Carwyn the way most of the other Lions do. He says he was good, but not great. He says he had better coaches in his time in rugby. He may have had something of an unhappy time on the field in New Zealand, but he gets universal credit from his fellow Lions for the way he conducted himself off it despite his Test ambitions crumbling around his ankles. He was wisecracking and upbeat. He felt it his duty to put a brave face on his disappointment for the good of his mates.

'Spence was a fantastic tourist, the kind that keeps the whole thing glued together,' said Gareth Edwards. 'He never let his head drop and he always kept everyone's spirits up. A great man. He used to make up little poems: "I'm not a pheasant plucker, I'm a pheasant plucker's son. When I'm not plucking pheasant . . ." and so on. The following year at Cardiff I was tackled by him. He clung to me, whispering as we went down to the bottom of a ruck, "D'ya know, I'm not a pheasant plucker, I'm a pheasant plucker's son . . ."'

Spencer never played in another Test after New Zealand. His international career came to an end at the age of twenty-four, but his work in administration carries on. When the Lions committee were looking for a person to manage the tour to New Zealand in 2017, they turned to John Spencer.

He wasn't around for a long time, but Arthur Lewis, the Welsh centre, could hardly have been around at a better time. He was twenty-eight when he made his debut in 1970, went on to win a Grand Slam in 1971, won three out of three in the truncated championship of 1972 and shared the championship in 1973. He played eleven Test matches for Wales and won nine of them. He was never going to break up the Dawes-Gibson midfield partnership in New Zealand, but he was a fine tourist nonetheless.

Chris Rea, the Scottish centre, had gone into the tour in great form, scoring in three consecutive Tests before heading to New Zealand. He was another victim of the immovable objects that were Dawes and Gibson. 'None of the backs got injured, which was very inconsiderate of them,' he joked years later. 'The worst of it was I'd had to sell my beloved MG Midget to go on the tour because I had to take four months unpaid leave.' Hampered by injury early in the tour, he found the summer a frustrating experience and, like Spencer, never played for his country again. He was twenty-seven and went on to become a journalist.

Gareth Edwards' partnership with Barry John was at the heart of the success, a half-back combination of the ages. When rugby people sit down to discuss the greatest players who ever picked up a rugby ball, Edwards is always in the conversation and, more often than not, he's chosen as the greatest of all time. His pace, strength, bravery, the length and accuracy of his passing, the quality of his leadership and his innate understanding of the game made him a legend.

From his first appearance in the Five Nations in 1967 to his last appearance in 1978, Edwards never missed a game. He won fifty-three caps for Wales, scored twenty tries and won three Grand Slams. He played in three Lions tours and won two of them – 1971 and 1974. He also scored the most beloved try in the game's history, for the Barbarians against New Zealand in 1973. In 2015, Gareth became Sir Gareth. He remains a revered character in world rugby.

In one sense it's incredible that a player of Chico Hopkins' quality only ever played in one Test for Wales in 1970 and one for the Lions in 1971 – and both of them were as a substitute. He was excellent in both games. It's incredible until you realise that his competitor for the number-nine jersey was Gareth Edwards, not just a supreme scrum-half but a supreme scrum-half who hardly ever got injured.

Chico was a huge character on tour, one half of a much-loved double act with Bob Hiller. He always believed he was good enough to get more caps, but it never worked out. 'There are no sour grapes because I had a great time,' he said. 'The game has been a godsend for me. I would have been a bastard recluse without it because I was a bit shy. And now people remember me because the name Chico sticks with them. There were better players than me around and people think "Who?" when you mention them. What more can a player want than to be remembered after all these years?'

Frank Laidlaw, the Scottish hooker, was a Lion in 1966, playing in two Tests in New Zealand. He was thirty by the time 1971 came along, was susceptible to knee ligament trouble and couldn't unseat John Pullin in the front row of the scrum. Laidlaw didn't win another cap for Scotland after the tour. He later became a proponent of Scientology.

John Pullin remained England's hooker for five more years, his Test career coming to an end in 1976 after forty-two caps for his country and seven for the Lions in 1968 and 1971. He played through a difficult era in English rugby and won just thirteen of those forty-two Tests, but amid those years there were some spectacular highs.

Only three England captains in history have led the side to victory in a Test in South Africa and Pullin did it first, in 1972. Will Carling and Martin Johnson did it later. Only two England captains in history have led the side to victory in New Zealand and, again, Pullin did it first in 1973, Johnson following on thirty years later. And there was another day for which Pullin will be forever remembered – in Ireland, at any rate. The 1972 Five Nations was interrupted by the Troubles in Northern Ireland. Citing security fears, Scotland and Wales refused to travel to Dublin to fulfil their fixtures and the concern was that, in 1973, England would follow suit.

Much to Ireland's relief and overwhelming appreciation, England made the trip. Pullin led them on to the field and all of Lansdowne Road rose as one to thank them. The applause went on and on. Some England players were close to tears, such was the emotion in the stadium. England lost the game, but in the post-match dinner Pullin made a speech and uttered a line that will be recalled for as long as the game is played in Ireland: 'We may not be any good, but at least we turn up.'

Stack Stevens, the Cornish farmer, was parachuted into the tour after Ray McLoughlin was injured in the Battle of Canterbury. He won twenty-five caps for England, the last of them in 1975. He had the distinction of being alongside John Pullin in the English front row on the day they beat South Africa in Johannesburg in 1972 and New Zealand in Auckland in 1973.

The Dublin publican, Sean Lynch, only had four caps to his name when he was selected for the Lions squad as back-up to the first-choice tighthead, Sandy Carmichael. All of that changed after Canterbury. Suddenly, Lynchy was set loose. He was hard and abrasive and an utter pest to the New Zealanders, a trait that cost him a punch in the mouth and fourteen stitches in the Maori game. Everybody on that tour has a Sean Lynch story, usually involving some mad capers while out on the town. On his rugby, he had a simple philosophy in New Zealand: 'I'd no interest in running around with the ball. My job was to give it back to the best backline in the world. Feed it out and let them do the rest. We knew where Barry John would kick the ball. He'd kick it on a sixpence. I knew without lifting my head where he'd land it and I'd speed to that breakdown.'

Lynch played seventeen times for Ireland, his final cap coming in 1974. He always was, and still is, an unassuming man, slow to talk up his role on the tour.

Ian McLauchlan picked a fine time to score the only try of his ten-year international career – the pivotal touchdown in the first Test in Dunedin. He may not have been Fergus Slattery's cup of tea, but Mighty Mouse, a nickname coined by Doug Smith, left an indelible mark on the tour in his head to heads with Jazz Muller in the Test series.

He always has – and always will – rail against the notion that he was second choice behind Ray McLoughlin until the Irishman's injury in Canterbury. He might have been a small prop, at about 5 ft 10 in, but he was utterly unyielding, very good technically and had a self-belief that was unshakeable no matter what kind of bruiser he went up against.

To hammer home the point about him deserving his place in the Test series in 1971 – injured rival or no injured rival – McLauchlan toured with the Lions again in 1974 and played in all four Tests against the Springbok captain, Hannes Marais. Once more, the Mouse prevailed. His Lions record reads played eight, won five, drew two, lost one. He made the absolute most out of his international career, only retiring in 1979 at the age of thirty-seven.

One of the saddest stories of 1971 was that of Sandy Carmichael, the formidable Scottish tighthead, who was invalided out of the tour after being targeted by the thugs of Canterbury. There was huge sympathy for Carmichael for the facial battering he took, huge anger towards those who did it and, also, huge confusion about why Sandy allowed it to happen without fighting back.

The Scot sucked up a massive amount of punishment, suffered a fractured cheekbone as a result and had to go home.

That was just part one of his Lions story. Part two happened three years later in South Africa. Carmichael was still a prop to be reckoned with, but a new kid called Fran Cotton had emerged on the stage by then and Sandy couldn't shift him from the Test team. Sandy was an unused substitute throughout the four-match series.

He played on until 1978 and with fifty caps for his country his place in the story of the Scottish game is assured. In a Lions context it's a tale of what might have been.

Ray McLoughlin didn't have just one rugby career, he had two. Between 1962 and 1966 he played eighteen times for Ireland and in three Tests for the Lions in New Zealand. He became known as a master thinker about the game and a technical wonder when it came to the intricacies of scrummaging and front-row play. He became Ireland captain in those years and sought to change the mindset of his players while making the preparation more focused.

McLoughlin had no truck with the Irish Rugby Football Union officials ruling the roost. He didn't want the blazers in team meetings, didn't want them on the team bus, didn't want them keeping the players awake at night with their boozing at the team hotel. McLoughlin was the first Irish captain to stand up to the union men and say that things had to change.

The IRFU looked on him and his modern methods with suspicion. Not long after, he lost the captaincy. Then he walked away from the international scene for five years while building a hugely successful business. He returned in 1971 and played another twenty-two times for Ireland. In New Zealand he was respected not just as a player but as the kind of rugby intellectual that Carwyn loved being around. Before punching Grizz Wyllie in the head in Canterbury and thereby putting himself out of the tour, McLoughlin was a key factor in the coaching of the Lions forwards.

He missed out on the glory, but he doesn't have many regrets. Weighing up his whole life – the forty caps for his country and the fortune he has made in business – he deems himself a very fortunate man.

When Carwyn needed replacements for his fallen front rows, one of the players he turned to was Welshman Geoff Evans – not a prop, but a second row. He got up to speed in his first game, when he had his eye cut open and had to leave the field. His best days were in the games against Hawke's Bay and Auckland. Evans won seven Welsh caps between 1970 and 1972.

Mike Roberts of London Welsh was chosen as the fourth lock, and in the early games on tour he was a fairly peripheral figure. When Carwyn lost Sandy Carmichael after Canterbury, he made Roberts an offer he couldn't refuse – he told him he was now under consideration as tighthead prop instead of a second row. A Grand Slam-winning lock was now forced to adapt to life in the front row as understudy to Sean Lynch.

He fared as well as Carwyn could have hoped. He was too tall and too long-backed to make an impression on the best scrummagers in New Zealand, but he coped admirably against all odds. His international career after 1971 was a strange experience. He missed all of 1972, played twice in 1973, once in 1975 and won his last cap four years later in 1979.

Gordon Brown – Broon frae Troon – never intended on being a rugby player. He was the son of a footballer and that's what he wanted to be, too. He was a goalkeeper and once explained the turning point in his sporting life.

'It was a West of Scotland Cup tie and the game had a huge following, around 2,000 there. We were 6–1 down – none of the goals my fault, of course – when their winger came homing in on goal. He went round me and I brought him down with a rugby tackle. Bedlam. The crowd was going mental, throwing coins and howling for my blood. There were two policemen there and for the first time in their lives they had to escort a player off the field. In the dressing room I could hear the voices outside planning dire things for me and I ran all the way home. The Monday night, I went to the rugby club and asked to play. I honestly thought I'd be safer.'

He was only twenty-three years old when he went on the Lions tour. 'At first he seemed baby-faced and rather too tender to stand up to the knocks of rugby, New Zealand style,' wrote the *Dominion*. That feeling didn't last all that long, of course.

Brown was a formidable lineout player, skilful with ball in hand, big and tough at 17 st and 6 ft 5 in and the kind of battler that won the absolute respect of Willie John McBride, the legend he played alongside in two of the Tests in New Zealand and in three more in South Africa four years later. Brown was a gregarious character, a much-loved man who went on a third Lions tour, back in New Zealand, in 1977, where he played his last Test match.

He played thirty times for Scotland and eight times for the Lions between 1969 and 1977. Brown was such a witty storyteller that he became a major hit on the after-dinner speaking circuit. It was in late 1999 that he started experiencing symptoms, as he put it, similar to a groin strain. He was soon diagnosed with non-Hodgkin's lymphoma. The chemotherapy began in 2000. 'I've been lucky,' he said in an interview at the time. 'Normally you only find out what people think of you when you actually die. I've found out and I'm still here. The number of people who have rung me up and said, "We love you Broonie."'

The big man passed away in March 2001. He was fifty-three years old.

Delme Thomas started in the first two Tests in New Zealand before losing his place in the second row to Gordon Brown. Thomas was a veteran of two Lions tours by then. He actually made his Lions debut before he made his Welsh debut. He had two Lions caps, from 1966, before he ever got the chance to wear the red of Wales. He wore it twenty-five times between 1966 and 1974. Stellar though his international career was, arguably his greatest day in rugby came when he captained Carwyn's Llanelli to victory over the touring All Blacks in 1972.

Mick Hipwell's best game in New Zealand also happened to be his last – Canterbury. The Irish back-row forward went on tour in great form but was unfortunate to sustain a cartilage injury in the first stage of the trip in Australia and he was fighting a fitness battle pretty much all the way after that. He was thirty-one years old and played the last of his dozen caps for Ireland in the spring of 1972.

A replacement on the 1968 Lions, Rodger Arneil repeated the trick in 1971 when coming in for the injured Mick Hipwell. The Scottish back row played with an industry that made him a success on the tour despite not making the Test team. For a short while it looked like he was going to force his way in, but it wasn't to be. It wasn't just the fifteen on the team that made the Lions great, it was also the quality of the back-up. Arneil played for Scotland for one more season and finished his international career in 1972 with twenty-two caps.

The All Blacks bookended Derek Quinnell's career, the third Test in New Zealand in 1971 being his first game of international rugby, when he was twenty-two years old, and a Test against the Kiwis in Cardiff in 1980 being his last. His role in silencing Sid Going in that third Test in Wellington has gone down in Lions legend. He didn't enjoy the best of luck on tour, a leg injury slowing his momentum early on. 'There was a suspicion that the Lions themselves didn't quite realise how good this scowling giant was,' wrote the *Dominion*. Quinnell's effectiveness in the back row was recognised soon enough. Carwyn gave him a specific job to stop Sid at Athletic Park and he carried it out to perfection. Quinnell played two Tests for the Lions in New Zealand in 1977 and two more in South Africa in 1980. He played twenty-three times for Wales.

John Taylor was another London Welsh man, a flanker who broke into the Wales team in 1967 at the age of twenty-one. He won twenty-six caps for his country and played in all four Tests in New Zealand, but he will be remembered for one game more than any other. It was the second round of matches in the Grand Slam season of 1971 and Wales were up against the wall against Scotland in front of a crowd of 105,000 at Murrayfield.

It was an epic Test. Wales had the lead, then Scotland had it, then Wales retook it, then Scotland took it back again. Taylor scored one of the Welsh tries that day but with just a few minutes left the Scots were ahead 18–14. Then Gerald Davies scored in the corner to make it 18–17 with the conversion to come.

Barry John was off the pitch injured, so the job, from the right-hand touchline, fell to the bearded Taylor. He banged it over, Wales won 19–18 and then went on to take the Grand Slam two games later. Taylor's kick is remembered as 'the greatest conversion since St Paul on the road to Damascus'. Taylor is also remembered for his principled stance on apartheid in South Africa. He turned down the chance to play against the Springboks on their tour to the UK and Ireland in 1969–70 and declined an invitation to tour

South Africa with the Lions in 1974. He won worldwide respect for both his rugby and his moral strength.

Fergus Slattery, the tearaway openside flanker from Dublin, was unlucky not make the Test side, but he would make up for it four years later when he played all four Tests in South Africa. He was a player of the highest class, a whirling dervish of boundless energy, physicality and skill. He was a strong character who didn't suffer fools. He spoke his mind from his first day in international rugby in 1970 to his last in 1984.

His fourteen-year span included sixty-one caps for Ireland and one of the most storied seasons in Irish rugby in 1982, a year that brought Ireland their first Triple Crown in thirty-three years. In any shortlist of the greats of Irish rugby, Slattery would be right up there.

Peter Dixon took a break from his studies at Oxford University to high-tail it to New Zealand as a rookie number eight-cum-flanker. The only international experience he had before he left was little more than an exhibition match between England and a President's XV at Twickenham in May 1971 – and given how it turned out, he could have done without it.

The President's side was star-studded and included four All Blacks: Brian Lochore, Colin Meads, Ian Kirkpatrick and Bryan Williams. In a 28–11 annihilation of the English, Williams scored three tries and Kirkpatrick got two. Little was known of Dixon before the tour, but he adapted to his surroundings and forced his way into the starting line-up for three Tests. He went on to captain England and won twenty-two caps between 1971 and 1978. His last cap was a 16–6 loss to New Zealand in November '78, but that wasn't quite the end of his story.

New Zealand returned to Britain in 1979 for an eleven-match tour. They won ten of them, including both Tests against

Scotland and England. The one they lost was against the North of England in Otley. The New Zealand side contained eleven of the players who would win at Twickenham a week later – among them Andy Dalton, Andy Haden, Graham Mourie, Murray Mexted, Stu Wilson and Bernie Fraser.

Peter Dixon was in North's back row. The New Zealanders may have known nothing of him when he first arrived in their country in 1971, but he won their respect that summer and won it all over again on that famous day in Otley eight years later.

When Mervyn Davies was picked to make his debut for London Welsh in 1968, having played third- and second-team rugby in the previous two weeks, a supposed sage among the selectors said that he wasn't much good but that at least he'd win some lineout ball. Three months later, Davies was playing for Wales.

He played thirty-eight times for his country and eight times for the victorious Lions of 1971 and 1974. Nicknamed Merve the Swerve after his deceptive running style, he changed the way number eights played the game. Before Davies' elan hit the scene, the number eight was considered a largely negative force whose principal function was as a destroyer of opposition attacks. He was a prodigious tackler but his skills set him apart. He was a great athlete with great hands. He became the template for all future number eights. He lost only eight games for Wales and won two Grand Slams, three Triple Crowns and five championships.

His career was cut short in 1976, not long after he captained Wales to the Grand Slam. While playing for Swansea in a Welsh Cup semi-final against Pontypool he suffered a brain haemorrhage and never played again. He was twenty-nine.

Originally a teacher, Davies' work took him into sales and then coaching and journalism. A poll of Welsh rugby supporters saw him voted as Wales' greatest ever captain and greatest ever number eight. After a long battle with cancer, Mervyn Davies died in March 2012. The flags at the Millennium Stadium flew at half mast as the world of rugby paid tribute to one of its most inspirational and influential talents.

It was only the force of Carwyn James' personality that persuaded Willie John McBride to go to New Zealand in 1971. The Ulsterman loved the concept of the Lions, but he was fed up with the defeats, the disorganisation and the politics that held the team back. He'd promised himself that after three tours, nine Tests, eight defeats and one draw his Lions adventure was over. Carwyn managed to change his mind.

'Even New Zealanders could share his delight when at long last he played in a victorious Test side,' reported the *Dominion*. If Dawes was captain, then McBride was the most brilliant back-up, the leader of the pack, a charismatic man for whom his players would have run through a brick wall. McBride became Ireland captain in 1973 at the height of the Troubles and firmly believed in rugby's capacity to bring people together.

'I had a guard sleeping outside my door at the Shelbourne Hotel,' he said. 'He was there because of threats. I said to one of them once, "How real is this threat?" And he said, "We don't know, but we can't take a chance."

'There were people down south saying, "What's that Protestant doing captaining Ireland?" and up here there were other people saying, for different reasons, "Why's he captaining an Irish team?" I couldn't win with either of them. It was always my belief that rugby people stood by each other. Throughout the murder and mayhem in Northern Ireland there wasn't a single game of rugby ever cancelled between a team from the north and a team from the south. We crossed over the border all the time to play each other and the game was a great unifier in tough times. It kept people together. It preached tolerance.'

Willie John didn't just win a series in New Zealand, he stayed on and captained the Lions to another series victory in South Africa three years later. It was his fifth tour, an achievement that was later recognised when he was voted rugby personality of the century by *Rugby World* magazine.

In all, he played sixty-three times for Ireland and won seventeen Test caps for the Lions before leaving the stage in 1975 at the age of thirty-four. He, like the team he played for, had become immortal.

EPILOGUE

'YOU WAIT UNTIL YOU PLAY . . .'
BY CARWYN JAMES

ANOTHER DAY, another place.

'Give me an L . . . give me an I . . . give me an O . . .'

Frightening!

'The Lions are here.'

Reassuring!

'It doesn't matter if it's two, three or twenty-three, we've got to beat them . . .'

Softer tones exuding authority.

'There'll be no excuses.'

Silence, a rush of blood.

'Get your bloody retaliation in first.'

'One for all and all for one.'

'Sounds like me in the front-row fraternity again.'

'And not a word, not one word to the ref, OK? OK, Robbo? . . . You'd better not.'

With a lilt, Robbo'll have a clinic. Robbo'll . . .

'Cut the cackle. Think nothing about it. Seven minutes, George? Seven minutes, lads. Think about it. Think, think, think.'

Silence. Thinks pregnant with tries, dropped goals, dropped passes. More thinks.

'All the best, Syd. Wings cover. Look after yourself, King. Drive them hard, Willie. Hit town, Sean. Mighty, compress – and less oscillating. Stick to him, Sloppy. Get there first, JT. OK, Gibbs, JPR, Gareth? All the best lads. And not a word to the ref.'

Another game. Just like the last one, but different.

Statistics, lots and lots of statistics. 'Three-one, John, right, Frank? Whose got the rucks? Thanks, Boss. Good lineout count, Del. Well done, Willie John; well done, Syd. Thanks.'

'President Sam, chairman Jim, gentlemen. Thank you for the game, for another hard game and the excellent spirit in which it was played. To the opposition may I say . . . And to my boys . . . which reminds me of the two nuns . . .'

Confronted by a large, heavy blazer badge and lapels plastered with mini ones:

'Did you enjoy it?'

'Oh yes, a good game.'

'Yes, it was a good game.'

'A very good game.'

'Do you think you deserved to win?'

'I don't know, really. But I suppose if you score thirty points more than the other team, I suppose, you know, you deserve a win.'

'Pity we missed that penalty.'

'Oh, yes, that penalty. Yes, that might have turned the game.'

'You think so?'

'Oh yes, it might well have turned the game. Still, it was a good game.'

'Yes, a very good game. But you wait until you play . . .'

And we wait, and we wait and we wait until we play, until we play, until we play . . . all twenty-four of them. Or was it twenty-six?

'Let's blow town.'
– Another day, another place.
– All three and a half months of it. And then, home.

BIBLIOGRAPHY

How the Lions Won: The Stories and Skills Behind Two Famous Victories. Terry O'Connor (ed). Collins, 1975.

The Victorious Lions: The 1971 British Isles Rugby Union Tour of Australia and New Zealand. John Reason. Rugby Books, 1971.

Fred the Needle: The Untold Story of Fred Allen. Alan Sayers and Les Watkins. Hodder Moa, 2011.

In Strength and Shadow: The Mervyn Davies Story. David Roach and Mervyn Davies. Mainstream Sport, 2012.

How to Watch a Game of Rugby. Spiro Bernard Zavos. Awa Press, 2012.

'Battling the Lions: The battle of Lancaster Park'. John Brooks. *New Zealand Herald*, 10 May 2005.

Behind the Lions: Playing Rugby for the British & Irish Lions. Stephen Jones, Tom English, Nick Cain and David Barnes with Peter Burns and John Griffiths. Arena Sport, 2016.

Behind the Silver Fern: Playing Rugby for New Zealand. Lynn McConnell and Tony Johnson. Arena Sport, 2016.

'John Dawes looks back at the historic 1971 Lions triumph in New Zealand'. *Wales Online*, 22 March 2013.

'Des Connor's 1971 Lions-bait remains absolutely priceless'. Frank Keating. *The Guardian*, 11 May 2011.

'Band of Brothers – Lions of '71 roar one more time'. John Taylor. *ESPN*, 28 May 2008.

The All Blacks. T. P. McLean. Sidgwick & Jackson, 1991.

The Rugby Union Writers' Club Pay Tribute to the 1971 British Lions in New Zealand. The Rugby Union Writers' Club, 1971.

Super Sid: The Story of the Great All Black. Bob Howitt. Rugby Press Ltd, 1978.

Mud in Your Eye: A Worm's Eye View of the Changing World of Rugby. Chris Laidlaw. Pelham Books, 1973.
Delme: The Autobiography by Delme Thomas. With Alun Gibbard. Y Lolfa Cyf, 2014.

Grizz: The Legend. Phil Gifford. Margin Release Ltd, 1991.

The World of Rugby: A History of Rugby Union Football. John Reason and Carwyn James.

Britain's Finest Lions. Lindsay Knight. *Dominion/Sunday Times NZ*, 1971.

Mighty Mouse. Ian McLauchlan. Stanley Paul, 1980.

Lions Rampant. Terry McLean. A. H. & A. W. Reed, 1971.

The Dawes Decades. David Parry-Jones. Seren, 2005.

The Lions Speak. John Reason (ed). Rugby Books, 1972.

Decade of the Dragon. John Taylor. Hodder & Stoughton, 1980.

The Roaring Lions. J. B. G. Thomas. Pelham Books, 1971.

Colin Meads All Black. Alex Veysey. Collins, 1974.

Broon from Troon. Gordon Brown. Stanley Paul, 1983.

Beegee: The Bryan Williams Story. Bob Howitt. Rugby Press Ltd, 1981.

Gerald Davies: An Autobiography. Gerald Davis. Allen & Unwin, 1979.

Barry John: The King. Barry John and Paul Abbandonato. Mainstream Publishing, 2000.

Welsh Greats: Carwyn James. Documentary, BBC Wales.

Gareth: The Autobiography of a Rugby Legend. Gareth Edwards. Arrow Books Ltd, 1979.

John Dawes: And the Legendary 1971 British Lions. Ross Reyburn. Y Lolfa Cyf, 2013.

Nobody Beats Us: The Inside Story of the 1970s Wales Rugby Team. David Tossell. Mainstream Publishing, 2011.

All Blacks versus British & Irish Lions Official Programme, First Test. 2005.

'Ken Going: The battle of his life'. Tim Eves. *The Northern Advocate,* 7 June 2008.

'Heart of the country: Still Going strong on the farm'. Bridget Carter. *New Zealand Herald*, 6 August 2003.

'The day Tauranga Domain hosted 23,000 rugby fans'. Peter White. *Bay of Plenty Times*, 29 August 2015.

'Lions in Bay's Domain'. Kelly Exelby. *Bay of Plenty Times*, 28 May 2005.

'Lions tour shows way to keep rugby interest high'. Sean Fitzpatrick. *New Zealand Herald*, 14 June 2009.

'1971 Lions heroes recall how they tamed mighty All Blacks'. Rory Keane. *Irish Examiner,* 10 September 2013.

'Henry early convert after consulting coach's bible'. Brendan Gallagher. *Telegraph*, 22 May 2001.

'The Henry law'. Wynne Gray. *New Zealand Herald*, 24 May, 2005.

'Mike Gibson: I'm not sure I'd have wanted to be a professional'. Paul Kimmage. *Irish Independent*, 07 February 2016.

'The Big Interview: Gareth Edwards'. Paul Kimmage. *The Sunday Times*, 25 March 2007.

'Battling the Lions: The whistle blowers'. Suzanne McFadden. *New Zealand Herald*, 10 May 2005.

'Dixon a low-key hero of legend'. Simon Turnbull. *The Independent*, 9 June 2001.

'A forbidding place to visit'. John Taylor. *ESPN*, 13 June 2014.

Fergie. Alex Veysey.

'Queensland's 1971 team are the only state side to beat the Lions'. Jim Tucker. *The Courier-Mail*, 02 June 2013.

'A beer with an All Black: Andy Leslie'. Adam Julian. *Clubrugby.co.nz*, 30 March 2015.

All Blacks Legends Series, Episode 4: Andy Leslie.

'Barry John: the Welsh wizard who retired too soon'. Paul Rees. *The Guardian*, 26 April 2012.

Barry John: The King. Documentary, BBC Wales.

'Kindred spirits bridging the passage of time'. *Irish Times*, 03 February 2007.

'Off with farm boots, on with rugby sprigs'. Frances Morton. *New Zealand Herald*, 29 May 2011.

'Pride of the Valleys'. Michael Brown. *New Zealand Herald*, 14 May 2005.

'Battling the Lions: The Weak Link'. John Brooks. *New Zealand Herald*, 10 May 2005.

'Colin Meads: Why the All Blacks must win'. *New Zealand Herald*, 10 May 2005.

Lions of Ireland. David Walmsley. Mainstream Sport, 2001.

Legends in Black: New Zealand Rugby Greats on Why We Win. Tom Johnson. Penguin New Zealand, 2014.

Lions of England. Peter Jackson. Mainstream Sport, 2005.

Laurie Mains. Bob Howitt and Robin McConnell. Rugby Publishing Ltd, 1996.

'Steve Hansen: An All Blacks coach must win every game – you don't have the luxury of being able to rebuild and lose'. Ian Chadband. *The Telegraph*, 29 November 2013.

'Will 2017 Lions tour of New Zealand be 1971 revisited?' *New Zealand Herald*, 29 November 2016.

'Steve Hansen's special bond with father Des, the man who moulded him'. Liam Napier. *Sunday Star Times*, October 9 2016.

'Local Lions no match in 1971'. allblacks.com.

'Greatest team's greatest moment was "the day it all came together"'. Brendan Gallagher. *The Telegraph*, 15 June 2005.

'Irish draw inspiration from new Kidd on the block'. Paul Trow. *The Independent*, 30 December 1995.

'Take heed New Zealand, the Lions are coming'. *New Zealand Herald*, 28 November 2016.

Referee. Humphrey Rainey. John McIndoe, 1982.

Giants of Scottish Rugby. Jeff Connor. Mainstream, 2000.

Meads. Brian Turner. Hodder Moa Beckett Publishers Limited, 2002.

All Blacks V Lions. Ron Palenski. Hodder Moa Beckett Publishers Limited, 2005.

Rugby World. August 1971.

Rugby World. September 1971.

Rugby World. October 1971.

The Barry John Story: An Autobiography. Barry John. Collins, 1974.

Mervyn Davies: No. 8. Mervyn Davies and David Parry-Jones. Pelham Books Ltd, 1977.

Lions of Wales: A Celebration of Welsh Rugby Legends. Peter Jackson. Mainstream , 1998.

We Beat the All Blacks. Documentary.

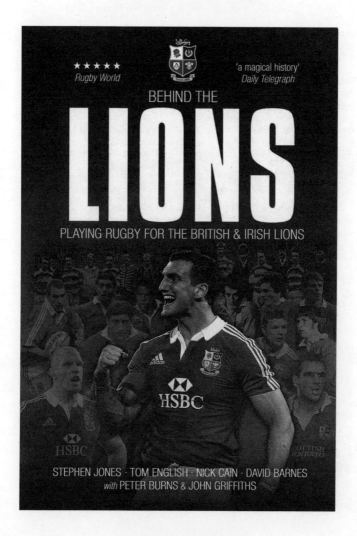

ALL BLACKS®

BEHIND THE

SILVER FERN

PLAYING RUGBY FOR NEW ZEALAND

TONY JOHNSON

LYNN McCONNELL

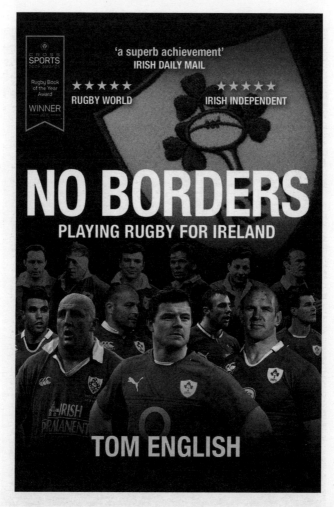

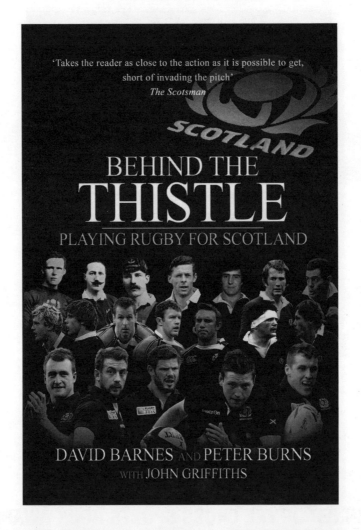

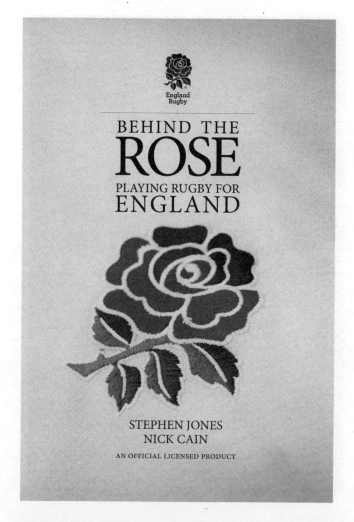

Whangarei

Auckland
Pukekohe

Hamilton

New Plymouth

Wanganui

Wellington

Greymouth

Tauranga

Gisborne

Napier

Palmerston North

Masterton
Blenheim

Christchurch

Timaru

Dunedin

Invercargill